# Introduction to Natural Language Semantics

CSLI Lecture Notes
Number 80

# Introduction to Natural Language Semantics

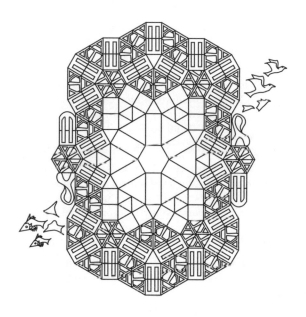

## Henriëtte de Swart

CSLI Publications
Center for the Study of Language and Information
Stanford, California

Copyright © 1998
CSLI Publications
Center for the Study of Language and Information
Leland Stanford Junior University
Printed in the United States
02 01 00 99 98      5 4 3 2 1

Library of Congress Cataloging-in-Publication Data

Swart, Henriëtte de, 1961–
Introduction to natural language semantics / Henriëtte de Swart.
p.    cm.   — (CSLI lecture notes ; no. 80)
Based on notes prepared for various introductory semantics classes taught by
the author at the University of Groningen and Stanford University, 1991–1997.
Includes bibliographical references and index.

ISBN 1-57586-139-9 (cloth : alk. paper).
ISBN 1-57586-138-0 (pbk. : alk. paper)

1. Semantics. 2. Semantics (Philosophy) I. Title. II. Series.
P325.S957   1998
401'.43—dc21
98-13781
CIP

∞ The acid-free paper used in this book meets the minimum requirements of
the American National Standard for Information Sciences—Permanence of
Paper for Printed Library Materials, ANSI Z39.48-1984.

# Contents

# List of Figures

# Preface

This textbook grew out of notes I prepared for my semantics classes over the last six years. At first, they were just meant for my own use, but over time, I received more and more requests from fellow semantics teachers for copies of my notes. In the end, I grew tired of sending .ps files all over the world, and was convinced that I should make them available to the general public. It took more time than I had anticipated to turn my loose notes into a real book, but I hope the result is worth it.

Given that the notes were not originally meant to be published, I freely used a great number of sources. There are quite a few good textbooks on semantics these days, and I am grateful to the authors of these books for the inspiration they gave me. The most important books I used are listed here (in alphabetical order):

E. Bach (1980). *Informal lectures on formal semantics*, Suny Press, Albany, NY.

R. Cann (1993). *Formal Semantics*, Cambridge University Press, Cambridge.

G. Chierchia and S. McConnell-Ginet (1990). *Meaning and grammar*, MIT Press, Cambridge, MA.

D. Cruse (1986). *Lexical semantics*, Cambridge University Press, Cambridge.

L.T.F. Gamut (1991). *Logic, language and meaning*, University of Chicago Press, Chicago. volume 1: Introduction to logic; volume 2: Intensional logic and logical grammar.

R. Larson and G. Segal (1995). *Knowledge of meaning* , MIT Press, Cambridge MA.

J. McCawley (1993). *Everything that linguists have always wanted to know about logic but were ashamed to ask*, University of Chicago Press, Chicago (second edition).

B. Partee and A. ter Meulen and R. Wall (1990). *Mathematical methods in linguistics* , Kluwer Academic Publishers, Dordrecht.

Every teacher knows that exercises constitute a crucial part of a textbook. Everyone who has ever had to prepare problem sets or exam questions also knows that it is really hard to design problems in such a way that they help the students digest the theory, test their understanding of the presented materials, and develop their creativity. Over the years, I wrote my own problem sets, partly based on ideas exposed in books and research articles. But I also used existing exercises from various textbooks. I decided to integrate them all into the published version for greater variety. A list of exercises borrowed or adapted from the literature (text books and/or research articles) is given here:

chapter 1: 2 builds on a paragraph in (Akmajian *et al.* 199:218).
3 is inspired by (Larson and Segal 1995).
4 (i) and (iii) are examples from (McCawley 1993:365).

chapter 2: 1 is from (Akmajian *et al.* 199:225).
2 is partially built on the Language Files.
3 is based on (Asher and Lascarides 1995).
4 is based on (Lyons 1995:62–65).
5 is built on (Akmajian *et al.* 199:48).
7 is inspired by and partially copied from (Chierchia and McConnell-Ginet 1990:27–28).
8 is adapted from (de Jong *et al.* 1990:10).

chapter 3: 1 is inspired by (Hobbs *et al.* 1993).
2 is based on (McCawley 1993:81–87).
3 is inspired by (Browne 1986).
4 is based on (Chierchia and McConnell-Ginet 1990:76–77).

chapter 4: 5  is adapted from (Partee *et al.* 1990:175–176).

6  is adapted from (Chierchia and McConnell-Ginet 1990:chapter 3).

7  is inspired by and partially copied from (Partee *et al.* 1990:179).

chapter 5: 5, 7 and 8 are new exercises, partly built on examples adapted from (Partee *et al.* 1990:176) and (McCawley 1993:246).

chapter 8: 1  is from (Partee *et al.* 1990:400).

2  (i) is from (Larson and Segal 1995:317).

6  is inspired by (Barwise and Cooper 1981).

7  is inspired by (Zwarts 1983).

chapter 9: 2  is based on (McCawley 1993:528–548).

I am grateful to all these authors for publishing their analyses and problems, and I hope they are pleased to know that others were inspired to use them.

The materials developed here were used in various introductory classes to semantics I taught at the University of Groningen and Stanford University between 1991 and 1997. They were also the basis for the class on quantification and anaphora I taught at the European Summer School in Language, Logic and Information at Copenhagen in the summer of 1993. Many thanks are due to all the participants for their questions, comments and remarks that helped shape the book. I would like to include a special thanks to my teaching assistants at Stanford: Jean Braithwaite, John Fry, Chris Manning, Patrick O'Neill, Marc Pauly, Christine Poulin and Suzanne Riehemann. They provided invaluable and cheerful help, and spent many hours grading homeworks, explaining problems to the students and answering their questions. Their enthusiasm and support made teaching Ling 130, Ling 230A and Ling 230B great fun! I would like to thank Tim Fernando for testing out the materials in this book at Carnegie Mellon University, and giving me feedback. I am grateful to Donka Farkas, Henk Verkuyl and Arto Anttila for reading the prefinal version of the manuscript, and providing helpful comments. Many thanks to Kyle Wohlmut for proofreading the book and designing the front page. The book would never have appeared in the form you see it now without the great editorial support of Stefan Kaufmann and the staff at CSLI Publications. Thank you, all of you!

Textbooks are never perfect, and this one certainly is not, but I keep working on improvements. Therefore, I would be grateful if you could point our errors, unclarities, omissions, etc. to me. You can send comments, reactions and questions to the following e-mail address: deswart@csli.stanford.edu. Your help is much appreciated!

# Chapter 1

# What is meaning?

The first question in approaching semantics as the study of meaning is: what is meaning? Another issue to be addressed is the relation between meaning, mind, and world, and its effect on the organization of a semantic theory. Finally, we will discuss the place of semantics in linguistic theory, and the borderline between semantics and pragmatics.

## 1.1 Language and meaning

*Semantics* is defined as the study of meaning expressed by elements of a language or combinations thereof. Utterances are not just noises or scribbles, they are used to convey information, they are linked with kinds of events, with states of mind, etc. Speaker and hearer use language to *communicate*. Typically, communication involves a message encoded by the sender into some kind of signal and sent through a channel to the receiver, who receives the signal and decodes the message. In a regular speech situation, there is a speaker who is the sender, and the message is what she wants to get across to the hearer, who is the receiver. The signal consists of sound waves, which encode words and sentences, the channel is the air, and the hearer decodes the sound waves.

Communication is only successful if the idea the hearer gets is the same as what the speaker intended the hearer to get. One requirement is that

1

speaker and hearer share a language, so that they know how to do the
encoding and decoding. This knowledge of the language system which
is stored in the brain is what Chomsky (1965) refers to as the speaker's
*competence*. Competence is contrasted with *performance*, which applies to
the use of the language system. Even people who master their language to
perfection make mistakes: they speak in ungrammatical sentences, stumble
over their words, or misinterpret perfectly grammatical sentences. Such
performance errors reflect the actual processes that go into production and
understanding of language. The notion of linguistic competence abstracts
away from the actual process to study the knowledge native speakers have
of their language as an abstract cognitive system. Linguistic competence
involves more than being able to make the right sounds. Parrots and certain
other birds can be taught to make articulate sounds, but they do not relate
these sounds to content. Because of that, we feel they are not competent
speakers of the language: the sounds they make do not convey information
and do not achieve communication. It is the fact that linguistic expressions
are not just *forms*, but have *content* which makes language such a suitable
tool for communication. Competent speakers are those who know not only
the forms and the contents, but also the link between them. It is the
task of a semanticist to describe the meaning of linguistic elements and to
study the principles which allow (and exclude) the assignment of meaning
to combinations of these elements. In addition, a complete and adequate
semantic theory characterizes the systematic meaning relations between
words and sentences of a language, and provides an account of the relations
between linguistic expressions and the things that they can be used to talk
about (i.e., the external world).

If we define semantics as the study of meaning, we should like to know
what exactly it means to *mean* something. The question of what the meaning of meaning is has been studied by philosophers of language as well as
linguists. The words *to mean* or *meaning* occur in all kinds of natural
language sentences, such as the ones listed in (1).

Dictionaries give *signify, import, denote, represent* as synonyms of *to
mean* and provide descriptions such as 'to be defined or described as, to
denote, to convey' for (1a)–(d), 'to convey the same sense as, to refer to
the same thing as' for (1e), 'to imply, to result in' for (1f, g), 'to design for
a certain purpose' for (1h), 'to intend to convey or indicate' for (1i, j), 'to
be of a specified importance or significance, to matter' for (1k), etc.

The noun *meaning* is described as 'something that is signified, something that one wishes to convey, especially by language' for (1l), 'something
that is felt to be the inner significance of something' for (1m). *Sense, significance, signification, acceptation* and *import* are given as synonyms.

In order to create some order in this diversity it is important to restrict

(1)  a.  The word "dog" means a certain species of mammal.
    b.  The red light means that you cannot go in.
    c.  Those clouds mean rain.
    d.  {a,b,c} means 'the set consisting of the elements a, b and c.'
    e.  The French word "chien" means "dog".
    f.  This will mean the end of our regime.
    g.  His losing his job means that he will have to look again.
    h.  This building is meant for storage.
    i.  I mean to help if I can.
    j.  What do you mean by that look?
    k.  The opinions of critics meant little to him.
    l.  Do you know the meaning of the word hypochondriac?
    m.  What is the meaning of life?

the notion of meaning in which we are interested. We will stay away from moral values such as the specified importance or the inner significance of things. This excludes examples like (1k) and (m) from our theory of meaning. Furthermore, we will ignore purposes and intentions, and thus leave cases like (1h), (i) and (j) outside the discussion. We will replace the informal use of *to mean* in (1f) and (g) by the formal term *to imply*. We will furthermore restrict ourselves to meaning conveyed by symbolic systems, which removes examples of 'natural' meaning like (1c). This leaves us with the cases in (1a), (b), (d), (e) and (l) and the paraphrases *to denote, to be described or defined as* and *sense, denotation, signification, acceptation* as the core meaning of meaning.

We will furthermore restrict our notion of language, because there are various kinds of languages:

(2)  a.  Natural languages such as English, Chinese, Sanskrit, sign languages like ASL (= American Sign Language), etc;
    b.  Complementary sign systems which function in communication, such as smiling, gesturing, shaking hands, etc;
    c.  Sign languages for specific purposes, such as traffic signs, secret codes, the Morse code, etc;
    d.  Formal languages such as algebraic languages, programming languages, first order predicate logic, etc.; and
    e.  languages or communication systems of other animals such as bees, dolphins, apes.

This list may not be exhaustive, but it shows that there is a lot of diversity in sign systems. They can all be said to have their own syntax and semantics. The overall theory which tries to develop a unifying analysis of these systems is called *semiotics*.

In this course, we will limit ourselves to natural language, so we will not try to account for examples like (1b), which involves a sign system like in (2c). Examples like (1d) have a special status, because the semantics of formal languages such as programming languages, logical languages, etc. is fully defined and specified as part of the description of the language when we learn it. This implies that there is a set of rules which (recursively) define the meaning of any well-formed expression in the language. We do not need to 'go out in the field and search for' the meaning of an expression, because it is already there and we have defined exactly what it is.

If things were as easy for the semantics of natural language, we would long have finished the job. (Un)fortunately, this is not the case. For one thing, determining the meaning of a natural language expression is an empirical matter. It turns out that it is not so easy to define a set of rules which recursively define the meaning of any well-formed expression of English, French, Chinese, Navajo, ASL, etc. Given that *direct interpretation* of natural language with respect to the outside world (or some model of it) is not always so easy, many semanticists opt for the *indirect* approach. We know that a translation can sometimes help us to determine the meaning of an expression. Suppose I speak French, but you don't, and we both speak English. In that case, I can teach you something about the meaning of a French expression by translating it into English. In such a setting, I could utter a sentence like (1e). If you know the meaning of the word *dog* in English, you have now learnt the meaning of the word *chien*, because my utterance established an equivalence relation between the two word meanings. The same 'trick' can be used with the translation of natural language into some formal language. Suppose I can describe the meaning of an English expression by translating it into an expression of a formal language. Because there will be a full and explicit interpretation procedure for the expressions in this formal language, I will immediately have grasped the meaning of the English expression. Of course, I will only have access to it in an indirect way, namely via a translation procedure, but as long as the translation is perfect, the exact meaning will be captured. But that is of course the critical point. It is essential to have a formal language which does indeed qualify as an adequate translation for English. As you may expect, this issue is far from trivial. The development of a family of formal languages which capture increasingly complex parts of the meaning of natural language runs through this book like a continuous thread.

## 1.2  Meaning, mind, and world

People hold different views on the relation between language, states of mind and the outside world. A *mentalistic* approach to meaning claims that words primarily stand for ideas (concepts, images, thoughts, ... ). This is an attractive view, for nobody will deny that we have mental representations and concepts, and that we reason with them. Language is in the brain, and for that reason linguistics is a branch of cognitive science, on a par with psychology and neuro-sciences. But it is not easy to build a psychologically realistic theory of meaning. A conceptual analysis works pretty well for names like *Pegasus* or *the Eiffel Tower*. They are the kind of words which immediately call up a mental image of the object. If we build into the theory a notion of *prototype*, we can extend this to common nouns such as *bird, dog, triangle* and verbs like *walk, kick, laugh*. For instance, a robin is a more typical bird than a penguin, so the mental image of the word *bird* will probably more closely resemble a robin, but this is not in any way incompatible with the existence of atypical birds like penguins. The mental approach is harder to apply to words that do not have clear conceptual content. We have difficulty defining the mental image associated with *only*, or *hello*. Another issue to worry about is the definition of meaning beyond the word level. We need to define mental operations which build complex concepts out of atomic ones in order to be able to assign a concept to a sentence, because sentences are clearly meaningful. We also have to avoid making mental concepts too private. The concepts and their modes of composition need to be intersubjective in order to allow communication between individuals. There are various proposals for mental operations of this kind. Fodor (1975) appeals to the notion of a language of thought to build the structure of more complex mental concepts. Johnson-Laird (1983) uses the notion of 'mental model' to describe complex mental structures. In a series of books and articles, Jackendoff develops a conceptual semantics which mixes ideas coming from predicate logic (see chapter 4), theories about thematic roles that are concerned with who is doing things (agent), and who or what is undergoing the action (patient), and psychological theories on (visual) perception (Jackendoff 1972, 1983, 1990). For instance, Jackendoff (1996) presents an analysis of the composition of verbs and their arguments which explains why the combination of *push* and *a cart* in the verb phrase *push a cart* introduces a spatial path along which the cart is moved indefinitely, whereas the combination of *eat* and *an apple* in the verb phrase *eat an apple* introduces a mapping from parts of the apple to parts of the event in such a way that an apple is gradually consumed in a finite period of time. Although analyses like these are an important step forward, the construction of complex concepts is a problem which has not

yet been entirely solved. It is not by itself impossible to define operations
on concepts, but we have to make sure those operations are as psychologically realistic as the atomic concepts. The question of what counts as a
psychologically realistic operation on conceptual meanings is not so easy
to answer.

An important problem for the mentalistic approach is that this approach
does not give us a clear view of the relation between words, concepts and the
outside world. Concepts stand for objects in the world derivatively, because
the ideas or concepts themselves stand for those objects. But this seems to
push the problem of external significance from expressions to ideas. As long
as we do not know how ideas classify objects in the outside world, this does
not help much. Many researchers working in the mentalistic approach are
less concerned with external reference than with cognitive representations,
so not everybody takes this to be a serious problem. For instance, Larson
and Segal (1995) make it the explicit aim of semantic theory to account
for the part of our linguistic knowledge which concerns meaning. Their
enterprise is rooted in the cognitivist perspective of generative grammar
(Chomsky 1986, Higginbotham 1985). However, we cannot deny that one
of the important characteristics of natural language expressions is that
they are *about* something. If I said 'The book is on the table' in a situation
where there is clearly a contextually relevant book visible on a contextually
relevant table, then this sentence would accurately describe the situation.
You would probably tell me that I am right. But if I removed the book from
the table, you would no longer agree with me if I uttered the same sentence.
People have quite solid intuitions about the relation of the sentence to the
two situations. This intuition of external reference is something we want
a semantic theory of natural language to capture. We use language to
communicate, to talk about things outside, about the way the world is (or
should be). This 'aboutness' of natural language suggests that meanings
are not just things in our head, something like a mental or conceptual
representation, but that they are somehow connected to the outside world.
In sum, language has content and this content is anchored to reality via
some aboutness relation.

Researchers who take the aboutness of language as a core property
in view of its relevance for communication have developed approaches to
meaning in which the main focus is on the external significance of language,
on its connection with the described world, rather than the describing mind.
In this view, sentences are classified by the way they describe things to be.
In a referential theory of meaning, the relation between linguistic expressions and things in the world is defined as a relation of *reference*. The
notion of reference has to be taken in a rather broad sense here. Words
*refer* to all kinds of things in the world: objects, properties of individ-

uals, relations between individuals, events and situations. An approach that establishes a direct relation between words and the objects they represent does not exclude that we also talk about non-existing objects such as Pegasus and Santa Claus, or the largest prime number or the present king of France. What is even more important is that it does not ignore the study of verbs expressing mental states and attitudes, such as hopes, beliefs, dreams. In fact, within the referential framework there is a considerable amount of linguistic and philosophical literature on the similarities and differences between such sentences as (3a) and (b):

(3)  a.  Bill Clinton gave a speech on television last night.
     b.  Sue dreamt she kissed Bill Clinton last night.

(3a) is a statement about the real world, and it is a matter of checking whether the sentence is true or false. In (3b) the situation is more complex. There are two individuals in the real world involved (Sue and Bill Clinton), there is a real world event (a dream) and there is an event in Sue's dreamworld (a kissing). (3b) is an example of the problem of *intensionality*: we refer to a world which is not the real world. Predicates like *to dream*, but also *to believe, to think* are called 'world creating' predicates, because they introduce their own possible 'world', which is not necessarily identical to the real one. The creativity of the human mind allows us to make these imaginary worlds as complex as we like (just think about fiction). Sentences like (3b) show that language also serves to communicate about mental states with other persons. In a referential theory of meaning, it is important to be able to represent information about mental states as well. But even the semantics of world creating predicates and other intensional expressions will ultimately be formulated in terms of reference, albeit reference at different indices. Not just the reference here and now in the real world comes into play, but the reference in other situations as well (see chapter 9 for more details).

Note that there is no implication that the representations in a referential theory of meaning have psychological import. The theory is used in explaining our knowledge of language, but makes no claim about how we know these things, what kind of knowledge this is, or how it is stored in the brain. It does not aim to be more than an account of what it is that we know when we know a language. In that sense, it aims at equivalence with, rather than identification of, our mental representations. As such, a referential theory of meaning does not claim to be psychologically realistic, but to be compatible with a theory which is.

Ideally, we would want to build a theory which combines insights from both the mentalistic and the referential theory and analyzes meanings as relations involving three things: expressions of language, objects in the world and mental states of the speaker and hearer. There is currently an attempt to bring the different frameworks closer together as a first step towards building a theory of that kind. See Gärdenfors (1994a, b), and Zwarts and Verkuyl (1994) for more discussion.

## 1.3 The place of semantics in linguistic theory

In linguistics, the term *grammar* is often used to describe what internal knowledge fluent speakers possess of their language–their *linguistic competence*. Whatever fluent speakers know of their language is a proper part of a description of that language, and belongs to the object of study of linguistic theory. Given that speakers know what the morphemes, words, sentences and discourses of their language mean, semantics must be a component of the grammar. Moreover, it was mentioned above that we use language to communicate, to talk about things in the outside world, to convey information about the way the world is (or should be). The 'aboutness' of language, and the important role that that notion plays in communication is one of the motivations to adopt a referential approach to meaning. The fact that communication consists in the transmission of information provides an additional argument in favor of the view that semantics is a genuine part of linguistic theory.

Quite generally, we can say that there are three essential ingredients to the use of language as a means of communication, namely:

(i) the linguistic expression(s) used

(ii) what the expression refers to
(objects, properties, relations, events, ... )

(iii) context

Syntactic research focusses primarily on (i), especially on the structure of larger units such as the sentence. One issue that syntacticians are interested in is word order. The English, Dutch and French embedded sentences in (4a–c) all have a subject, a verb and a direct object, but the order of the words is systematically different in the three languages:

(4)   a.   (I saw that) the student wore a red sweater [English]
      b.   (Ik zag dat) de student een rode trui droeg [Dutch]
          (J'ai vu que) l'étudiant portait un pull rouge [French]

The subject in (4a–c) consists of a noun (N) and a determiner (Det). The combination of these two words builds a complete nominal constituent, called a noun phrase (NP). In all three languages, the determiner is placed left of the noun. The rest of the sentence says something about the subject. We call this the verbal predicate or the verb phrase (VP). The VP in (4a–c) consists of a verb (V) and a direct object (an NP). The object is a more complex noun phrase than the subject, because it also contains an adjective. Both English and Dutch place the adjective between the determiner and the noun. French places most (but not all) adjectives after the noun. If we look now at the order of the subject (S), the verb (V) and the object (O), we observe that the order of these elements in English and French is SVO, whereas the Dutch order is SOV. Syntacticians work on theories which capture the differences and similarities between the structure of phrases and sentences in the languages of the world.

Semantic research focusses on the relation between (i) and (ii), in particular on the meaning which arises out of the combination of more elementary expressions into groups of words and sentences. If we look at the examples in (4) again, we observe that they all express the same meaning: there is a certain individual who is characterized as a student, and this individual has the property of carrying a red sweater. This is a complex property which can be further analyzed into a relational expression (the verb) and the object the student has a relation with (a red sweater). The object has to have a combination of two properties: it has to be a sweater, and it has to be red. Although the order of the words in (4a–c) is different, the procedures which combine the meanings of the elements into a more complex meaning are the same. This underlines the observation that all languages are equal in that they have the same communicative possibilities. As a result, semantic variation is more constrained than syntactic variation.

It is the introduction of structure which takes semantic theory beyond the definition of the meaning of a list of words. This view on the relation between syntax and semantics reflects the intuition that it may be possible– and even fruitful to some degree–to study structure without reference to meaning. For instance, there may be elements which are indispensible for the well-formedness of a complex expression, but which do not themselves contribute essentially to the interpretation. Although we can study structure without meaning, we cannot study meaning without structure. A meaning is always the meaning of something, and that something must be a syntactic expression. Preferably this expression is syntactically well-formed, but with examples like (5) communication can be successful even if there is a grammatical error:

(5)  a.   *I aren't tired.
     b.   *La porte est ouvert.                          [French]
          the-[fem] door is open-[masc]

   Given that syntactically ill-formed sentences are often interpretable, we cannot claim that such expressions do not have meaning. But the more general claim stands, namely that for complex expressions there can be no meaning without structure. Semantics is always relational, and as a result, semantics always needs syntax. However, if we are interested in language as a means of communication, we do not want to do pure syntax, just in order to do syntax. In this perspective, it is not very useful to develop a grammar without an interpretation of the expressions built up by the syntax. The conclusion must be that we do not want to develop a grammar without interpretation, and that syntax and semantics go hand in hand. This is a core element in the view of grammar developed by Montague (1973), which is known as *Montague grammar*. Other theories of grammar have inherited the idea that syntax and semantics are closely tied together, for instance Head Driven Phrase Structure Grammar (HPSG) (Pollard and Sag 1994) and Lexical Functional Grammar (LFG) (Dalrymple et al. 1995).

   *Pragmatics* studies the relation between (i) + (ii) and (iii) and focuses thereby on language in the context of use. Communication often goes well beyond the meaning of what is said. Suppose someone utters (6):

(6) It's warm in here.

   If this is uttered when speaker and hearer have just entered a tropical greenhouse in the middle of a cold winter, the speaker probably just makes a (correct) observation about the difference in temperature inside and outside. In such a context (6) is used as a descriptive statement. But if someone comes to my house on a hot summer day and utters the same sentence, I will probably take that to mean that the speaker does not appreciate the temperature inside the house. This may lead me to turn on the air conditioning or to open a window to have some fresh air. So there is a difference between *sentences* and *utterances*: one and the same sentence uttered in two different contexts constitutes two utterances, and the information these utterances get across may be quite different. Given that the context of use determines to a considerable degree the way linguistic meaning works out in a particular situation, we distinguish between *sentence meaning* and *utterance* or *speaker's meaning*. Any act of communication takes place in a specific context, so communication always relies on utterance meaning. On the other hand, our linguistic capacity is clearly independent of any specific context in which we utter a sentence. The study of the interpretation of sentences belongs to grammar. Semantics is thus about the study of literal, context-independent meaning. *Pragmatics* is interested in how sentences work out in context, and is therefore concerned with utterance meaning. This includes the study of nonliteral meaning such as irony (7a) and metaphor (7b, c):

(7)  a.  Oh, that's just great! (upon discovering your bike has a flat tire when you are in a hurry to get home)
b.  She is a real treasure.
c.  They just wouldn't swallow our idea.

There are systematic ways in which hearers build up ironical and metaphorical meanings when the literal interpretation of a sentence is clearly inadequate in the context. Knowledge of the world, conceptual schemas that describe stereotypical courses of events (scripts or frames), and well-known figures of speech are used as interpretation strategies that build up contextualized (utterance) meaning on the basis of literal (sentence) meaning. For more discussion, see Searle (1979), Lakoff and Johnson (1980).

The notion of context includes the 'setting', that is the time and location of the utterance, which involves the language user in the role of speaker and hearer. The crucial role of the context of use is visible in the interpretation of deictic elements such as *I, here, now* (Levinson 1983). The following example about deixis is from Barwise and Perry (1983). Suppose Alex utters (8), speaking to Bertha, and Bertha uses the same words, talking to Alex:

(8)  I am right, you are wrong.
a.  Alex to Bertha: Alex is right, Bertha is wrong.
b.  Bertha to Alex: Bertha is right, Alex is wrong.

The two people talking to each other use exactly the same words, but they obviously disagree forcefully with each other. Alex and Bertha make rather different claims about the world: what Alex said will be true if Alex is right and Bertha is wrong, whereas what Bertha said will be true if Alex is wrong and Bertha is right (compare 8a and b). These different claims are the different interpretations of the utterances. But the meaning of the sentence they both used did not change. Even though the two utterances have the same sentence meaning, the utterance meaning is different, because the reference of *I* and *you* changes from one utterance to the next. Deixis shows that utterance meaning cannot be fully determined by sentence meaning. We need to take into account certain features of the speech situation which directly affect the reference of a deictic expression. The interpretation of tense and temporal expressions such as *yesterday, last week* is also deictic and crucially dependent on the setting:

(9) Last week I played tennis with Chris.

We calculate the reference of *last week* as 'one week back in time from now', and whether the sentence is true or false depends on where the 'now' of the utterance is located in time. Every moment the reference of *now* changes. Yet the word does not change its meaning when it changes its reference. If it did, we could never find out what it means, and we couldn't understand what the speaker was trying to communicate. The context-dependent character of deictic expressions makes their analysis essentially a pragmatic matter (see Levinson 1983 for more discussion).

Context can also be more generally the real world or the fictional world the expression is related to. World knowledge often comes in when we discuss notions like coherence. For a long time, world knowledge was like a pragmatic wastebasket into which everything was thrown which couldn't be explained by syntactic or semantic rules. More recently, researchers have started sorting out some of the contents of this wastebasket, as it turned out to contain valuable information necessary to build machines which can model natural language understanding (think of applications in the areas of artificial intelligence and machine translation). A typical kind of puzzle in this respect is *anaphora resolution*. An *anaphor* is an incomplete expression which depends for its interpretation on some other element in the sentence or in the context. The expression the anaphor is dependent on is called the *antecedent*. For instance, the antecedent of an anaphoric pronoun like *he, she, they* tells us which individual(s) the pronoun refers to. Anaphora resolution is the process which involves finding the right antecedent for the anaphor, so that we resolve the identity of the individual(s) the pronoun stands in for. In some cases, the referent of the pronoun is fixed by the utterance situation. Consider (10):

(10) (Jane pointing to Bill): "He is the one I saw on the night of the party."

Jane's pointing gesture picks out the reference of the pronoun *he*. Because the referent is directly determined by the situation of utterance, we talk about a deictic interpretation of the pronoun. Unlike the first and second person pronouns *I* and *you*, third person pronouns are not inherently deictic. In the absence of a pointing gesture, the referent of the pronoun is usually determined by the linguistic context. We call this an anaphoric interpretation of the pronoun. In the easiest case, there is only one appropriate antecedent available in the context, as in (11):

(11) Jane$_i$ came home around five. Bill stood up and greeted her$_i$.

The pronoun *her* points to a female referent. In (11), there is only one female referent in the discourse, and the pronoun is naturally linked to Jane. The subscript $i$ on the proper name and the pronoun is a syntactic device which is commonly used in linguistics to describe the (semantic) link between the anaphor and its antecedent. Other cases are more complex; compare (11) and (12):

(12)   a.   I took my daughter$_i$ to the dentist$_j$ this morning. She$_j$ told her$_i$ it wouldn't hurt too much, but she$_j$ would give her$_i$ a pain killer anyway.

        b.   I took my daughter$_i$ to the dentist$_j$ this morning. She$_i$ asked her$_j$ if it would hurt and how long it would take.

In (12) there are two potential referents for each of the occurrences of the pronouns *she* and *her* and no grammatical rule determines the linking. General knowledge about the relation between dentists and their patients predicts a certain behavior for each of the participants. The notion of *script* or *frame* is often brought in to describe such fixed patterns of behavior for certain common real life situations. Our knowledge of this stereotypical behavior determines the preferential coindexing in (12a) and (b). Note that the indices only indicate the result of the pronoun resolution process: they show how the pronouns are resolved, not how we achieved this. Typically, a mixture of linguistic and non-linguistic knowledge comes in to determine where the indices should go.

Not all world knowledge is located in scripts or frames. The rules which determine the preferential coindexing in (13) are dependent on specific knowledge about a particular person. The following example is from Kameyama (1996):

(13)   a.   John hit Bill. *He* was severely injured.

        b.   John hit Arnold Schwarzenegger. *He* was severely injured.

In (13a), the preferred reading is that Bill was injured because of John hitting him. A hearer who does not know who Arnold Schwarzenegger is will interpret (13b) no differently from (13a). But those of us who know Arnold as a strong, almost invincible superhuman individual will tend to take John as the injured person in (13b). Because we know Arnold is stronger than the average person, we jump to the conclusion that John will probably suffer for his attack.

Computational linguists are interested in combining linguistic and world knowledge to develop algorithms for anaphora resolution that solve puzzles like the ones in (12) and (13). In this book, we will mostly limit ourselves to (some of) the grammatical rules that govern the anaphor-antecedent relation (see in particular chapter 5 and chapter 6. In some sense, we try to maximally exploit linguistic knowledge before giving in to 'knowledge of the world'. Whether this is the most efficient strategy from a computational point of view is open to debate.

## 1.4 Exercises

Exercises marked with an exclamation mark (!) are for discussion in class or section.

(1)! Explain why communication is likely not to be successful in the following situations in terms of encoding and decoding of the message sent by the speaker and received by the hearer by means of some signal travelling through some channel:

   (i) Context: semantics class at Stanford university, 3rd week of the quarter, so far all lectures have been taught in English. Utterance: 'Je suis votre nouveau prof de sémantique. Ouvrez vos livres à la page 23 s'il vous plaît.'

   (ii) Context: audience of deaf people at an ASL meeting. Utterance (in English): 'We all want to encourage the use of ASL in a larger community.'

   (iii) Context: exhausted visitor arrives at destination after a long trip. Dialogue:
      * (visitor to host): 'I am really thirsty.'
      * (host to visitor): 'Are you? I am sorry to hear that.'

   (iv) Context: Alice visits Humpty Dumpty. Dialogue (Humpty Dumpty starts): 'There's glory for you!' 'I don't know what you mean by 'glory',' Alice said.
   Humpty Dumpty smiled contemptuously. 'Of course you don't—till I tell you. I meant 'There's a nice knock-down argument for you!' '
   'But 'glory' doesn't mean 'a nice knock-down argument', ' Alice objected.
   'When *I* use a word, ' Humpty Dumpty said, in rather a scornful tone, 'it means just what I choose it to mean—neither more nor less.'
   'The question is.' said Alice, 'whether you *can* make words mean so many different things.'

(2)! Putnam (1975, 1988) notes that elm trees are not maple trees, and that most speakers know that elm trees are not maple trees—in other words, they know that *elm* does not mean the same as *maple*. Yet many of these same speakers cannot tell an elm tree from a maple tree; the knowledge they have in their heads is not sufficient to differentiate these kinds of trees. The same is true for many other *natural kind terms*—common nouns that denote kinds of things in nature, such as aluminum versus molybdenum, gold versus pyrite ('fool's gold'), diamonds versus zircons. We are all confident that these pairs of words are not synonymous, yet many people's concepts contain no information sufficient to distinguish one member of each pair from the other. Thus, it is clear that normal speakers do not have a determinate concept of the things these words denote. Explain the problems this raises for (i) a mentalistic theory of meaning and (ii) a referential theory of meaning. Putnam suggests that there is a 'division of linguistic labor' in language, in that normal speakers depend on and defer to 'experts' in these matters. To determine whether a tree really is an elm or a maple, one consults a tree specialist. To determine whether a metal is gold or pyrite, one consults a metallurgist. And so on. These experts have procedures, based on scientific understanding, for determining the category of the object. With respect to these terms, then, reference is in part a social phenomenon. Explain how the appeal to specialists helps us to solve the problem of the meaning of elms trees and maple trees, diamonds and zircons, etc. in the perspective of (i) a mental theory of meaning and (ii) a referential theory of meaning.

(3)! The examples in (i)–(iii) are all odd as sentences of English. (i) is syntactically ill-formed and semantically uninterpretable. (ii) is syntactically well-formed, but semantically anomalous. Is the oddness of (iii) due to syntactic or semantic problems? Motivate your answer.

   (i) Jimmy Sara to herself asked kiss.

   (ii) The blue sky asked a myth to kiss itself.

   (iii) Sara asked Jimmy to kiss herself.

(4) Describe how scripts or frames figure in the interpretation of the following sentences. Explain why these examples involve definite descriptions, rather than pronouns:

   (i) The last time I ate here, I had to wait 15 minutes before *the waiter* brought me *the check*.

(ii) When Ted was driving home yesterday, he had to step on *the brake* suddenly, and *his head* went through *the windshield*.

(ii) Whenever I teach freshman algebra, *the girls* do better than *the boys*.

(5) Consider the implications in (i) through (vi). Are they to be accounted for by linguistic theory alone, or by linguistic theory in conjunction with other theories? Explain which parts of linguistic theory come into play in the analysis, and which other theories (if appropriate).

  (i) 'To Harry, Bill gave a shirt' implies 'Bill gave Harry a shirt'.

 (ii) 'John invited Mary' implies 'Mary was invited by John'.

(iii) 'Eva got up late' implies 'Eva did not get up early'.

(iv) 'Steve is human' implies 'Steve is a mammal'.

 (v) 'Steven is a jerk' uttered by Harry implies 'Harry thinks Steven is an annoying person'.

(vi) Communication between Bill (speaker) and Mindy (hearer) on Tuesday morning: 'I would like to invite you to the party tonight' implies 'Bill would like to invite Mindy to the party on Tuesday night'.

# Chapter 2

# Desiderata for a theory of meaning

Now that we have defined semantics as the study of meaning expressed by elements of a language or combinations thereof, we can investigate the issues a semantic theory should address. First we need to know what the meanings of words in the language are. Then we need to find a way to semantically combine elements of a language and build up complex meanings. We will make some decisions as to the organization of our semantic theory, and introduce the principle of compositionality of meaning and a strict distinction between object language and metalanguage.

## 2.1   A structured lexicon

If we think about meaning in a 'naive' pre-theoretic way, the first thing which comes to mind is the meaning of *words*. In learning a foreign language, we think we learn the syntax by studying a grammar book and the semantics by learning the vocabulary, the *lexicon* of the language. In fact, we can already study meaning below the word level. The conventional view of linguistics has it that phonology studies the clustering of acoustic properties into minimally distinctive units, the phonemes. The minimal meaning-carrying elements of language are morphemes, which are clusterings of phonemes. Sometimes words as such are minimal meaning-carrying elements. Examples are *moon* or *table*. Sometimes words are built up from more than one morpheme, so in *tables* we have both the root *table* and an inflectional morpheme, the plurality marker -*s*. In *performed* we have both the root *perform*- and the past tense marker -*ed*. Usually, morphemes are called inflectional when they don't change the category (part of speech) of the base morpheme. For instance, both *table* and *tables* are nouns. In contrast, derivational morphemes often change the category of the base morpheme: *to perform* is a verb, but *performance* is a noun. And from the verb *to count* we can derive the adjective *countable* by adding the derivational morpheme -*able*. We can even go further and derive the noun *countability*, which consists of three different morphemes. The meaning of such complex words is derived in a systematic way from the morphemes they are composed of. The root *perform* has the same meaning in *performance, performer, performed*, etc. Such words are said to be in the same paradigm. The inflectional morpheme -*s* functions as a plurality marker in *tables, girls, linguists*, etc. Similarly, the derivational morpheme -*er* refers to the agent of the action in *performer, writer, murderer*, etc. rather

The meaning of words and relations between words are studied in lexical semantics (Cruse 1986, Lyons 1995). Notions which play a role here are ambiguity (1a), synonymy (1b), antonymy (1c), hyponymy (often creating a taxonomy, also called an *isa*-hierarchy) (1d). Predicates can be classified as symmetric (1e) or as converse predicates (1f):

(1)  a.  bank, punch, pitcher
     b.  beautiful–lovely, mercury–quicksilver, big–large
     c.  male–female, dead–alive, happy–sad, tall–short
     d.  a german shepherd is a dog, is a mammal, is a living being
         a dandelion is a flower, is a plant, is a living being
     e.  Alex is married to Bertha ⟷ Bertha is married to Alex
         Max is dancing with Sue ⟷ Sue is dancing with Max
     f.  Alex is the husband of Bertha ⟷ Bertha is the wife of
         Alex
         Sue sold a book to Bill ⟷ Bill bought a book from Sue

The notions of symmetry and converse relation will be made more precise in chapter 4, but the intuitive meaning of these concepts should be clear from the examples in (1e) and (1f). If a relation holds between two objects or individuals $a$ and $b$, its converse relation holds between $b$ and $a$. If the same relation that holds between $a$ and $b$ holds between $b$ and $a$, the predicate is symmetric. Properties like these are used in semantic networks to describe meaningful relations between lexical items. Semantic networks provide a much richer model of the human speaker's knowledge than dictionaries because of the structure they impose on the lexicon.

The lexicon can be further structured by using semantic features such as [± ADULT], [± MALE], [± CAUSE ], etc. This allows us to classify the relations/differences between items such as:

(2)  a.  [± ADULT] woman/girl, cat/kitten, cow/calf
     b.  [± MALE] king/queen, uncle/aunt, bachelor/spinster
     c.  [± CAUSE] kill/die, keep/stay, feed/eat

The decomposition of the meaning of words into semantic features is often called a decompositional analysis. The decomposition into semantic features can be very helpful in describing the relations in a relatively well structured and closed domain. A good example are kinship relations, where features like [± ADULT] and [± MALE] allow us to distinguish different family members. In this domain, we also find a nice application of symmetric and converse relations, as illustrated by (1e) and (f) respectively. The problem with features is that they may end up being rather abstract notions, as in (2c). The semantics of causation is a problem in and of itself. More generally, we should wonder whether the decomposition analysis captures the full range of syntactic and semantic properties of the expression. In the literature, this issue has been extensively discussed in relation to the analysis of verbs like *kill* as 'cause to cease to be alive' or *open* as 'cause to be open'. In section 2.2, we will see that these expressions are not really synonymous.

More generally, the question arises how many features we need in the description of natural language, and how 'atomic' they are. Ideally, a decompositional analysis should be based on a relatively small and and least finite set of features. In reality, it seems that we need another feature for every state that is described by an adjective or a noun. Aside from the general features [± MALE], [± ADULT], etc. there always seems to be a residue of meaning that needs a very specific description. (2a) analyzes a girl as a young woman, a kitten as a young cat, a calf as a young cow. The notions of womanhood, cathood, or cowhood do not seem to be further reducible. The set of atomic features that would be necessary to describe such lexical items is quite big.

In order to avoid endless discussions on the nature and number of semantic features, many modern theories of lexical semantics abandon the use of lexical decomposition in favor of more direct relations between concepts. An approach which is close in spirit to the feature analysis, but which avoids the problem of the residual meaning involves the introduction of meaning postulates. Meaning postulates formulate constraints on the relations between lexical items by limiting the class of admissible models one can use for the interpretation of the language. The notion of model of interpretation will be formally introduced in chapter 4 below. What we can say informally is that a model gives us a picture of the part of the world against which we want to evaluate the linguistic expression. The restriction to admissible models which satisfy semantic constraints on lexical items implies that we cannot come up with an interpretation for a sentence involving *kill* or *keep* without respecting the causative meaning component of the verb, because our interpretation function will rule out such interpretations as inadmissible in the model. Meaning postulates and similar notions are thus abstract characterizations of the speaker's knowledge which are used to structure lexical information.

Structured approaches to the lexicon can also capture certain semantic intuitions about the well-formedness of linguistic expressions. A lexical decomposition approach can explain the following semantic anomalies in terms of conflicting features:

(3)  a.  My uncle is pregnant.
     b.  This stone is dead.
     c.  My husband is a bachelor.

An approach in terms of meaning postulates or general constraints would rule out these sentences because they cannot be interpreted in a model which respects the lexical properties of the words involved.

The results of lexical semantics play an important role in psychology and cognitive science (think about language processing and knowledge representation). However, it is clear that we have to go beyond the meaning of words if we want to grasp the meaning of sentences. If all we knew was that *Jim* and *Sally* are proper names referring to individuals and *to hit* is a relation of striking, we would be unable to describe the difference in meaning between (4a) and (4b):

(4)  a.  Jim hit Sally.
     b.  Sally hit Jim.

We conclude that the meaning of a sentence is not only determined by the meaning of the words of which it is composed, but also by its grammatical structure. In (4), the word order rules of English determine which NP is the subject and which one the object of the sentence. The grammatical structure relates to the *argument structure* of the verb. The argument structure is specified in terms of *thematic roles* of the participants in the action. In (4), the subject maps onto the agent of the action (the 'hitter'), and the object onto the patient (the 'hittee'). The influence of grammatical structure on sentence meaning implies that the scope of a semantic theory of natural language must go beyond lexical semantics. The emphasis of the rest of this book will be on the semantics of phrases and sentences, more than on the semantics of words. However, we will presuppose a lexicon that is structured by means of meaning postulates, and use that as the basis of our model. An important motivation in favor of this view is the observation that there are interesting connections between argument structure and grammatical structure, which suggest that we have to take the idea of 'projection' from the lexicon seriously. The intuition that the thematic roles are somehow tied to argument positions in the syntactic structure is the basis of the projection principle of generative grammar (Chomsky 1982). Grammarians hold different views about the division of labor between the lexicon and the syntax. More radically lexicalist theories are developed by LFG and HPSG. The reader is referred to Neidler (1996) and Sadler (1996) for a general overview of the principles of LFG and Dalrymple et al. 1995 for a collection of papers. An introduction to HPSG as developed by Pollard and Sag (1994) is presented by Cooper (1996). Strong connections between lexical semantics and syntactic structure are also found in the work by Jackendoff (1983, 1990), Dowty (1991), Goldberg (1995), Levin and Rappaport Hovav (1995) and others.

When semanticists turned their attention from the meaning of words to the meaning of sentences (see section 2.2 below), lexical semantics was no longer the focus of attention. However, with the rise of computational linguistics, lexical semantics made an important comeback. The importance of a structured lexicon in natural language understanding, automatic translation, and artifical intelligence stimulated fruitful research on the integration of lexical properties into a more general theory of grammatical and encyclopedic knowledge. Examples are the work by Kamp and Roßdeutscher (1994), Pustejovsky (1995), Saint-Dizier and Viegas (1995), etc.

## 2.2   From words to sentences: a historical intermezzo

If we adopt a historical perspective, we observe that for a long time the meaning of words was all there was in a linguistic approach to meaning. It is important to see why it took linguists so long to realize that the study of meaning goes beyond lexical semantics in order to appreciate the developments in semantic theory.

In the 19th century, the approach to language was strongly influenced by biological—in particular Darwinistic—principles. This favored a view of language as an organism and stimulated research about the classification of languages, which is quite understandable given the surge of interest in the Indo-European language family at that time. It further generated research about language change, the origin of natural language and the coming into being and extinction of languages. Bréal's (1899) *Essai de Sémantique* still reflects this focus on language development, but it is the first extensive study of meaning in its own right. Bréal's book is about word meaning and contains much information on how words change their reference over time. An English example of narrowing the meaning of a word over time is *meat*. Originally *meat* meant any solid consumable food, but now it is used to refer only to the edible flesh of animals. A word that became broader in use is *cool*. *Cool* refers to a low temperature, but was also in use as a slang word. As such, it was part of the professional jargon of jazz musicians, and referred to a specific artistic style of jazz. With the passage of time, the word has come to be applied to almost anything conceivable, not just music. But it still indicates approval of the thing in question, and it is still part of an informal speech style.

Once we get a feeling for the linguistic work of the 19th century, we start to appreciate the importance of Ferdinand de Saussure's Course in General Linguistics (1916) for its distinction between the diachronic and the synchronic study of language. Diachronic means 'across time', so this branch of linguistic research concentrates on the shifts and mutations of language over the years and centuries. Bréal's work can thus be characterized as a diachronic investigation of the meaning of words. Synchronic means 'with time', so in this perspective researchers study the structure of a language as a coherent, functioning system of communication at some frozen moment in time. For instance, a dictionary may make some occasional remarks about the archaic use of a certain word, but it essentially serves to specify the current meaning of the word at the time the dictionary is written. Accordingly, a dictionary from around 1997 will typically describe *meat* as 'edible flesh of an animal'. From Saussure onwards, linguistics has been strongly dominated by synchronic research. This textbook is also synchronic in nature.

Saussure introduced the notion of *signe* ('sign') as a combination of a *signifiant* (form, sound pattern) and a *signifié* (meaning, concept). He emphasized that the relation between signifiant and signifié is arbitrary and based on convention . There is nothing inherent about dogs which motivates the English calling them 'dogs'. This is confirmed by the fact that the French refer to a dog as *un chien*, whereas the Germans use *ein Hund*. Not only is the relation between the sound and the meaning of a word conventional, the same is true for the grammatical structure of a natural language. If we assume that the core of a transitive sentence consists of a verb (V), a subject (S) and an object (O), there are in principle six different orders in which they can occur: VSO, SVO, OSV, etc. Given that we find all six orders realized in natural languages around the world (albeit not with the same frequency), the conclusion must be that there is no intrinsic natural order for verbs and their arguments. Communication can rely on conventionality because language is a social construct.

Saussure further established a distinction between *langue* ('language') and *parole* ('speech'). By *langue* Saussure meant the language faculty, or language as a linguistic structure, a linguistic system shared by a language community. The notion of *parole* refers to the combinations through which the individual speaker uses the code provided by the language to express his own thoughts. The true object of linguistic study is the *langue*, not the *parole*. Saussure pointed out that language is more than a list of words or signs. He characterized language as a system and highlights the relations between signs. He distinguished between 'paradigmatic' and 'syntagmatic' relations. The former focus on relations of signs with other signs in a paradigm (compare this to what we have been saying about paradigms and semantic networks in section 2.1 above), and the latter on the relations of signs with other signs in their structural environment (phrases and sentences). Syntagmatic relations play a role in the study of inflectional and derivational morphology, of complex word formation and of phrases which consist of fixed combinations of words such as *s'il vous plaît* 'if you please', so they are clearly part of the *langue*. Sentences seem to be on the borderline of language and speech for Saussure. On the one hand, sentences uttered by individual speakers have a high degree of freedom of combination of words and phrases, which is a characteristic of speech. On the other hand, sentences are constructed on regular patterns, the types of which belong to the langue. As a result of the emphasis on signs, the European research of the first half of the 20th century mainly studied the paradigmatic relations and the 'local' syntagmatic relations between signs. It is not until the rise of generative grammar that the sentence as a whole became the centerpiece of linguistics. Chomsky's distinction between competence and performance, introduced in chapter 1 is closely related to Saussure's distinction between langue and parole. However, the construction of well-formed sentences is clearly part of the native speaker's knowledge of his/her native language in Chomsky's view. This generated new research with a strong emphasis on the structure of phrases and sentences.

In the United States, the linguistic research around the turn of the century was also influenced by the biological approach to language, but the most important things that separated the American linguists from their European colleagues were the emphasis on field work and the interest in the variety of languages, which arose out of the study of native American languages. Boas and his students studied languages 'in their natural habitat', and because of the absence of written records, the focus was naturally on synchronic, rather than diachronic research.

As far as semantics is concerned, the most influential linguist was probably Bloomfield, whose behaviorism dominated the linguistic scene in the second quarter of the 20th century (see Bloomfield 1933, 1936). Behaviorism is a school of psychology that rejects the study of the mind as unscientific. All animal and human behavior should instead be explained in terms of stimulus-response conditioning. Bloomfield was influenced by Saussure's work, which established the link between European and American research. Bloomfield's interest in American Indian languages concerned the phonological and morphological structure, not its mental or cultural aspects. But unlike Saussure, Bloomfield rejected the study of linguistic meaning altogether, on the grounds that it required introspection and was thus not rigorous enough to allow scientific investigation.

Neither the European nor the American linguists had much to say about syntax, the structure of sentences. A full-fledged theory of syntax only started to emerge with generative grammar in the 1950's/1960's. Given the anti-mental, positivist attitude of those days, it is not surprising that the early days of generative grammar were devoted to phonology, morphology and syntax. Sound patterns, phrase structure rules and transformations were 'objective' enough to fit into a behaviorist-type theory, but meaning was still too 'subjective' to be a respectable discipline. Chomsky (1957, 1965) managed to bring parts of the study of meaning back into linguistics by focusing on semantic issues which can be explained in syntactic terms. For instance, the ambiguity in a sentence like 'Flying planes can be dangerous' can be resolved by assigning the sentence two different syntactic structures (see the discussion of the sentences in (10) below for further illustration of this point). Also, Chomsky used transformations on syntactic structures and specifically discussed the effect of transformations on the meaning of the sentence. The revived interest in meaning led to the development of interpretive semantics (Katz and Fodor 1964) and from there to generative semantics, with Postal, McCawley, Lakoff and Ross as the main leading figures in the second half of the '60s. The core idea of an interpretive semantics is that we first develop syntactic structures that represent sentences and then turn these structures into semantic representations. Generative semantics on the other hand, develops devices that generate meanings and map these meanings onto syntactic structures. Lexical decomposition as introduced in section 2.1 above was used to identify the components of meaning. The basic components were put together to project meaning onto structurally complex expressions. E.g. *to kill* was analyzed as 'cause to die' and *to die* as 'cease to be alive'. The lexical item was derived from these components by means of projection rules, which built on a fully explicit syntactic structure. This meant for instance that the meaning components 'cause' and 'open' were combined in a tree-like structure, and used as the basis to build up the syntactic and semantic representation of a sentence like 'John opened the door'. Thus, there was no distinction between building up the meaning of lexical items and the meaning of sentences (see Fodor 1977 for an overview of semantic theory in generative grammar and Harris 1993 for a historical perspective).

Generative semantics failed for a number of reasons. Partly, the theory was just too vague, and the researchers involved did not manage to build an overall, systematic theory of meaning. Partly, there were serious problems with the basic ideas, in particular with the fact that generative semantics did not establish a firm distinction between syntax and the lexicon. The notion of lexical insertion in a transformational grammar raised problems for such minimal pairs as (5):

(5)  a.   John cleaned the jacket again.
     b.   John caused the jacket to be clean again.

Suppose that John's jacket was bought new, and in a clean state, but no one ever cleaned the jacket before John bought it. It eventually got dirty, and John cleaned it. Then it would seem that (5a) is false, while (5b) is true. So in a case like (5), both the complex predicate construction and the lexicalized verb are possible, but they differ in meaning. Similar differences in meaning exist between a verb like *to remind* and its lexical decomposition as 'to strike as similar'. If they were really equivalent, we would expect (6b) to be as contradictory as (6a), but it is not:

(6)  a.   Jane strikes me as being similar to Hillary Clinton, but Jane does not strike me as being similar to Hillary Clinton.
     b.   Jane reminds me of Hillary Clinton, but Jane does not strike me as being similar to Hillary Clinton.

A person can remind me of someone else without striking me as being similar to that person. Although the meanings are close, they are not strictly equivalent, which explains why (6a), but not (6b) leads to a contradictory statement.

In other cases, one or the other construction may not be acceptable. Consider (7):

(7)  a.   Andrew caused Xander to die on Sunday by stabbing him on Saturday.
     b.   *Andrew killed Xander on Sunday by stabbing him on Saturday.

(7a) is perfectly acceptable, but (7b) is semantically anomalous. (7a) expresses that Xander's death took place on Sunday, and was caused by Andrew stabbing him on Saturday. With *cause to die*, each of the two adverbial phrases can attach to the verb it modifies. With the verb *to kill*, however, we do not have access to the processes of causing and dying separately. The delay in (7) between the cause and the effect makes it impossible to use the single verb *kill*.

The difference between pairs like those in (8) also needs to be explained:

(8)   a.   Xander died in agony.
      b.   *Xander ceased to be alive in agony.

If we analyze *to die* as 'cease to be alive', we cannot explain why one can die in agony, but not cease to be alive in agony. The adverbial modifier *in agony* characterizes the way in which Xander undergoes the process of leaving his earthly body. The comparison of (8a) and (b) suggests that *to die*, but not its proposed lexical decomposition, covers the process leading up to the moment of death as well as the actual change from being alive to being not alive.

In the late '60s, Chomsky started arguing against transformational analyses within the lexicon, such as the derivation of nominalizations like *refusal* from the verb *refuse*. The general idea was to disallow transformations to change the syntactic category of an expression. In Chomsky's view, lexical items are to be considered as atoms, and morphological relations such as those between verbs and nominalizations are not to be governed by transformations. Accordingly, Chomsky (1970) introduced a strict separation between syntax and the lexicon. This move oriented generative grammar away from the transformational style projection rules developed by generative semantics. The hypothesis of lexical integrity put an end to the explosion of uncontrollable transformations and led researchers to formulate constraints on transformations. However, it also led to a view according to which syntax was considered the core of grammar and semantics was more marginal. The only aspects of meaning incorporated in the later developments of generative grammar were those which could somehow be reduced to syntax. Semantics was strictly taken as interpretive semantics. As we saw above, this means that we first develop syntactic structures that represent sentences and then turn these structures into semantic representations. The interpretation of a sentence is thus built on top of the complete structure. Note that this is not the only view we can have of the relation between syntax and semantics. As we briefly discussed in section 1.3 above, and as we will see in more detail in section 2.4.1 below, Montague grammar builds up syntactic structure and semantic interpretation in parallel at every stage of the derivation. However, an interpretive semantics fits in better with the overall design of generative grammar, and both interpretive and generative semanticists crucially sought to establish a semantic theory as an integral component of a theory of (generative) grammar. The failure of generative semantics, and the strong emphasis on syntactic structure in the interpretive approach to semantics led most linguists to give higher priority to the study of synax. As a result, the study of meaning was again marginalized in linguistics, notwithstanding the important contributions made by the authors mentioned, and closely related work by Gruber (1965), Fillmore (1968), and others.

It seems then that, for some reason or other, linguists have often been hesitant to consider the study of meaning as an integral part of the theory of grammar, especially when the study of meaning carries us beyond lexical semantics. Therefore it is perhaps not surprising that the study of the meaning of larger structures of natural language has been strongly influenced by philosophical and logical traditions of semantics. With the formalization of propositional and predicate logic around the turn of the century, logicians had powerful tools to offer to anyone interested in the meaning of natural language. We will have more to say about this type of approach in later chapters.

## 2.3   Meaning at the sentence level

With the failure of generative semantics in the back of our mind we see that it is a real step forward to extend the study of meaning to larger structural units such as entire sentences. Since sentences are composed of words and phrases, we can expect certain semantic properties and relations of words and phrases to carry over to sentences. However, as traditional grammarians put it, a sentence (as opposed to a single word or phrase) expresses a 'complete thought'.

This suggests that sentences have a unique function over and beyond the words that make up the sentence, and that we may expect to find semantic properties and relations that are unique to sentences.

### 2.3.1   Similarities between meaning at the word level and meaning at the sentence level

First, we observe that the same principles which play a role in lexical semantics are important at the sentence-level. For instance, sentences can also be synonymyous (9):

(9)   a.   It is easy to please John.
      b.   John is easy to please.

The sentences in (9) differ in syntactic structure, but there is no difference in meaning between them. Thus they are appropriately characterized as synonymous. Similarly, it is easy to see that sentences can be ambiguous, just like words can be ambiguous. Examples are in (10):

(10) a. The bat was found in the attic.
　　 b. Intelligent students and faculty members presented papers at the conference.
　　 c. Mary made her dress correctly.
　　 d. A student accompanied every visitor.

(10a) is an example of lexical ambiguity: the noun *bat* can describe a nocturnal flying mammal with long forelimbs and digits that support a thin wing membrane, or it can refer to a stick or club for striking the ball in baseball or a similar game.

The sentence is ambiguous because the word *bat* is ambiguous. *Lexical ambiguity* is highly dependent on the language involved. A translation of the sentence into another language might force you to actually use two different lexical items. French for instance uses the two words *chauve-souris* and *batte* to refer to the flying mammal and the stick, respectively. Lexical ambiguities raise considerable problems for natural language processing and automatic translation: the program has to come with instructions on how to choose the right word in the right context. In many cases, it will help to look at the meaning of other words in the sentence, e.g:

(11) a. The sheep were in the pen.
　　 b. I left the pen on the table.

It is quite unlikely that sheep are found in writing instruments, and an enclosure for animals is not normally something one can leave on a table. However, as (10a) illustrates, not all sentences provide enough information to disambiguate the word. Both the flying mammal and the stick can reasonably be expected to be found in an attic. In such cases, we have to consider the larger linguistic context in order to determine which interpretation to choose. The interested reader is referred to Hobbs et al. (1993) and Asher and Lascarides (1995) for more discussion of lexical disambiguation in a discourse context.

(10b) is an example of structural or *syntactic ambiguity*. There are different ways in which we can organize the words into constituents, and they lead to distinct interpretations. We can represent the groupings with brackets, and show that different bracketings give rise to distinct syntactic structures. For example (11a), this is illustrated in (12):

(12)   a.   [[Intelligent students] and faculty members] presented papers at the conference.

          b.   [Intelligent [students and faculty members]] presented papers at the conference.

(12a) takes *intelligent* to modify the students. We read *and* as conjoining the intelligent students with the faculty members. This means that we do not say anything about the intelligence of faculty members. (12b) first conjoins the students and the faculty, and take *intelligent* to be a modifier of the complex noun. This configuration requires both the students and the faculty members to be intelligent. The ambiguity spelled out in (11a) is a structural ambiguity because the source of the different meanings is the syntactic structure assigned to the sentence.

(11c) illustrates a combination of syntactic and lexical ambiguity. The two interpretations are associated with quite different syntactic structures. In one case *her dress* is like *her skirt*, and the adverb *correctly* modifies the verb *make* and the sentence expresses that the way in which Mary made the dress is correct. In the other case *her dress* is like *her put on clothes*, and the adverb *correctly* modifies the verb *to dress*, so that the sentence involves Mary ordering a female person to dress in a correct way.

(11d) illustrates that sentences can be ambiguous even though there is no ambiguity in lexical items or in syntactic structure. (10d) can mean that there is one specific student who accompanied every visitor, or that every visitor is accompanied by a (possibly different) student. The ambiguity is characterized as a difference in scope. In chapter 4, the notion of scope will get a formal characterization. Informally, we can say that scope is a relational notion, where the interpretation of one expression depends on another one in a certain way. If the students in (11d) vary with the visitors, we say that *every visitor* has scope over *a student*. If we hold the student fixed, and make *every visitor* the dependent element, we say that *a student* has scope over *every visitor*. The difference in scope does not correspond with an ambiguity in any of the lexical items involved. It does not correlate either with distinct bracketings similar to the structures illustrated in (12). Purely *semantic ambiguities* of this kind are a notorious problem for any theory of meaning, because of the difficult questions they raise about the relation between syntax and semantics. Not surprisingly therefore, scope ambiguities play an important role in linguistic theory, and we will spend much of chapter 5) on discussion of this issue. Scope relations illustrate a certain dependency of one expression on another. Other kinds of dependencies involve anaphorical relations. As already pointed out in chapter 1, they raise similar problems about the relation between syntax, semantics and pragmatics. In section 2.3.2 we will look somewhat more precisely at some problems in the syntax-semantics interface.

## 2.3.2 Syntax-semantics interface

One general difference between studies in the meaning of words and studies of meaning at the sentence-level is the focus on content words or open-class forms like *bird, blue, write* in the former, and the emphasis on function words or closed-class forms like *the, and, because, to* in the latter. Roughly, content words are like the bricks with which you build a house, whereas function words are like the cement used to hold them together. In many cases, the structural properties of sentences determine their meaning to a considerable degree, and function words play an important role in the grammatical structure. As a result, some of the properties of natural language a semanticist is interested in are studied by syntacticians as well. One of the shared topics concerns anaphoric relations. In chapter 1, we already pointed out that pronouns are semantically incomplete in the sense that their meaning cannot be fully determined by looking at the expression itself. In order to interpret an anaphor, we need to find its antecedent. In many cases, there are strict syntactic constraints on the domain in which we can look for the antecedent of an anaphor. Some straightforward cases of anaphor-antecedent dependencies within the sentence are given by the reflexive and personal pronouns in (13):

(13)    a.   Hans shaves himself.
           b.   Hans thinks that he is brilliant.

In (13a), the reflexive pronoun *himself* is dependent for its interpretation on the subject Hans. The sentence cannot be used to express that someone other than Hans was shaved. Given that the reflexive pronoun must refer to the same individual as the subject, we say that the reflexive pronoun is obligatorily *coreferential* with *Hans*. For the personal pronoun in (13b) there is no such obligation. In a discussion about the winner of this year's Nobel prize in physics, someone can utter (13) to express the idea that Hans thinks this year's winner of the Nobel prize in physics is brilliant. We call this the deictic interpretation of the pronoun, for it can refer to anyone who is salient in the context or the situation. However, the sentence can also be used to mean that Hans thinks of himself as a brilliant person. We conclude that the personal pronoun *he* in (13b) can but need not be coreferential with the subject of the main clause. As pointed out in chapter 1, the correct identification of the antecedent of a pronoun involves a process of anaphora resolution. As we have already seen, it is current practice in linguistics to use subscripts to indicate the relation between anaphor and antecedent by co-indexing the two expressions:

(14)  a.  Hans$_i$ shaves himself$_i$.
      b.  Hans$_i$ thinks that he$_i$ is brilliant.

Co-indexing is a syntactic device, but it has consequences for the interpretation. If a reflexive or a personal pronoun is co-indexed with a proper name as in (14), it is interpreted as being coreferential with the individual the proper name refers to. Co-indexing cannot always be interpreted as coreferentiality. This would not be appropriate in cases like (15):

(15)  a.  [Every linguist]$_i$ thinks that he$_i$ is brilliant.
      b.  Nobody$_i$ hates himself$_i$.

An expression like *every linguist* does not refer to a particular individual, so the pronoun *he* cannot be taken to refer to the same individual. This may be even clearer from an NP like *nobody* in (15b). Such expressions as *every linguist* and *nobody* are traditionally referred to as *quantificational* or *quantified* NPs, because they involve quantities rather than qualities. They say something about a the number of objects concerned and do not refer to particular individuals. The co-indexing in (15) cannot be interpreted as co-referentiality, because there is no individual both the antecedent and the anaphoric pronoun can refer to. We say that in such cases co-indexing indicates *binding*. Binding means that the reference of the pronoun varies systematically with the choice of the individual determined by the quantifier. For instance, suppose that our set of linguists consists of Mary, Sue and Bill. In that context, we can spell out (15a) as saying that Mary thinks that Mary is brilliant, Sue thinks that Sue is brilliant, and Bill thinks that Bill is brilliant. Similarly, (15b) means that Mary does not hate Mary, Sue does not hate Sue, Bill does not hate Bill, and for any other individual we can come up with, it is true that that individual does not hate himself or herself. The semantics of quantification and binding will be explained in more formal detail in chapter 4.

Coreferentiality and binding are clearly semantic notions: they say something about semantic relationships at the sentence level. On the other hand, it is well-known that the possibility of anaphoric relations is severely constrained by the syntax. We already observed that the relation between the reflexive pronoun and the subject in (13a) is much tighter than the relation between the personal pronoun and the subject in (13b).[1] Further

---

[1] This is an important reason for syntacticians to distinguish between *anaphors* like reflexives and reciprocals and *pronouns* such as *he, she, him, her*. Reflexives and reciprocals are obligatorily anaphoric, whereas personal pronouns always have the option of getting a deictic interpretation, as we observed above. Given that as semanticists we are interested in the constraints on the meaning of these expressions, we will not take up the syntactic terminology. For us, both *he* and *himself* are syntactically pronouns, and semantically either deictic or anaphoric expressions.

syntactic and semantic constraints involve the position of the anaphor with respect to its antecedent, compare (15) and (16):

(16)  a.   *Himself$_i$ shaves Hans$_i$.
      b.   *He$_i$ thinks that Hans$_i$ is brilliant.
      c.   His$_i$ mother always supports Hans$_i$.
      d.   When he$_i$ is tired, Hans$_i$ is often in a bad mood.
      e.   *His$_i$ mother loves every linguist$_i$.
      f.   *When he$_i$ is tired, every linguist$_i$ is in a bad mood.

(16a) and (b) suggest that an anaphor cannot precede its antecedent. However, (16c) and (d) show that this is too restrictive. Moreover, the contrast between (16c, d) and (e, f) points to further differences between coreference and binding. Work in syntactic theory has shown that hierarchy is more important than left-right order in the relation between an anaphor and its antecedent. This results in the claim that anaphors cannot *c-command* their antecedents. C-command is a relation defined on tree-like syntactic structures. An expression A c-commands an expression B if every branching node dominating A also dominates B. Intuitively, this requires A to be at least as high in the tree as B.[2] According to this definition, the subject c-commands the object in (16a) as shown in figure 2.1. However, the possessive pronoun in (16c) does not c-command the object in figure 2.2.

If we assume a syntactic constraint in terms of c-command, we can rule out the coindexing in (16a) as an ungrammatical antecedent-anaphor relation. We need to appeal to a semantic constraint in order to exclude cases in which a bound anaphor precedes but does not c-command its binder (16e,f), and accept cases in which the same syntactic structure is interpreted as coreferentiality (16c,d). The constraints on the antecedent-anaphor relation illustrate that semantic notions like coreferentiality and binding cannot be studied independently of the syntactic structure of the sentence.

### 2.3.3   Semantic inference

Aside from these syntax-semantics interface issues, there are aspects of meaning at the sentence level that are more exclusively of interest for semanticists. One of these properties is the notion of *truth*. Truth is only defined at the sentence level. Words and phrases have meanings and denotations, but only sentences are used to say something which is true or false.

---

[2]Instead of imposing configurational restrictions on binding, it is also possible to define constraints on lists of arguments structures in lexicalist theories such as HPSG. The result is essentially the same.

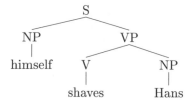

Figure 2.1: Reflexive pronoun that c-commands its antecedent

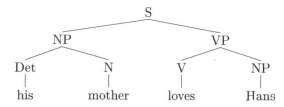

Figure 2.2: Pronoun not related by c-command to its antecedent

The interest in truth is motivated by our choice to develop a referential theory of meaning. In chapter 1 we observed that sentences say something about situations in the real world. A sentence is true if it correctly describes a particular situation, it is false if it does not. For instance, the sentence 'The door is open' is true in a certain context if the relevant door is indeed open, and false if the door is closed. Our desire to capture the aboutness of natural languages means that we want a theory of truth to be part of our theory of meaning. Note however, that truth is not to be confused with meaning: we know what the meaning is of a sentence, even if we are unable to determine its truth value. A blind-folded person may not be able to verify whether or not the door is open, but he/she has not therefore lost the meaning of the sentence 'The door is open'. As semanticists, we are not so much interested in actual truth or falsity, but in the conditions under which a sentence is true. If we know the meaning of a sentence like 'The door is open', we know what the world must look like in order to make the sentence true. Sentence meaning is thus more adequately formulated in terms of truth conditions. A theory of truth and truth conditions is used to determine the meaning of expressions which typically involve structural information relating sentences, such as the connectives *not, and, but*. Consider for instance the sentences in (17):

(17)  a.  Susan is not rich.
      b.  Carole lives in Paris, and Dave lives in London.
      c.  Ella likes spinach, but Phil prefers carrots.

The meaning of the words *not, and* and *but* is crucial to understand the meaning of the complex sentences in which they occur. (17a) is true if and only if the sentence 'Susan is rich' is false. Thus we can derive the truth value of the negative sentence in (17a) from its affirmative counterpart. Similarly, (17b) is true if and only if both the sentences 'Carole lives in Paris' and 'Dave lives in London' are true. We observe that the meaning of *not* and *and* can be strictly defined in terms of the truth value of the sentence(s) they combine with. Such connectives are called *truth-functional* connectives. The issues of truth, truth conditions, and the semantic constribution of connectives like *not, and*, etc. are taken up in more detail in chapter 3.

The meaning of *but* in (17c) is more complex. Truth-functionally, *but* is like *and* in that the sentences that are related by the connective both have to be true in order for the complex sentence to be true. However, *but* adds an element of contrast between the two sentences. The contrastive nature of *but* cannot be captured in terms of truth conditions, but it is characterized as a presupposition. Before we can define the notion of presupposition, we have to say a few words about truth relations more in general.

We do not only want truth properties, but also truth relations to fall within the scope of semantics. The central truth relation defined over sentences is *entailment*. One sentence is said to entail another sentence if the truth of the first guarantees the truth of the second, and the falsity of the second guarantees the falsity of the first. Entailment is the crucial property in inference patterns. For instance, if (18a) and (18b) are true of the same individual, we also know that (18c) is true:

(18)   a.   Hans is German.
       b.   Hans is a linguist.
       c.   Hans is a German linguist.
       d.   Hans is a German linguist, but he is not German.

We can say that (18a) and (b) together *entail* (18c), because the situation described by (18a) and (b) together is sufficient to describe the situation in (18c). In other words, whenever (18a) and (b) are true, (18c) must be true as well. (18c) all by itself entails both (18a) and (18b): the information that (18c) conveys is contained in the information that (18a) and (18b) contain. Note also that an utterance like (18d) is contradictory: if the first conjunct is true, the second conjunct can never be. Another example of entailment is given in (19):

(19)   a.   The children sang and danced.
       b.   The children sang.

The truth of (19a) allows us to conclude that (19b) is true. The falsity of (19b) guarantees the falsity of (19a).

Entailment is a semantic and not a syntactic notion. Sentences which are syntactically similar to the ones in (18) and (19) need not have the same entailment patterns. For instance, (20a) does not entail (20b), and neither does (21a) entail (21b):

(20)   a.   Hans is an alleged linguist.
        b.   Hans is a linguist and Hans is alleged.

(21)   a.   Few children sang and danced.
        b.   Few children sang and few children danced.

Entailment is a very strong version of what we can also call *implication* or *inference*. But the notions of implication and inference are sometimes used rather loosely to describe a situation in which one statement follows from another. We will only use entailment in the strict sense of semantic inference or preservation of truth in which it is defined here. Chapter 3 develops a formal definition of entailment in propositional logic.

A notion which is closely related to entailment is *presupposition*. Just like entailments, presuppositions are a kind of implication. If A presupposes B, then A not only implies B but also implies that the truth of B is somehow taken for granted, or is treated as uncontroversial. The term pre-supposition reflects the idea that the implication is background information, already part of the knowledge shared by speaker and hearer when the presupposition carrying expression is uttered in the discourse. Some examples will help to clarify the distinction between presupposition and entailment. For instance, (22a) presupposes (22b):

(22)   a.   Paul stopped smoking.
        b.   Paul smoked.

One can hardly stop smoking if one did not smoke before. A felicitous context in which we say about Paul that he stopped smoking is thus one in which both speaker and hearer know that Paul used to be a smoker before. Therefore, we say that for $x$ to stop V-ing presupposes that $x$ V-ed before.

We may wonder how we know that the relating between to stop V-ing and V-ing is one of presupposition or of entailment. We can test this by looking at embedded contexts. Embedding of the presupposition-carrying expression under different operations often maintains the presupposition. For instance, all the sentences in (23) preserve the presupposition that Paul smoked before:

(23) a. Paul stopped smoking.
     b. Paul didn't stop smoking.
     c. Did Paul stop smoking?
     d. I regret that Paul stopped smoking.

Given that the negative and interrogative sentences (23b) and (c) carry the same presupposition as the affirmative sentence (23a), we say that negation and interrogation are presupposition preserving environments. The presupposition is also preserved when the sentence is embedded under a predicate like *regret* (23d). Embedded contexts show that entailments and presuppositions are not the same. The examples in (23) show that presuppositions are typically preserved under negation and interrogation. Of course this is not true for entailment, because entailment is strictly defined in terms of preservation of truth. The difference is illustrated in (24). (24a) presupposes and entails (24c), whereas (24b) presupposes, but does not entail (24c):

(24) a. It was Jane who brought a cake.
     b. Was it Jane who brought a cake?
     c. Someone brought a cake.

A further difference between entailments and presuppositions is that semantics inferences are 'hard' implications that cannot simply be dropped. The entailment relation between (24a) and (24c) means that the truth of (24a) makes it impossible to claim the falsity of (24c). Presuppositions can be cancelled in certain contexts, though. (23b) is normally used to express the fact that Paul used to smoke before (presupposition), and hasn't stopped. However, (23b) can also express a meta-linguistic negation, as Horn (1989) calls it. Under that interpretation, negation is used to deny the truth of the presupposition: Paul didn't stop smoking, because he never smoked in the first place, so how could you claim he stopped. The fact that we can cancel a presupposition shows that this notion is weaker than that of entailment.

The cases we looked at so far showed that presuppositions were preserved in contexts in which entailments are lost. This might lead the reader to think that entailments are somehow subsumed under presuppositions. This is not the case. In (25), we see an example of an entailment relation which does not correspond with a presupposition:

(25) a. Jane bought a cake.
     b. Someone bought a cake.

(25a) entails, but does not presuppose (25b). That is, we do not need to have background knowledge about there being someone who bought a cake in order to felicitously interpret (25a).

Summing up, we define entailment as semantic inference, that is, preservation of truth. Presuppositions are background assumptions which guarantee the felicity of an utterance in a certain context. Both notions are defined as implications, which means that they overlap to some degree. However, we can keep them apart if we realize two things: unlike presuppositions, entailments do not have anything to do with background assumptions. Unlike entailments, presuppositions survive in certain embedded contexts.

Another notion of inference which is weaker than entailment, but relevant for the analysis of natural language is the notion of *implicature* introduced by Grice (1975). Some examples are given in (26):

(26) a. A is writing a testimonial about a pupil who is a candidate for a philosophy job and his letter reads as follows: 'Dear Sir, Mr. X's command of English is excellent, and his attention at tutorials has been regular. Yours, etc.'
*implicature:* X is not a great philosopher, don't hire him!
   b. Some students passed the exam.
*implicature:* Not all students passed the exam.
   c. Some students passed the exam. In fact, all did.

An implicature is clearly weaker than an entailment, because it is a non-logical inference, which comes about as a result of embedding the statement in a particular conversational context. Implicatures can typically be cancelled or suspended without generating a contradiction, as illustrated by (26c). Entailments cannot be cancelled or suspended in this way. In this book, we study only the strong form of implication we defined as entailment above. But it is important to realize that there are other, related notions of semantic and pragmatic inference. There is an extensive literature on presuppositions and implicatures. The reader is referred to Levinson (1983) for a general overview of pragmatic inference, and to Horn (1996) and Beaver (1997) for recent discussion of issues in the study of presuppositions and implicatures.

# 2.4 Constraints on a theory of meaning

## 2.4.1 Compositionality

It is a general property of natural languages that the number of sentences they can generate is infinite. This implies that the set of meanings is infinite as well. We can always construct a more complex sentence, for instance by embedding:

(27)   a.   Joan left.
     b.   Mary saw that Joan left.
     c.   Anne thought that Mary saw that Joan left.
     d.   Jane knew that Anne thought that Mary saw that Joan left.
     e.   ...

This example shows that the set of natural language sentences is in principle infinite. It also shows that natural language is *recursive*: at a certain point you can apply the same mechanism over and over again. This implies that it is impossible to give an exhaustive list of the sentences of a language, and therefore of the meanings of a language. One of the consequences of this observation is that a semantic theory that accounts for meaning relations at the sentence level cannot be formulated in the style of a feature based network. A feature-based theory adopts a relatively small, but at least finite set of features. A finite list of features is incapable of describing the infinite set of natural language meanings. The potential *infinity* and *creativity* is the main argument in favor of the view of syntax as a finite set of recursive rules for the generation of sentences. This is very similar to the fact that you may never have added up 1,437,952 and 21,840 in your life, but you can nevertheless tell that the correct outcome is 1,459,792, because you know something about numbers and you have an *algorithm* or rule for addition. In the same way, we have an algorithm for building larger linguistic units such as constituents and sentences out of words and morphemes. The argument is valid for semantics as well as for syntax. We need systematic ways to build up the meaning of a sentence out of the words and morphemes which compose it and the way they are combined. For instance, *tables, houses, books, students* all combine a noun with the morpheme *-s* to build a plural noun. We want to formulate this as a syntactic and a semantic rule of composition, rather than giving an exhaustive list of all the individual cases. Similarly, we want to generalize over cases like (28a) and (28b), and claim that in both cases the subject is assigned a certain property:

(28)   a.   Joan left.
     b.   Joan read a book.

In (28a), the property Joan has is given by an intransitive verb, so we can directly look up its meaning in the lexicon. In (28b), Joan has a complex property which needs to be further analyzed into a transitive verb and an object. However, syntactically and semantically the basic verb phrase (VP) *left* functions in the same way as the complex VP *read a book*. If we can build up the meaning of the complex VP in a compositional way, we can end up giving it a semantic representation which is of the same type as the semantic representation of the simple VP in (28a).

And if we wish to cross sentence boundaries and study discourse, we need an extension of the algorithm which builds up sentences in order to to build up the meaning of a sequence of sentences from the composing sentences and the way they are put together. This is why most semantic theories are built on the principle of *compositionality of meaning*:

- *Principle of Compositionality of Meaning*
  The meaning of the whole is a function of the meaning of its parts and the way they are put together

This heuristic principle reflects the intuition that complex meanings are not arbitrary, but can be systematically derived from their parts. If we accept the principle of compositionality, we need to formulate the rules which determine how meanings are put together to form larger units. The simplest way to define a compositional interpretation is to let the semantics run parallel to the syntax. After all, we know that we need a finite set of recursive rules to define all the possible well-formed expressions of a language. If every syntactic rule which tells us how to combine linguistic expressions to build a more complex expression has a corresponding semantic rule which defines the interpretation of the complex expression from the constituent parts, we have a fully compositional theory of meaning.

If we want to use the notion of compositionality of meaning in our study of the semantics of natural language (see Janssen 1997 for some arguments pro and contra), this deeply influences our view of linguistic theory. In particular, we need a syntactic theory which is set up in such a way that we can formulate (semantic) rules of interpretation for every (syntactic) construction rule. This is not something all syntactic theories allow us to do. Although the idea of syntax and semantics going hand in hand is at the heart of logical grammars like Montague grammar, most generative grammars in the Chomskyan tradition build up an entire syntactic tree before interpretation enters the picture. We have referred to this above as an interpretive semantics. As we will see later, the specific relation that a theory of grammar postulates between the syntax and the semantics of sentences has important consequences for the treatment of certain semantic phenomena, such as scope ambiguities (see chapter 5).

## 2.4.2   Object language and metalanguage

One of the problems which arise when we talk about language is that we have to use ... language. This leads to potentially confusing situations, as shown by (29a) and (29b):

(29)  a.   January has 31 days.
     b.   January has 7 letters.

(29a) is a normal statement about the month January, that is, about the abstract object denoted by the expression *January*. (29b) takes the same expression as a *name*, a linguistic object about which we state something at a meta-level. This means that we have to distinguish two different functions of language when we use language to talk about language. We have the *object language* (the language we talk about), and the *metalanguage* (the language in which we talk about the object language). One way to distinguish elements from object and metalanguage within one sentence is by typographic means as in (30a) or (30b):

(30)  a.   *January* has 7 letters.
     b.   'January' has 7 letters.

Expressions can be turned into names by putting them between quotation marks or writing them in italics. In these cases this works fine, but in other contexts the combination of object language and metalanguage in one utterance can lead to paradoxes such as the one in (31):

(31)   Sentence (31) is false.

This sentence can be neither true or false: if (31) is false, it should be true that (31) is false, but then, if it is true that (31) is false, then what the sentence states must be true and false at the same time. The paradox in (31) is known as the problem of self-reference, and was already known by the Stoics, Greek philosophers of around 400 B.C. It arises because the expression *sentence (31)* is embedded in a statement about itself which involves a truth predicate. A solution to the paradox was formulated by Tarski (1944), who introduced the methodological distinction between the object language and the metalanguage. Tarski's solution is to rule out the possibility that an object language contains self-referential expressions and that it contains its own truth predicate. If we define the truth predicate in a metalanguage different from the object language, paradoxes like the one in (31) no longer arise, because the sentence is not well-formed. For more discussion of the problems of self-reference and the related 'liar' paradox, see Barwise and Etchemendy (1987).

    Given that we are interested in a theory of truth as part of our theory of meaning, the paradoxes of self-reference require us to observe the distinction between metalanguage and object language. This means that we have to have a metalanguage which is different from the object language. Natural languages are rich enough to be able to say things about (other) natural languages, so in principle we could choose English, French, Russian, ... as a metalanguage to talk about the object language French, Russian, English, .... However, this is not usually the way we go about things. One reason is that we do not have as yet a complete analysis of the syntax and semantics of any natural language. But the truth of the semantic claims we want to make can only be established if we have at our disposal an explicit characterization of the metalanguage which is our 'tool' for the description of the object language. To phrase things in a very pessimistic way, this would mean that, as long as linguistics hasn't completed the syntactic and semantic description of any natural language, the vagueness of one natural language would only be translated into the vagueness of another one. Another important argument is that natural languages are ambiguous. That is, one (possibly complex) expression sometimes has more than one meaning (compare the ambiguous sentences in (10) again). Ambiguity is an interesting property of natural language, which we want to study as semanticists. But in order to make the different interpretations of an expression clear, we want to have a way to express them. If we use another natural language as a metalanguage, we might be in trouble, because they could also have ambiguities, which we would have to analyze in another language, which again, etc. The result is clearly an infinite regression. Therefore, it is useful to use a precise and unambiguous language as our metalanguage. This is why semanticists often use formal languages as the metalanguage. The languages of algebra and logic are fully explicit and unambiguous, so we know exactly which expressions do and do not constitute well-formed expressions and what will be the interpretation they get. They are also fully compositional and allow recursion. This gives us a very powerful mechanism to describe natural language. Some of the most widely used formal languages are propositional logic and first order predicate logic. We will discuss their properties and their use in the analysis of the meaning of natural language expresssions in chapters 3 to 5 below.

## 2.5 Exercises

(1)! Suppose someone were to claim the following: "Given some combination of phonemes, we can *never* predict the meaning of the combination; given some combination of morphemes, we can *sometimes* predict the meaning of the combination; given some combination of words into a sentence, if we know the words and their grammatical relations, we can *always* predict the meaning of the sentence." Criticize or defend this claim in terms of evidence presented in this chapter and your own ideas. Motivate your argument with real language examples.

(2)! Compound words such as *high chair*, *sailboat* or *outhouse* show a high degree of nonarbitrariness in their form-meaning connection. Comment on the way the meaning of these words is built up. Is is possible to derive the meaning in a fully compositional way? Not all compound words show complete nonarbitrariness in their meaning-form connection (anymore). Think about the color of objects we call *blueprints*, what we find in a *bathroom*, what the *landlord* owns, etc. Explain the relation between arbitrariness and non-arbitrariness of the meaning-form relation in these examples.

(3)! The word *bar* is ambiguous.

   (i) Describe the two (major) senses of the word *bar*.

Consider the disambiguation of the word *bar* in the context of the discourse in (I):

I   a. The judge asked where the defendant was.
    b. The barrister apologized and said he was at the pub across the street.
    c. The court bailiff found him slumped underneath the bar.

Answer the following questions:

   (ii) Sentence (Ic) all by itself could still be ambiguous. Explain informally, but as precisely as possible why *bar* cannot have the courtroom sense given the context set up by (Ia) and (b), but must have the pub sense here.

   (iii) Explain why a theory that takes domain information (e.g., associations between words that appear closely together) would predict that the courtroom sense of *bar* would be preferred here.

   (iv) Explain why a theory which takes only domain information cannot explain the difference between the preferred interpretations of (I) and (II):

II   a. The judge asked where the defendant was.
     b. The barrister apologised, and said he was at the pub across the street.
     c. But suddenly, his whereabouts were revealed by a loud snore.
     d. The court bailiff found him slumped underneath the bar.

(4) Synonymy is rarely absolute in the sense that the two expressions are identical in all their meanings and synonymous in all contexts. For each of the pairs of expressions in (i)–(iii), give an example in which the meaning of the two expressions is not fully identical in some context and an example of a context in which the use of one of the two expressions is not likely or even impossible.

(i)! big/large

(ii) fragrance/smell

(iii) unmarried/not married

(5) English has a prefix -un, whose use is illustrated in the following lists:

List A

| true | — | untrue |
| likely | — | unlikely |
| natural | — | unnatural |
| acceptable | — | unacceptable |

List B

| tie | — | untie |
| cover | — | uncover |
| dress | — | undress |
| fold | — | unfold |

In what way does the prefix un change the meaning of the word that it attaches to in lists A and B? In both cases, describe the meaning change as carefully as possible, and comment on differences in the meaning change you find between lists A and B.

(6) The sentences in (i) through (iv) are all ambiguous:

(i)! He fed her dog biscuits.

(ii) I'd like you to take out the garbage.

(iii) Susan didn't buy two books.

(iv) Jane told me that she was very unhappy.

Give unambiguous paraphrases of the two (or more) different readings each sentence has. Explain whether the ambiguity is syntactic, semantic or pragmatic in nature (or a combination of any of these kinds of ambiguities).

(7) Consider the following pairs of sentences:

(i)! a. That John was assaulted scared Mary.
    b. John was assaulted.

(ii) a. Is John not aware that Mary is pregnant?
    b. Mary is pregnant.

(iii) a. Some Italian is a violinist
     b. Bernardo is an Italian violinist.

(iv) a. If I discover that Mary is in New York, I will get angry.
     b. Mary is in New York.

(v) a. It is possible that Clinton will return to Arkansas.
    b. Clinton was in Arkansas before.

There is a relation of presupposition and/or entailment between the (a) and (b) sentences in some of these pairs. Say which relation(s) hold(s) (if there is one), and explain in a few lines why it is an entailment or a presupposition.

(8) Underline the elements of the object language (if there are any) in (i)–(v):

(i)! Keynes rhymes with brains.

(ii) He is a linguist.

(iii) He is a personal pronoun.

(iv) The sentence he is a personal pronoun has five words.

(v) Snow is white is true if and only if snow is white.

# Chapter 3

# Connectives, truth, and truth conditions

We use logical languages as metalanguages to talk about natural language. This lecture introduces the syntax and semantics of propositional logic. We adopt the correspondence theory of truth and discuss the notions of truth in a model and truth conditions for propositions. Furthermore, we will see how propositional logic handles tautological/contradictory statements and how relations between propositions (inference patterns) are accounted for.

## 3.1    Reasoning patterns

We use logical languages as metalanguages to talk about natural language. As logic is often defined as the science of reasoning, it is not surprising that one of its central concerns is the study of valid arguments. Such a reasoning pattern is structured as a series of one or more propositions which constitute the *premises*, followed by a *conclusion*. In a valid argument, the truth of the premises guarantees the truth of the conclusion: if the premises are all true, then the conclusion must be true as well. The validity of an argument is independent from the actual truth or falsity of the premises. It is the form of the reasoning pattern which determines validity, not the content of the premises or the conclusion. The language of *propositional logic* is useful to analyze inference patterns such as:

(1)  a.  If it snows, it is cold.
         It snows.
         Therefore: it is cold.

     b.  If John is in love, he is happy.
         John is not happy.
         Therefore: John is not in love.

The examples in (1) involve *syllogisms*, which typically consist of two premises followed by a conclusion. The examples in (1) suggest that at least certain valid arguments are concerned with relations between sentences, and not with the internal structure of sentences. In other words, for any two sentences $S_1$ and $S_2$, we can construct valid arguments of the form:

(2)  a.  If $S_1$, then $S_2$.
         $S_1$.
         Therefore: $S_2$.

     b.  If $S_1$, then $S_2$.
         It is not the case that $S_2$.
         Therefore: It is not the case that $S_1$.

Propositional logic is designed to deal with patterns like the ones in (2). These arguments typically involve sentential connectives like *not, or, if ... then*, etc. The validity of the natural language argument in (1) is accounted for by providing a translation of the argument into propositional logic. This will look like a somewhat more formal version of (2). If the translation is a perfect match, the proof that the argument is valid (or invalid) in propositional logic extends to the proof of the validity (or invalidity) of the argument in natural language. Another advantage of a propositional logical translation is that it highlights the underlying form of the natural language reasoning patterns in contexts like (1), as illustrated by the more general format of (2).

Like any language, a propositional logical language comes with a *syntax* and a *semantics*, so we distinguish between form and content. On the syntactic side, we find notions like the *atoms* (primitives) of the language, the rules for the construction of (atomic and complex) *well-formed formulas* (abbreviated as wff), and *rules of inference* which allow the construction of *proofs* from premises. As far as the semantics is concerned, we need to define truth, truth conditions, entailment and the general notion of interpretation of propositions in a model.

## 3.2 Syntax of propositional logic: propositions and connectives

The *syntax* of propositional logic involves a set of primitives and a set of (recursive) construction rules which define well-formed formulas. We assume an infinite basic vocabulary of atomic propositions represented by the symbols $p$, $q, r, s \ldots$ Atomic propositions correspond to simple, non-complex (declarative) sentences such as those in (3):

(3)  a.  It is raining.
     b.  Mary is intelligent.

The following definition tells us what counts as a well-formed formula in propositional logic. ($\phi, \psi, \ldots$ are used as meta-variables over propositions):

- Syntax

  (i)  Any atomic proposition is itself a well-formed formula (wff).

  (ii)  If $\phi$ is a wff, then $\neg\phi$ is a wff.

  (iii)  If $\phi$ and $\psi$ are wff, then $(\phi \wedge \psi)$, $(\phi \vee \psi)$, $(\phi \to \psi)$ and $(\phi \leftrightarrow \psi)$ are wff.

  (iv)  Nothing else is a wff.

$\neg\phi$ is said to be the negation of $\phi$. $(\phi \wedge \psi)$ is the conjunction of $\phi$ and $\psi$. $(\phi \vee \psi)$ is the disjunction of $\phi$ and $\psi$. $(\phi \to \psi)$ is the conditional and roughly corresponds to '$\phi$ implies $\psi$', or 'if $\phi$ then $\psi$'. Finally, $(\phi \leftrightarrow \psi)$ is the bi-conditional, which means that $\phi$ implies $\psi$ and vice versa, or '$\phi$ if and only if (iff) $\psi$'. This informal description of the meaning of the connectives is just for convenience. A formal definition of the semantics of the connectives is provided in 3.4 below. The set of syntactic rules recursively defines the full set of well-formed formulas in the language of propositional logic in an explicit and unambiguous way. In order to get a feeling for the generative capacity of these rules, here are some examples of what formulas of propositional logic may look like:

(4)  a.  $(p \vee \neg q)$
     b.  $\neg (p \wedge \neg q)$
     c.  $((((p \wedge q) \vee \neg r) \to s) \leftrightarrow t)$

And some examples of what they may **not** look like:

(5)  a.  $\vee q$
     b.  $\neg \wedge p q$
     c.  $p \vee q \to r$

(5a) is bad because disjunction is a two-place connective, and this formula is missing a disjunct. (5b) is ill-formed because negation can only operate on propositions, not on other connectives. Furthermore, a connective like conjunction can have only one propositional variable on each side. The problem with (5c) is that we do not know whether the disjunction of $p$ and $q$ constitutes the antecedent of the conditional, or whether the conditional as a whole is the second disjunct in the formula. This shows that the brackets in formulas of propositional logic are important. For instance, (6a) and (b) are both well-formed formulas, but they are different in form and meaning:

(6)  a.  $(p \lor (q \to r))$
     b.  $((p \lor q) \to r)$

As a general rule, we put brackets around two-place connectives, but not around the one-place connective negation.

## 3.3   Semantics of propositional logic: truth, and truth conditions

Propositions do not always correspond to one and only one sentence. Synonymous sentences such as (7a) and (7b) express the same proposition:

(7)  a.  Paris is the capital of France.
     b.  Paris is France's capital.

Ambiguous sentences such as (8) express different propositions:

(8) Mary said that John saw her dress.

Atomic propositions describe states of affairs, that is, situations which may or may not be the case in a particular context. The semantics of propositional logic is thus defined in terms of *truth values*. Every atomic proposition can take one of two truth values: 1 (true) or 0 (false). A proposition is true if and only if (iff) it correctly describes some state of affairs. This theory of truth was developed by Tarski (1944). It is referred to as the *correspondence theory of truth*, because it defines truth of a proposition in terms of its correspondence with the facts in the outside world. That is, the sentence 'it is raining' is true iff it is raining. The correspondence theory of truth relates language and reality, and is thus typically part of a referential theory of meaning.

Atomic propositions are expressed by declarative sentences that make statements. Of course, natural language has many sentences which cannot be said to be true or false. Consider for instance questions, imperatives and exclamatives:

(9)  a.  Did Eve pass the semantics exam?
     b.  Who opened the door?
     c.  Stop talking!
     d.  What a mess!

Sentences like these are neither true nor false: they just don't express atomic propositions that have a truth-value. This does not imply that they are *meaningless*: they clearly do have a well-determined meaning. It also does not mean that semantics has nothing to say about the meaning of these sentences. One way of looking at the interpretation of questions is to say that they denote a context-dependent proposition (Groenendijk and Stokhof 1984). In this perspective, (9a) denotes the proposition that Eve passed her semantics exam in a context in which it is true that Eve passed her semantics exam. In a context in which Eve did not pass her semantics exam, it will denote the proposition that Eve did not pass her semantics exam. This view also helps to determine the interpretation of question embedding predicates such as *know* or *wonder*:

(10)  a.  I know whether Eve passed her semantics exam.
      b.  I wonder whether Eve passed her semantics exam.

This is not the only way we can approach questions. We could also assume that questions denote the set of the possible answers to the question (as argued by Hamblin 1973) or the set of the true answers to the question (as proposed by Karttunen 1977). What all these analyses have in common is that they attempt to relate the meaning of questions to (sets of) propositions (see Higginbotham 1996 and Groenendijk and Stokhof 1997 for more discussion of this point). Even the semantics of non-declarative sentences thus makes crucial use of the notion of proposition. This does not mean that propositional logic itself has much to say about these issues. In order to provide a full and correct semantics of questions, imperatives and exclamatives, we need a better understanding of their performative character. After all they are *speech acts*: they perform the action of questioning, ordering or exclamation by means of natural language (Austin 1962, Searle 1969). It is certainly not impossible to work out an interesting semantics of sentences other than declaratives, but it is clear that, whatever we want to say about the semantics of questions, imperatives and exclamatives, we need more powerful mechanisms than propositional logic. We will limit ourselves in this book to the more basic cases of declarative sentences. This means that all the sentences we take into consideration denote propositions.

Some propositions will always be true, no matter what the external circumstances look like. We call them *tautologies*. Some examples:

(11)   a.   Every man is a man.
        b.   A bachelor is unmarried.
        c.   It is raining or it is not raining.

(11a) and (11b) are always true because of the predicate-argument structure of the sentences. This is something which cannot be handled by propositional logic. The tautological character of (11b) is explained by lexical-semantic properties of the predicates involved. The common noun *bachelor* already bears the feature [– MARRIED], so it is redundant to predicate this as a property of the individual involved. In chapter 4, we will see that we can describe the tautological character of (11a) in predicate logic. (11c) is tautologous because of the contribution of the connective. This is something propositional logic can explain, as we will see in section 3.4.3 below.

Other sentences of natural language correspond to propositions that are always false, whatever the factual situation in the outside world may be. We call them *contradictions*:

(12)   a.   Every man is not a man.
        b.   A bachelor is married.
        c.   It is raining and it is not raining.

The contradictions in (12a) and (b) are to be explained in terms of predicate-argument structure. The contradiction in (12b) is again a result of the lexical-semantic properties of the predicates involved. The contradictory nature of (12a) follows from basic assumptions of predicate logic, as will be explained in chapter 4. Only the contradiction in (12c) is within the scope of propositional logic.

Tautologies and contradictions are not often used in daily conversation, although they can occur and have specific meaning effects, as illustrated by the following examples:

(13)   a.   War is war.
        b.   To be or not to be, that is the question.

A tautology like (13a) can be uttered to underline some of the unavoidable consequences of war (e.g. casualties). The famous question in (13b) says it all. However, the specific uses of the tautologies in (13) are part of the utterance (or speaker) meaning rather than the linguistic meaning of the sentence. As such, their study is part of pragmatics, and not of semantics. Most sentences in everyday discourse will be neither tautologies nor contradictions: they will be true in some situations, false in others. We call them *contingent statements* or simply *contingencies*. Some examples:

(14)  a.  It is raining.
      b.  Noam is a linguist.
      c.  Susan is in the office and Fred is in the garden.

In most places, it is likely to rain on some days, but not on others. For practical purposes, it can be quite useful to know whether it is raining or not, say, today. If it does, you should think of bringing an umbrella; if it does not, you should complain about the drought. This kind of information is dependent on what the real world looks like. However, it is independent of the meaning of the words and of the sentence itself. That is, the meaning of the sentence in (14a) is the same on days that it rains and on days that is doesn't. Speakers of a language know the meaning of a sentence in their language even if they cannot tell the truth or falsity of the proposition expressed by that sentence in a particular context. For example, (14b) has a clear meaning to me, irrespective of whether I do or do not know that Noam is a linguist.

As we already briefly argued in chapter 2, semanticists are not really interested in whether it is raining or not today, and whether Noam is really a linguist, a plumber or a physicist. Similar remarks can be made for (14c). We may not know whether it is true that Susan is in the office and Fred is in the garden. However, we know that in order for (14c) to be true, both statements have to be true. The distinction between truth and meaning implies that we are not so much interested in actual truth, but in *truth conditions*. In order to know the meaning of a sentence, we need to know what the world must look like if the sentence is to have the value 'true'. Truth conditions are the conditions which need to be met for there to be an appropriate correspondence between the proposition expressed by the sentence and the state of affairs in the world. Now, the outside world is big and complex, and we do not have full information about everything that is going on everywhere on the earth. Therefore we do not usually evaluate the truth of a sentence with respect to the whole world, but with respect to some *model* of the world. The advantage of working with models is that they are defined in a precise way. We know exactly who is there, what properties every individual has, what is going on, etc., because the model provides a description of the denotations of all the lexical items of the (object) language. This idea will be developed in more detail in chapter 4, where we will provide a precise model-theoretic interpretation of proper names, common names, intransitive and transitive verbs, a number of determiners, etc. In this chapter, we only look at the meaning of sentences as a whole. In this perspective, we say that (14a) is true iff it is raining in our model and (14b) is true iff the individual named Noam in our universe of discourse has the property of being a linguist according to our model. (14c) will be true iff it is true in the model that Susan is in the office *and* Fred is in the garden, etc. The truth conditions specified by our model-theoretic interpretation hold independently of any model, but the interpretation of particular sentences may be carried out only with respect to some particular model. For any expression $\alpha$ we write the interpretation (or denotation) of $\alpha$ with respect to a model $M$ as $[\![\alpha]\!]^M$.

If $\alpha$ is a sentence which expresses an atomic proposition, its interpretation in the model is a truth value. The assignment of truth values to propositions is handled by a valuation function $V$. Quite generally, a function is defined as a special kind of binary relation between two sets, called the domain and the range of the function. A function pairs each argument in its domain with just one element in its range. A valuation function $V$ has a set of propositions as its domain and a set of truth values as its range. $V$ assigns to a proposition the value 1 (true) if and only if the proposition corresponds with the facts in the model. A valuation $V$ which assigns to a proposition the value 0 (false) implies that the proposition does not correspond with the facts in the model. Since $V$ is a function, all propositions have exactly one truth value in the model $M$.

## 3.4 Sentential connectives

The truth value of a complex formula is compositionally determined by the truth values of its syntactic components and the syntactic structure of the complex formula (i.e. its connectives and their arrangement in the formula).

### 3.4.1 Negation

Negation reverses the truth value of the statement to which it is attached. If $\phi$ is true then $\neg\phi$ is false, and the other way around. For instance, if 'it is raining' is true, then 'it isn't raining' is false. The effect of connectives on the truth value of the basic proposition can be represented in a *truth table*:

(15)

| $\phi$ | $\neg\phi$ |
|--------|------------|
| 0      | 1          |
| 1      | 0          |

The first column contains the possible truth values of the atomic proposition $\phi$, and the second column gives the truth value of $\neg\phi$ as a derivation of the truth value of $\phi$. The horizontal rows give the connection between the truth values of $\phi$ and $\neg\phi$ for each possible assignment of truth to $\phi$. For one-place connectives, there are only two 'logical' ways in which the truth value of a modified formula can be derived from the original formula: we can keep the truth values the same (this is the semantics of the identity function), or we can reverse them (this is the semantics of the negation operator $\neg$). If we combine more propositions and more connectives, the number of colums will grow with every additional operation. The number of rows will increase with the number of (atomic) propositions involved, as all the possible combinations of the truth values of the different propositions need to be considered. Examples of complex truth tables are given in (25) and (33) below.

## 3.4.2 Conjunction

A conjunction $(\phi \wedge \psi)$ is true iff both conjuncts are true. For instance:

(16) Ann is rich and Mason is poor.

The conjunction in (16) is true iff it is true that Ann is rich and it is also true that Mason is poor. The truth table of conjunction correctly reflects the intuition that the complex statement is false whenever one of the conjuncts is false:

(17)

| $\phi$ | $\psi$ | $\phi \wedge \psi$ |
|---|---|---|
| 1 | 1 | 1 |
| 1 | 0 | 0 |
| 0 | 1 | 0 |
| 0 | 0 | 0 |

Predicate logical conjunction does not always correspond to conjunction in natural language. Conjunction often carries a temporal connotation which is absent from the logical connective. Compare:

(18)  a.  Jenny got married and got pregnant.
      b.  Jenny got pregnant and got married.

(18a) and (18b) strongly suggest a different order in which the events occur. The propositional logical connective thus conveys less information than its natural language counterpart. This is true for other cases as well. In translating from English into propositional logic, the sentential connectives *but* and *even though* are often rendered as conjunction. Thus both (19a) and (19b) translate as (19c):

(19)  a.  Jane snores, but John sleeps well.
      b.  Even though Jane snores, John sleeps well.
      c.  $(p \wedge q)$ where
          $p = $ Jane snores            and
          $q = $ John sleeps well

However, the connective $\wedge$ of propositional logic carries none of the connotations of contrast or unexpectedness of the English connectives. The observations made with respect to (18) and (19) raise the question whether propositional logical $\wedge$ is an adequate translation of natural language *and*. The question is important, for if the answer is 'no', we cannot use the propositional logical structure of valid and invalid arguments to account for the validity and invalidity of reasoning patterns formulated in natural language. In this book, we will assume that the answer to the question is 'yes'. The connective $\wedge$ provides a good translation for English *and, but, though* as far as the validity of arguments is concerned, because this notion is strictly limited to the truth-conditional import of the propositions. The propositional connective $\wedge$ correctly captures the intuition that in all the cases in (18) and (19) both conjuncts must be true in order to make the complex statement true. The other meaningful aspects of the sentences in (18) and (19) are derived from other sources. For instance, the notion of contrast inherent in *but* is characterized as a presupposition, as we already pointed out in chapter 2. Furthermore, we know that Grice (1975) formulates a maxim of cooperative conversation which recommends speakers to be orderly. The order in which the events are presented then generates the *implicature* that this is indeed the order in which they happened (see section 2.3.3 for the notion of implicature). The implicature is a suggested inference, but not a strictly logical entailment. The implicature explains the difference in meaning (if not truth conditions) between (18a) and (b): given that we have two possible orders of the conjuncts, the choice between them acquires a meaning in context. The contrastive aspect of the meaning of *but* and *even though* in (19) is often handled by treating it as presuppositional. If we use *but* rather than *and*, we presuppose or take for granted that we want to contrast the two propositions. If we accept this division of labor between truth conditions and presuppositions, we can retain (19c) as the correct translation of all the sentences in (18) and (19) with their respective interpretation of $p$ and $q$.

Unlike its counterpart in propositional logic, the English connective *and* can be used to conjoin nouns, noun phrases, adjectives, verb phrases, etc. as well as sentences, as illustrated in (20):

(20)   a.   John and Mary sang.
        b.   Jane smokes and drinks.
        c.   Competent women and men occupy all the important positions in this firm.
        d.   Jane bought an exciting and controversial book on semantics.

These sentences cannot be directly translated into propositional logic, because the logical connectives are defined as operators over propositions. Sometimes, sentences containing phrasal conjunction can be treated as elliptical forms of sentential conjunction, e.g.:

(21)   a.   John and Mary sang.
        b.   John sang and Mary sang.
        c.   $(p \land q)$ where
           $p =$ John sang         and
           $q =$ Mary sang

(21a) may be regarded as an abbreviated form of (21b) and can thus be translated as (21c). Not all cases of phrasal conjunction can be treated in this way, as the following examples show:

(22)   a.   John and Mary met in New York.
        b.   Mary mixed red and blue paint.
        c.   At most two children sang and danced.

The subject in (22a) gets a collective, rather than a distributive reading: it is the group (collection) of John and Mary which is involved in the meeting, for an individual cannot meet. Something similar is true for (22b), where the mixture becomes like a new individual. In order to account for the use of *and* in contexts like (22a) and (b), we need to set up our model in such a way that we do not only have atomic individuals like John and Mary, but also complex individuals like groups. Semantic theories of plurals and groups have been developed by Scha (1981), Link (1983), Lasersohn (1995), Schwarzschild (1996) and others. A discussion of their proposals is outside the scope of this book, but see Link (1991), Landman (1996) and Lønning (1997) for recent overviews.

The problem with (22c) is that it is not equivalent to the conjunction of 'at most two children sang' and 'at most two children danced'. We will look more closely at instances of conjunction involving complex NPs like the ones in (21c) and (22c) in chapter 8. At that point, we will be able to derive the difference between (21) and (22) from the semantic properties of the NPs involved. We conclude from the examples in (21) and (22) that we should always be careful in translating natural language expressions into propositional logic, for English *and* does not always have the same meaning as the propositional connective ∧.

### 3.4.3 Disjunction

A disjunction $(\phi \lor \psi)$ is true whenever at least one of the disjuncts is true. This leads to the following truth table:

(23)

| $\phi$ | $\psi$ | $\phi \lor \psi$ |
|---|---|---|
| 1 | 1 | 1 |
| 1 | 0 | 1 |
| 0 | 1 | 1 |
| 0 | 0 | 0 |

The truth table gives the definition of inclusive *or*, which makes a complex sentence come out true when both disjuncts are true. However, in many contexts we feel that English *or* has an exclusive sense, which excludes the possibility that both disjuncts are true, for instance:

(24)  a.  Do you want tea or coffee?
      b.  All entrees are served with soup or salad.

Again, the question arises whether we want the exclusive interpretation to be part of the truth conditions (and make the top row of the truth-table 1–1–0 rather than 1–1–1), or whether we explain the meaning effects of (24a) and (b) in some other way. Although other choices are possible, we take the meaning effects in (24) to be an effect of pragmatics, rather than truth-conditional semantics. The preference for an exclusive interpretation is an implicature in the sense of Grice (1975). It arises from the maxim of Quantity, which requires the speaker to say as much as she can. As Horn (1972) points out, a disjunctive statement is weaker than a conjunctive one. If the speaker knew that both propositions were true, it would be more informative to use a conjunction, rather than a disjunction. The use of a disjunction suggests that the speaker does not have evidence that both disjuncts are true. This triggers the implicature that one of the disjuncts is likely to be false. This corresponds to the exclusive interpretation of *or*. The Gricean requirements on cooperative discourse then state that a disjunctive statement is most felicitously used in situations in which it is indeed the case that only one of them is true. Truth-conditionally, however, disjunction is defined as inclusive disjunction, so that the complex sentence comes out true if both disjuncts are true. One of the reasons is that an appropriate division of labor between semantics and pragmatics can take care of the overall preference for an exclusive interpretation. Another reason is that the inclusive use of disjunction is in fact just as common in natural language, as the following sentences illustrate:

(25)  a.   At present we invite all passengers who need some extra help, or who are travelling with small children, to board the aircraft.
      b.   At the party, Sue did not talk to either Fred or Jane.

(25a) is a typical pre-boarding call for an airline flight. If we would read *or* in (25a) as exclusive *or*, it would be forbidden for passengers who are travelling with small children *and* who need some extra help to board the aircraft at this time. That is certainly not the intention of this message, which is to consider cases in which either one or both of the propositions are true. (25b) embeds a disjunction under negation. The default interpretation is that neither Fred nor Jane was in conversation with Sue. This interpretation corresponds to the negation of inclusive *or*, as illustrated by the truth table in (26):

(26)

| $\phi$ | $\psi$ | $\phi \vee \psi$ | $\neg(\phi \vee \psi)$ |
|---|---|---|---|
| 1 | 1 | 1 | 0 |
| 1 | 0 | 1 | 0 |
| 0 | 1 | 1 | 0 |
| 0 | 0 | 0 | 1 |

If we would read *either ... or* in (25b) as exclusive disjunction, the sentence would come true if Sue talked to neither Fred nor Jane or if she talked to both of them. Intuitively, however, the sentence is false if Sue talked to both Fred and Jane. This shows that the inclusive interpretation is the truth-conditionally correct interpretation of *or* in all contexts. Strengthening to exclusive *or* is an implicature which arises in certain, but not all contexts.

Similar remarks about phrasal disjunction can be made here as in the case of phrasal conjunction. The disjunction of two proper names in (27a) is equivalent to the disjunction of two propositions in (27b):

(27)  a.   John or Mary will pick you up.
      b.   John will pick you up or Mary will pick you up.

In other cases, the disjunction of constituents does not correspond to a disjunction of propositions. An example is (28a):

(28)       A doctor or a dentist can write prescriptions.
  a.   $(p \lor q)$
  b.   $(p \land q)$ where
       $p =$ a doctor can write prescriptions          and
       $q =$ a dentist can write prescriptions

The intended interpretation is that *both* doctors *and* dentists can write prescriptions. Thus, the correct translation of (28) is the conjunction statement in (28b), rather than the disjunction statement in (28a). Examples like (28) illustrate once more how careful we have to be in relating natural language disjunction to the propositional logic connective $\lor$.

## 3.4.4   Conditional and bi-conditional

A conditional formula $\phi \rightarrow \psi$ is false only if the antecedent is true and the consequent is not:

(29) If it snows, it is cold.

(29) is clearly falsified by a situation in which there is snow, but we do not feel it is cold. On the other hand, if it does not snow, but it is cold anyhow, this does not falsify the conditional. It may be cold for other reasons (e.g. because it is below freezing), which does not affect the relation between it snowing and it being cold. This intuition about the meaning of *if ... then* constructions is captured by the following truth table:

(30)

| $\phi$ | $\psi$ | $\phi \rightarrow \psi$ |
|---|---|---|
| 1 | 1 | 1 |
| 1 | 0 | 0 |
| 0 | 1 | 1 |
| 0 | 0 | 1 |

For many people, the truth conditions of the conditional in (30) are counterintuitive at first sight. For most examples of *if ... then* constructions we encounter in real-life conversation, the truth value of the sentence is straightforward when the antecedent is true, but our intuitions are less clear when the antecedent is false. Consider:

(31)  a.   If it starts raining, we'll go home.
      b.   If you water them once a week, these plants will grow very big.

(31a) comes out true in a context in which it starts raining and we go home, and it comes out false in a context in which it starts raining and

we do not go home for some reason. But what about a context in which
it doesn't rain? We are hesitant to say the conditional is true in such
contexts. However, we certainly do not want to commit ourselves to the
falsity of the conditional in situations in which it doesn't rain. Given that
we do not have the value 'undefined' in propositional logic, our best bet
is to say the conditional is true if it doesn't rain, whether we go home or
not. The idea is that the conditional is verified as long as it is not falsified,
because we use binary truth values. (31b) is even trickier. We know that
plants die if they don't get water, so in a context in which the antecedent
is false, there is no chance of the consequent coming out true. The specific
contents of the propositions and causal relations between them do not affect
the truth-conditional import of the *if ... then* connective, though. Again,
there is a division of labor between truth conditions and other aspects of
meaning, such as causality.

   A bi-conditional $\phi \leftrightarrow \psi$ is paraphrased as 'if and only if'. The truth
conditions of the bi-conditional require both parts to have the same truth-
value:

(32)  Jane will go to the party if and only if Joan goes.

   (32) is true iff both Jane and Joan go to the party or if neither of them
goes. The truth-table for the bi-conditional is as follows:

(33)

| $\phi$ | $\psi$ | $\phi \leftrightarrow \psi$ |
|---|---|---|
| 1 | 1 | 1 |
| 1 | 0 | 0 |
| 0 | 1 | 0 |
| 0 | 0 | 1 |

   The five sentential connectives $\neg, \wedge, \vee, \rightarrow, \leftrightarrow$ exhaust the basic connectives of propositional logic.

## 3.4.5  Complex truth tables

More complex formulas can also be represented in truth tables. The number
of columns depends on the number of connectives present in the formula.
The number of rows in the truth table is determined by the requirement
that all possible combinations of truth values of atomic statements must
be considered. For instance, the truth table for $((\phi \wedge \psi) \rightarrow \neg(\phi \vee \chi))$ is
given in (34).

One interesting aspect of truth tables is that they allow us to determine
whether a formula is a tautology, a contradiction or a contingency. A statement is a tautology if the last column in the truth table contains nothing

(34)

| $\phi$ | $\psi$ | $\chi$ | $(\phi \wedge \psi)$ | $(\phi \vee \chi)$ | $\neg(\phi \vee \chi)$ | $((\phi \vee \psi) \rightarrow \neg(\phi \vee \chi))$ |
|---|---|---|---|---|---|---|
| 1 | 1 | 1 | 1 | 1 | 0 | 0 |
| 1 | 1 | 0 | 1 | 1 | 0 | 0 |
| 1 | 0 | 1 | 0 | 1 | 0 | 1 |
| 1 | 0 | 0 | 0 | 1 | 0 | 1 |
| 0 | 1 | 1 | 0 | 1 | 0 | 1 |
| 0 | 1 | 0 | 0 | 0 | 1 | 1 |
| 0 | 0 | 1 | 0 | 1 | 0 | 1 |
| 0 | 0 | 0 | 0 | 0 | 1 | 1 |

but ones. That is, the statement is always true, independently of the initial assignment of truth values to its atomic statements. Such statements are true simply because of the meaning of the connectives. A statement is called a contradiction if the last column in the corresponding truth table contains nothing but zeros. That is, it is always false, no matter what truth values are assigned to its atomic statements. All statements with both ones and zeros in the final column of their truth table are contingencies. Their truth or falsity depends on the truth value assigned to the atomic statements they are built upon. For instance, the truth tables for $(\phi \vee \neg\phi)$ , $(\phi \wedge \neg\phi)$ and $(\phi \rightarrow \psi) \leftrightarrow \neg(\phi \wedge \neg\psi)$ are the following:

(35) tautology:

| $\phi$ | $\neg\phi$ | $(\phi \vee \neg\phi)$ |
|---|---|---|
| 1 | 0 | 1 |
| 0 | 1 | 1 |

This table accounts for the tautological nature of (10c) above.

(36) contradiction:

| $\phi$ | $\neg\phi$ | $(\phi \wedge \neg\phi)$ |
|---|---|---|
| 1 | 0 | 0 |
| 0 | 1 | 0 |

This table accounts for the contradictory nature of (11c) above.

(37) tautology:

| $\phi$ | $\psi$ | $\neg\psi$ | $(\phi \to \psi)$ | $(\phi \vee \psi)$ | $\neg(\phi \vee \psi)$ | $((\phi \to \psi) \leftrightarrow \neg(\phi \vee \neg\psi))$ |
|---|---|---|---|---|---|---|
| 1 | 1 | 0 | 1 | 0 | 1 | 1 |
| 1 | 0 | 1 | 0 | 1 | 0 | 1 |
| 0 | 1 | 0 | 1 | 0 | 1 | 1 |
| 0 | 0 | 1 | 1 | 0 | 1 | 1 |

## 3.4.6  Interdefinability and logical equivalence

In previous sections we have introduced five connectives of propositional logic: negation, conjunction, disjunction, conditional, bi-conditional. Although it is convenient to have a notation for all these connectives, it turns out that we need only negation and one other connective to define the full range of well-formed expressions. This is because connectives can be defined in terms of each other. In order to show this, we need to introduce the notion of *logical equivalence*:

- Logical equivalence:
  If a biconditional proposition $\phi \leftrightarrow \psi$ is a tautology, then the two constituent propositions so connected are logically equivalent. This is written as $\phi \Leftrightarrow \psi$.

Logical equivalence is thus semantically defined in terms of the biconditional. The way in which the connectives of propositional logic are related to each other is expressed by the following laws:

- DeMorgan's laws

  (i) $\neg (\phi \vee \psi) \Leftrightarrow (\neg \phi \wedge \neg \psi)$

  (ii) $\neg (\phi \wedge \psi) \Leftrightarrow (\neg \phi \vee \neg \psi)$

- Conditional laws

  (i) $(\phi \rightarrow \psi) \Leftrightarrow (\neg \phi \vee \psi)$

  (ii) $(\phi \rightarrow \psi) \Leftrightarrow (\neg \psi \rightarrow \neg \phi)$

  (iii) $(\phi \rightarrow \psi) \Leftrightarrow \neg (\phi \wedge \neg \psi)$

- Bi-conditional laws

  (i) $(\phi \leftrightarrow \psi) \Leftrightarrow ((\phi \rightarrow \psi) \wedge (\psi \rightarrow \phi))$

  (ii) $(\phi \leftrightarrow \psi) \Leftrightarrow ((\neg \phi \wedge \neg \psi) \vee (\phi \wedge \psi))$

The interdefinability of connectives often comes in useful when one tries to simplify complex formulas by rewriting them in a more transparent way.

There are more laws of propositional logic which describe various properties of connectives and relations between them. The most important ones are the commutative laws, the associative laws, the distributive laws and the complement laws:

- Commutative laws

  (i) $(\phi \vee \psi) \Leftrightarrow (\psi \vee \phi)$

  (ii) $(\phi \wedge \psi) \Leftrightarrow (\psi \wedge \phi)$

- Associative laws

  (i) $((\phi \vee \psi) \vee \chi) \Leftrightarrow (\phi \vee (\psi \vee \chi))$

  (ii) $((\phi \wedge \psi) \wedge \chi) \Leftrightarrow (\phi \wedge (\psi \wedge \chi))$

- Distributive laws

  (i) $(\phi \vee (\psi \wedge \chi)) \Leftrightarrow ((\phi \vee \psi) \wedge (\phi \vee \chi))$

  (ii) $(\phi \wedge (\psi \vee \chi)) \Leftrightarrow ((\phi \wedge \psi) \vee (\phi \wedge \chi))$

- Complement law

  (i) $\neg \neg \phi \Leftrightarrow \phi$

The commutative laws tell us that the order of the propositions is irrelevant for the truth value of a disjunctive or a conjunctive statement. The associative laws tell us that we can freely rebracket if the complex statement involves just conjunctions or just disjunctions. The distributive laws regulate rebracketing of complex statements that involve a mixture of disjunction and conjunction. The complement law is valid in propositional logic, because this is a two-valued logic in which propositions can be either true or false, but not undefined. Again, these laws often come in handy when one tries to come up with a simpler translation for a sentence.

## 3.5    Back to inference patterns

A condition we impose on valuation functions V is that we only accept those that respect the interpretation of the connectives as given by the truth tables. This is reflected in the following rules for the interpretation of the connectives:

- Semantics of connectives

| (i) | $V(\neg\phi) = 1$ iff $V(\phi) = 0$ |
| (ii) | $V(\phi \wedge \psi) = 1$ iff $V(\phi) = 1$ and $V(\psi) = 1$ |
| (iii) | $V(\phi \vee \psi) = 1$ iff $V(\phi) = 1$ or $V(\psi) = 1$ |
| (iv) | $V(\phi \rightarrow \psi) = 1$ iff $V(\phi) = 0$ or $V(\psi) = 1$ |
| (v) | $V(\phi \leftrightarrow \psi) = 1$ iff $V(\phi) = V(\psi)$ |

Insofar as propositional logic provides an adequate translation of the natural language connectives *not, and, or, if ... then* and *if and only if*, we have now fixed the truth-conditional meaning of these expressions in a precise way. We can furthermore give an exact account of the tautological/contradictory/contingent nature of sentences involving these connectives in terms of truth tables. This explains our semantic intuitions about sentences like (10c), (11c) and (12c).

We have shown how statements are combined syntactically, how truth tables represent the semantics of connectives and how we use them to compute the truth value of complex statements. We are now ready to take up an analysis of valid patterns of reasoning, because this constitutes one of the interesting properties of propositional logic.

The first notion we want to define as a formal property of propositional logic is the notion of entailment or logical consequence between propositions

- $\phi$ entails $\psi$ iff for every valuation V, if $V(\phi) = 1$ then $V(\psi) = 1$.

Remember that the valuation function V maps propositions onto the set of truth-values 0 and 1. For instance $(\phi \wedge \psi)$ entails $\phi$ (and it also entails $\psi$). $(\phi \vee \psi)$ does not entail $\phi$ (or $\psi$ for that matter), but $\phi$ entails $\phi \vee \psi$, and so does $\psi$. The way to verify these claims is to write out the truth table for the corresponding conditional and verify that the final column consists entirely of 1's, which proves that the conditional statement is a tautology. Propositional logic is thus a good tool to describe *inference patterns* between sentences.

Inference patterns involve implicational relations between propositions. As pointed out in section 3.1 above, an *argument* consists of a number of statements called *premises* which are assumed to be true, even if just for the sake of the argument, and a *conclusion*. The truth of the conclusion is to follow necessarily from the assumed truth of the premises if the reasoning pattern is valid. We are interested in characterizing the valid forms of argumentation by defining a number of inference rules which guarantee truth preservation (but which may or may not preserve falsehood). An argument is *valid* if and only if there is no uniform assignment of truth values to its atomic statements which makes all the premises true, but its conclusion false; if there is such an assignment, we call the argument *invalid*. The criterion for validity can be formulated differently, but equivalently, by requiring that, if $P_1, P_2, \ldots, P_n$ are the premises and Q is the conclusion, the statement $((P_1 \wedge P_2 \wedge \ldots \wedge P_n) \to Q)$ is a tautology. We can see the connection if we realize that a conditional is tautologous in case it is impossible to combine a true antecedent with a false conclusion. The relation between logical consequence and implication explains why we write $((P_1 \wedge P_2 \wedge \ldots \wedge P_n) \Rightarrow Q)$ to indicate that $Q$ is a logical consequence of the conjunction of $P_1$ through $P_n$. In other words, the premises taken together entail the conclusion.

There are a number of valid *inference rules* formulated in propositional logic, which we can use to explain the validity of reasoning patterns in natural language. Typically, these inference rules are written in such a way that the premises are separated from the conclusion by a horizontal line:

(38)       Modus Ponens:                    Modus Tollens:

$$P \to Q$$
$$\underline{P}$$
$$Q$$

$$P \to Q$$
$$\underline{\neg Q}$$
$$\neg P$$

Hypothetical syllogism:       Disjunctive syllogism:

$$P \to Q$$
$$\frac{Q \to R}{P \to R}$$

$$P \vee Q$$
$$\frac{\neg P}{Q}$$

The following reasoning patterns are natural language examples of the propositional logical schemata above:

(39)  If John loves Mary, Mary is happy.
      John loves Mary.
      _____
      Mary is happy.

(40)  If John loves Mary, Mary is happy.
      Mary is not happy.
      _____
      John does not love Mary.

(41)  If Fred lives in Paris, then Fred lives in France.
      If Fred lives in France then Fred lives in Europe.
      _____
      If Fred lives in Paris, Fred lives in Europe.

(42)  Fred lives in Paris or Fred lives in London.
      Fred does not live in Paris.
      _____
      Fred lives in London.

Rules of inference are used to prove that a certain argument is or is not valid in propositional logic. We can use the formal proof to show why natural language reasoning patterns which exemplify the logical pattern are (in)valid.

## 3.6  Summary

In this chapter we presented the basic notions of propositional logic with a strong emphasis on its application to the analysis of natural language. We observed that the notion of truth in a model helps us capture the aboutness of natural language. Furthermore, truth-conditional connectives can be used to describe relations between propositions, and to define the notion of entailment. The translation of natural language sentences into propositional logic gives us insight into valid reasoning patterns. The interested reader is referred to Partee, ter Meulen and Wall (1990), Gamut (1991, volume 1), Cann (1993) and McCawley (1993) for extensive discussion of propositional logic and predicate logic (see chapter 4) in relation to the semantics of natural language.

The following presents a summary of the syntax and the semantics of a propositional logic $L$. As expected, the interpretation procedure is fully compositional and recursive. As a result, the truth value of a complex proposition is fully detemined by the truth values of the composing propositions and the connective that is used to put them together. The syntax rquires the definition of a vocabulary and of syntactic rules which generate well-formed formulas of $L$. The vocabulary consists of:

(i) a set of atomic propositions represented by the symbols $p, q, r, s \ldots$;

(ii) propositional connectives: $\neg, \wedge, \vee, \rightarrow, \leftrightarrow$;

(iii) brackets: (,), (also square: [ and ]).

The syntactic rules generate the set of well-formed formulas of $L$ in the following way:

- Syntax

    (i) Any atomic proposition is itself a well-formed formula (wff).
    (ii) If $\phi$ is a wff, then $\neg\phi$ is a wff.
    (iii) If $\phi$ and $\psi$ are wff, then $(\phi \wedge \psi)$, $(\phi \vee \psi)$, $(\phi \rightarrow \psi)$ and $(\phi \leftrightarrow \psi)$ are wff.
    (iv) Nothing else is a wff.

The first rule establishes that atomic propositions are well-formed formulas. The next two rules state how we can form complex well-formed propositions out of other (atomic or complex) propositions. These rules encode the recursion step and make sure that an infinite set of well-formulas is generated. The third rule guarantees that the rules in (i)–(iii) are the only way in which well-formed formulas can be construed.

The interpretation procedure of the language $L$ evaluates the well-formed formulas with respect to the model $M$. The assignment of truth values to propositions is handled by the valuation function $V$. Since $V$ is a function, all atomic propositions have one and no more than one truth value in the model $M$. Furthermore:

- Semantics

    (i)      $V(\neg\phi) = 1$ iff $V(\phi) = 0$
    (ii)     $V(\phi \wedge \psi) = 1$ iff $V(\phi) = 1$ and $V(\psi) = 1$
    (iii)    $V(\phi \vee \psi) = 1$ iff $V(\phi) = 1$ or $V(\psi) = 1$
    (iv)     $V(\phi \rightarrow \psi) = 1$ iff $V(\phi) = 0$ or $V(\psi) = 1$
    (v)      $V(\phi \leftrightarrow \psi) = 1$ iff $V(\phi) = V(\psi)$

The two sets of rules together fully specify the syntax and semantics of a propositional logical language $L$.

## 3.7   Exercises

(1)! Explain why the following syllogism is not a valid reasoning pattern:

> If it rains, the streets are wet some time afterwards.
> The streets are wet.
> ———————————————————————
> It rained some time before.

The pattern is called *abduction*, which is defined as inference to the best explanation. Explain why abduction is often used in our daily life, even though the argument is not valid. Explain how the syllogism above is related to the following inference:

> The streets are wet.
> ———————————————
> It must have rained.

What does a computer have to learn in order to 'understand' abductive arguments? Give another example of abduction which is likely to work in some appropriate daily life situation.

(2)! In propositional logic, 'if $p$ then $q$' and '$p$ only if $q$' have the same truth conditions. Both express implication, and the only difference is that in the former, the subordinating conjunction *if* attaches to the antecedent, whereas in the latter, the conjunction *only if* attaches to the consequent.

> 2.1 Show the equivalence of 'if $p$ then $q$' and '$p$ only if $q$' by writing out the truth tables of *if ... then* and *only if*.

This result predicts an equivalence between 'if $p$ then $q$' and '$p$ only if $q$' that is indeed found in certain cases. Consider (i):

> (i) a. If all men are mortal, then Aristotle is mortal.
>     b. All men are mortal only if Aristotle is mortal.

In many other cases, however, equivalence fails badly. Consider (ii) through (v). In (ii) and (iii), the sentences with *if* are normal, but the ones with *only if* are bizarre:

> (ii) a. If you're boiled in oil, you'll die.
>      b. You'll be boiled in oil only if you die.
> (iii) a. If Mike straightens his tie once more, I'll kill him.
>       b. Mike will straighten his tie once more only if I kill him.

> 2.2 Explain why the predicted equivalence fails in the cases (ii) and (iii). Hint: conditionals in natural language often establish a

temporal and/or causal relation between the two clauses. What happens if we assume that *only if* constructions reverses the temporal/causal relations expressed by the *if . . . then* construction?

In (iv) and (v) it is the sentence with *only if* which is natural, while the one with *if . . . then* is not. The sentences in (c) are a better paraphrase of the meaning of the (a)-sentences than the ones in (b):

(iv) a. I'll leave only if you have somebody to take my place.
   b. If I leave, you'll have somebody to take my place.
   c. If you don't have somebody to take my place, I won't leave.

(v)  a. You're in danger only if the police start tapping your phone.
   b. If you're in danger, the police start tapping your phone.
   c. If the police don't start tapping your phone, you're not in danger.

2.3 Give the truth table of 'if not $q$ then not $p$'. Comment on the similarities/differences between this truth table and the ones given in 2.1.

2.4 Explain why the predicted equivalence between the (a)- and (b)-sentences fails in the cases (iv) and (v). Hint: again, keep in mind the temporal/causal relations between the clauses. Note further that *only* typically has the meaning *nothing except*. E.g. *only John* means 'no one except John'. Show how the combination of this meaning of *only* with the *if*-clauses leads to the (a)-sentences being closer in meaning to the (c)-sentences than to the (b)-sentences.

(3)! Let $\vee$ be the standard inclusive *or* and $+$ the exclusive one (*and* is expressed with $\wedge$). If *or* in natural language is ambiguous, a sentence like (ia), expressed more idiomatically in (ib), would be ambiguous in four ways; it would have the four readings given in (ii):

(i) a. Bill smokes, or Bill drinks, or Bill smokes and drinks.
   b. Bill smokes or drinks or both.

(ii) $p = $ Bill smokes, $q = $ Bill drinks
   a.  $[[p \vee q] \vee [p \wedge q]]$      c.  $[[p + q] + [p \wedge q]]$
   b.  $[[p + q] \vee [p \wedge q]]$      d.  $[[p \vee q] + [p \wedge q]]$

Consider now (iiia) and (iiib):

(iii)  a.  $[p \vee q]$      b.  $[p + q]$

Prove that (iia–c) are all equivalent to (iiia), and that (iid) is equivalent to (iiib). What does this result show about the hypothesis that *or* is ambiguous between an inclusive and an exclusive reading?

(4) Sentence (i) is ambiguous. Represent the two readings of (i) in propositional logic, giving the key to the propositional variables you are using. Compute the truth value of sentence (i) under both readings in the situations 1–3:

    (i) It is not the case that Jack is singing or Jill is dancing.
    situation 1: Jack is singing; Jill is dancing.
    situation 2: Jack is not singing; Jill is not dancing.
    situation 3: Jack is singing; Jill is not dancing.

(5) Translate the following sentences into propositional logic. Give the key for the translation:

    (i)! Although it was extremely cold, Sally did not stay indoors.

    (ii)! Jim has been elected president, or Sally has been elected, and a new era has begun.

    (iii) If Sally brought an umbrella, but Jim did not, they will stay dry.

    (iv) Sally only goes to the party if Jim does not go.

    (v) Mary goes to the party if Bill does, and the other way around.

    (vi) You don't mean it, and if you do, I don't believe you.

    (vii) We are going unless it is raining.

(6) Show that the pairs of sentences in (i)–(v) are logically equivalent by going through the following steps. Translate the sentences into formulas of propositional logic, and give the key for the translation. Prove that the propositional logical formulas are logically equivalent. Use truth tables for the proof.

    (i)! a. It is raining.
        b. It is not the case that it is not raining.

    (ii) a. If it is snowing, it is cold.
        b. Either it is not snowing, or it is cold.

    (iii) a. If it is raining, it is not hot.
        b. If it is hot, it is not raining.

(iv) a. If either Jim or Sally is late, dad will be furious.

b. If Jim is late, dad will be furious and if Sally is late, dad will be furious.

(v) a. Bill is singing and Jim or Sally is dancing.

b. Bill is singing and Jim is dancing or Bill is singing and Sally is dancing.

(7) Translate the following arguments into propositional logic. Give the key for the translation. Write out the truth-table for the argument by translating the premises as the antecedent of a conditional and the conclusion as the consequent. If the argument is valid, explain which rule of inference it instantiates. If the argument is not valid, explain why this is the case by giving a counterexample.

(i)! Either the butler or the gardener murdered the countess.
The butler did not murder the countess.
_____
The gardener murdered the countess.

(ii) If the butler murdered the countess he must feel guilty now.
If the butler feels guilty, he will go into hiding.
_____
If the butler murdered the countess, he will go into hiding.

(iii) If the gardener murdered the countess he must feel guilty now.
The gardener did not murder the countess.
_____
The gardener does not feel guilty now.

(iv) The gardener only feels guilty if he murdered the countess.
The gardener did not murder the countess.
_____
The gardener does not feel guilty now.

# Chapter 4

# Predication and quantification

Propositional logic is insufficient, because it cannot account for inference patterns which depend on information below the sentence level. In this chapter we introduce the syntax and semantics of (first-order) predicate logic as an extension of propositional logic. Predicate-argument structures and statements involving existential/universal quantifiers allow us to describe a large number of natural language constructions and inference patterns.

## 4.1 Predicates and arguments

### 4.1.1 Below the propositional level

Propositional logic is a helpful tool in decribing natural language, but it is too limited in scope to do everything. In particular, it cannot be used to describe inference patterns which are based on the internal structure of propositions, because propositional variables are the 'atoms' of the language. As a consequence, there are many valid inference patterns in natural language that cannot be expressed in propositional logic. Consider for example the famous classical syllogism:

(1)     Every man is mortal.
        Socrates is a man.
        Therefore: Socrates is mortal.

This argument in intuitively valid, but we cannot express its validity
in propositional logic. The reason is that the validity of (1) is not based
on the properties of logical connectives relating propositions, but depends
on the internal structure of the propositions involved. This shows that in
order to analyze natural language, we need to go below the propositional
level.

Although intuitions about the validity of syllogisms like (1) and similar
ones have been around since the classical Greek philosophers studied them,
no formal system capturing them was developed until the late 19th century. In particular multiple quantification (sentences involving more than
one quantifier such as 'Everybody loves someone') was a nagging problem. The German philosopher Gottlob Frege worked out a system in which
predicates were expressions with 'open places' which could be filled by arguments that function as 'placeholders' (see Frege 1879). That way it became
possible to analyze not only predicate-argument structures like 'Socrates is
mortal', but also quantified statements such as 'Every man is mortal' and
sentences involving multiple quantifiers such as 'Everybody loves someone.'
In fact, Frege's system generates statements with as many predicates and
quantifiers as you like. This system is now known as first-order predicate
logic. It is a 'first-order' logic because predication and quantification always
range over individuals and not over higher-order entities like properties and
relations. In order to understand how first-order predicate logic works, we
have to know how the different elements of a sentence are combined in such
a way that they form propositions. We know that simple, declarative sentences correspond to propositions and denote truth values. If we want to
determine how nouns, verbs, adjectives, etc. build up propositions, we have
to find out what corresponds with the semantic values of these expressions
in predicate logic.

   It is often said that a proper name refers to or denotes the person who
bears that name. In predicate logic we have terms like $s$, $j$, $f$, which are
called *individual constants*. They denote specific individuals and can be
used to give the interpretation of proper names such as Socrates, Jane and
Fred. Other noun phrases which refer to individuals are definite descriptions, such as *the moon, the queen of Holland, the winner of the game*.
These expressions uniquely pick out certain individuals: there is only one
moon we can see from the earth, so that is 'the' moon; there is only one
person who can be queen of Holland at any time, so that is 'the' queen of
Holland, etc. Not all definite descriptions are uniquely describing in this

way: noun phrases like *the blackboard, the roof, the book* are only uniquely describing within a properly defined context, not in the world as a whole. Heim (1991) develops a proposal along these lines.

Sentences do not only consist of proper nouns or even full noun phrases—they typically also contain a verbal part, the *predicate*. In the example in (1) above, 'Socrates is a man' and 'Socrates is mortal' are propositions which describe a property of Socrates. Verb phrases in general correspond to *properties* of individuals. They translate into *predicate constants*, which are identified by predicate letters $P, Q, R, \ldots$ Common nouns like *student, table*, certain adjectives like *red, Spanish*, and intransitive verbs like *laugh, be happy* denote one-place predicates, because they combine with one argument to describe properties of an individual. In languages like English, the argument of a one-place predicate is given by the NP in subject position. We also find two-place predicates such as *love, hit, invite, brother-of*. For transitive verbs in languages like English, the two arguments are typically provided by the subject and the object. Two-place predicates describe relations between individuals and denote sets of pairs of individuals, namely those sets of pairs which stand in the love, hit, invite, brother-of relation to each other. We even have three-place predicates such as *give, introduce, lie between*, which typically involve a subject, an object and an indirect object. Three-place predicates decribe relations between triples of individuals. The intuitive relations between predicates and individuals are made more precise by the syntax and semantics of predicate-argument structures developed in sections 4.1.2 and 4.1.3.

## 4.1.2  The syntax of predicates and arguments

In propositional logic, atomic propositions are referred to by the propositional variables $p, q, r, \ldots$. Predicate logic allows us to describe the internal structure of such atomic propositions as the composition of a *predicate* and a number of *terms*, which function as the *arguments* of the predicate. The predicate is Frege's expression with one ore more 'open places'. Terms are Frege's 'placeholders' that fill the open places in the predicate). Predicates are specified as one-place, two-place, $\ldots$ , $n$-place, according to the number of terms they require to form a statement. They are abbreviated with capital letters $P, Q, R$, etc. The argument places of an $n$-place predicate can be filled in by individual constants. Individual constants are always written with small letters $a, b, c$, etc. The combination of predicates with their arguments is referred to as a *predicate-argument structure*. For instance:

(2)   a.   Socrates is mortal.
           Mortal$(s)$
           M$(s)$

     b.   Jane loves Fred.
           Love$(j, f)$
           L$(j, f)$

     c.   Stanford lies in between San Francisco and San Jose.
           Lie-between$(s, f, j)$
           B$(s, f, j)$

The sentence in (2a) denotes a proposition which can be spelled out as Mortal$(s)$ or M$(s)$. The proposition ascribes to Socrates the property of being mortal. (2b) expresses the fact that Jane stands in the *love* relation to Fred. Note that the order of the arguments is important: Love$(f, j)$ is not equivalent to Love$(j, f)$. This is as it should be, because if Jane loves Fred, it is not necessarily the case that he loves her in return. The left-right order in the arguments of the predicate-logical formula corresponds to the order of subject, direct object, indirect object, ... in the natural language sentence. This then provides the link between lexical semantics (the $n$-place nature of the predicate) and syntactic structure (the syntactic function of the terms in the sentence).

The extension to $n$-place predicates is trivial from (2c) onwards: one can always add more arguments. In natural language, predicates with more than three or four arguments are extremely rare, but the logic supports predicate-argument structures with an arbitrary number of argument positions. The examples in (2) illustrate that the combination of an $n$-place predicate with $n$ individual constants leads to an atomic proposition. Semantically, the combination of predicates and arguments relies on the notion of *predication*. Predication involves the combination of individuals with properties and relations to describe states of affairs: the predicate *mortal* in (2a) predicates something of Socrates. The predicate *Love* in (2b) establishes a certain relation between Jane and Fred. Predication is the heart of the semantics of predicate-argument structures as defined in section 4.1.3.

Everything we learnt from propositional logic carries over to predicate logic. We know that we can combine atomic statements by means of sentential connectives such as negation, conjunction, etc. Given that the combination of a predicate with the appropriate number of arguments defines an atomic proposition, this means that the following formulas are well-formed, and can be used to translate the relevant sentences of English:

(3)    a.    Milly doesn't swim.
    $\neg$ Swim($m$)

      b.    Milly doesn't swim, but Jane does (swim).
    $\neg$ Swim($m$) $\wedge$ Swim($j$)

      c.    If Copenhagen is nice, Milly is happy.
    Nice($c$) $\rightarrow$ Happy($m$)

Predicate logic can thus be viewed as an extension of propositional logic, where propositions get a more fine-grained analysis.

## 4.1.3    The semantics of predicate-argument structures

As with propositional logic, a statement in the predicate calculus bears one of the truth values 1 (true) or 0 (false). Given that we maintain a compositional theory of meaning, we want the truth value of a statement composed of predicates and terms to be determined by the semantic values of its components. This requires us to give an interpretation of proper names and other referential expressions, of $n$-place predicate constants, and of the way they are combined in predicate-argument structures.

Individual constants *name* the individuals in the universe of discourse in the model. Each proper name is connected to exactly one individual. For names like John and Mary, no unique reference seems to be possible, for we usually know more than one person who is called such-and-such. If names do not refer uniquely in daily life, we can always switch to unique identifiers like social security numbers to distinguish two individuals. This move allows us to preserve the idea that names are *rigid designators* and refer uniquely. The notion of individual is a primitive in our semantics. This means that we will not try to define what individuals are exactly: we just assume that we have a set of entities which make up the *universe of discourse U* of the model *M*. Anyone who is familiar with the philosophical literature on individuation knows that this is a simplification. There are all kinds of puzzles about individuals. Consider for instance the relation between individuals and the material they are made of. If you look at baby pictures of yourself, you will find that you may have trouble recognizing yourself. Furthermore, there is hardly anything which materially links you to that baby: most of your cells renew themselves regularly, and over the years your body material is nearly completely changed. However, we consider this development as irrelevant for individuation and maintain there is a chain of events which historically links you to that baby: you are still you, and you keep the same name (and social security number) over the years. Thus it is not entirely unreasonable to view individuals as a primitive in our theory.

The interpretation of a formal language has to include a specification of what constants in the language refers to. This is done by means of the interpretation function $I$, which assigns to each individual and $n$-place predicate constant an appropriate denotation in the model $M$. If $\alpha$ is an individual constant, the interpretation function $I$ maps $\alpha$ onto one of the entities of the universe of discourse $U$ of the model $M$: $I(\alpha) \in U$. We can draw a Venn diagram as in figure 4.1 to represent the universe and let constants refer to elements of the universe of discourse.

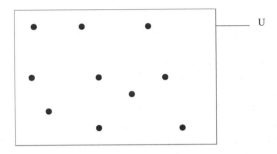

Figure 4.1: Universe of discourse $U$

Properties can be viewed in different ways. It is important to realize that they stand for concepts and are thus essentially *intensional* notions. An intensional definition of properties provides the necessary and sufficient characteristics an entity has to have in order to qualify as having this property. For instance, we define *orange* as a color in between red and yellow, and *rice* as an edible grain. But as we already noticed, it is not always easy to provide such an intensional definition for such complex concepts as an elm and an oak. In such cases, you may have to be a specialist in order to define exactly the right criteria which set one property aside from other, related properties. However, many people will still be able to recognize a particular individual as an elm, and another one as an oak. This suggests an alternative way of defining properties, namely by listing the individuals that have the property in question. We can get a pretty good feeling for what *orange* means if we know that this shirt is orange, these flowers are orange, this fruit is orange, etc. The listing approach is called the *extensional* interpretation of properties and it is the one adopted by predicate logic. In the extensional approach, one-place properties are modeled as sets of individuals: the property of being orange describes the set of individuals that are orange. Similarly, the property of being mortal picks out the set of individuals in the universe of discourse that have the property of being mortal. More formally: for $\alpha$ a one-place predicate, the interpretation function $I$ maps $\alpha$ onto a subset of the universe of discourse $U$: $I(\alpha) \subseteq U$. For instance, if the interpretation of the predicate *mortal* in our model is the set of individuals in $U$ that have the property of being mortal, we can write that as $[\![ \text{Mortal} ]\!]^M = \{x \in U \mid \text{Mortal}(x)\}$. This is represented in the Venn diagram in figure 4.2.

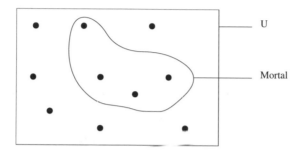

Figure 4.2: The interpretation of one-place predicates

This approach is adopted for properties like *laugh, walk*, but it also applies to common nouns like *linguist, student, table* and adjectives like *red, German*: they all denote sets of individuals which have the property of laughing, walking, being a linguist, being red, etc. One of the potential problems with the extensional approach is that two different properties that happen to have the same extension in the model get the same interpretation. For instance, if it turns out that all orange objects are round and all round objects are orange, then the two adjectives *orange* and *round* pick out the same set of individuals in the universe of discourse. Under the extensional interpretation, we cannot distinguish the two properties, we need an intensional definition. Your first reaction might be that this is a pretty rare case. Usually, we will be dealing with a model in which we find orange objects that are not all round, and round objects that are not all orange. That is why the extensional interpretation we adopt here provides an adequate description of large fragments of natural language. However, we will find that in certain contexts, we cannot get around the issue of extensionality. The questions this raises will be briefly addressed in chapter 7 and will be discussed more extensively in chapter 9.

Two-place predicates such as *love, talk-to, eat, mother-of* do not denote sets of individuals, but sets of ordered pairs of individuals, namely all those pairs which stand in the loving, talking-to, eating or mother-of relation. In general, we can form ordered pairs from two sets $A$ and $B$ by taking an element of $A$ as the first member of the pair and an element of $B$ as the second member. The so-called Cartesian product of $A$ and $B$, written

$A \times B$, is the set consisting of all those pairs. In the case at hand, we always take the members of the ordered pair (or triple, or $n$-tuple, see below) to be elements of the universe of discourse $U$. This allows us to formulate the interpretation of two-place predicates in terms of the Cartesian product $U \times U$. More precisely: for $\alpha$ a two-place predicate, the interpretation function $I$ maps $\alpha$ onto a set of ordered pairs of elements of $U$: $I(\alpha) \subseteq U \times U$. For instance $[\![ \text{ love } ]\!]^M = \{\langle x, y \rangle \in U \times U \mid \text{Love}(x, y)\}$.

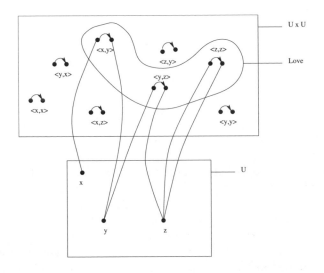

Figure 4.3: The interpretation of two-place predicates

We can easily extend this idea to predicates with more argument positions. For three-place predicates we need a set of ordered triples, for $n$-place predicates a set of ordered $n$-tuples. So for $\alpha$ an $n$-place predicate, the interpretation function $I$ maps $\alpha$ onto an ordered $n$-tuple of elements of $U$: $I(\alpha) \subseteq U^n$. The interpretation of an $n$-ary relation $R$ is then written as: $[\![ \text{ R } ]\!]^M = \{\langle x_1, \dots, x_n \rangle \in U^n \mid R(x_1, \dots, x_n)\}$.

Now that we know how the interpretation of proper names and $n$-place predicates is defined in predicate-logic, we should determine the way they are put together to form a proposition. Remember that the meaning of a proposition is a truth value. If the proposition involves a predicate-argument structure, the mode of combination of which is defined as a predication relation, then this implies that we need to define when the combination of the predicate and its arguments leads to a true proposition. The semantics of predication is defined in terms of *set membership*. If an $n$-place predicate applies to $n$ arguments, the proposition is true if and only if the denotation of the arguments is a member of the denotation of the predicate. For instance, a proposition like 'Chris is happy' is true iff the entity the individual constant $c$ refers to in the universe of discourse $U$ of the model $M$ is a member of the set $H$ of happy individuals:

(4) a. Chris is happy.
    b. $V_M(\text{Happy}(c)) = 1$ iff $I(c) \in I(H)$; also written as $I(c) \in \{x \mid \text{Happy}(x)\}$

The general interpretation of predication as set-membership is defined as follows:

- Predication as set-membership:
  If $X(x_1 \ldots x_n)$ is an atomic proposition, and $x_1 \ldots x_n$ are individual constants, then $V_M(X(x_1 \ldots x_n)) = 1$ if and only if $\langle I(x_1) \ldots I(x_n) \rangle \in I(X)$

This completes the semantics of predicate-argument structures based on the combination of predicates and individual constants.

## 4.1.4 Semantic properties of relations

Now that we have provided an interpretation of $n$-place predicates in terms of $n$-place relations, we can apply the well-known theory of relations to lexical-semantic properties of natural language predicates. We specifically required the pairs in the interpretation of $n$-place relations to be ordered, because it is not generally the case that an individual $x$ who stands in a relation $R$ to another individual $y$ guarantees that $y$ also stands in the relation $R$ to $x$. As pointed out above, if Jane loves Fred it is not so sure that Fred will love her in return:

(5) a. Jane loves Fred $\nleftrightarrow$ Fred loves Jane
    b. $\text{Love}(j, f) \nleftrightarrow \text{Love}(f, j)$

This is reflected in our semantics by the fact that $\langle j, f \rangle$ is different from $\langle f, j \rangle$, and one pair can be a member of the relation even if the other one is not. In fact, the definition of *converse relation* is based on reversal of the arguments of a relation. Examples of converse relations were already given in section 2.1 above. Some more examples are in (6):

(6) a. Alex is the husband of Bertha $\longleftrightarrow$ Bertha is the wife of Alex
    b. The lamp is above the table $\longleftrightarrow$ The table is below the lamp
    c. The $u$ follows the $q$ in the word *quiz* $\longleftrightarrow$ The $q$ precedes the $u$ in the word *quiz*

If a relation $R$ holds between $x$ and $y$, then its converse $R'$ holds between $y$ and $x$: $R(x, y) \leftrightarrow R'(y, x)$. In natural language, we find converse relations in lexical pairs as illustrated by (6). At a more general level, passive formation in a language like English can be viewed as a grammaticalized way to define the converse relation of a predicate. Consider the passive form of (7a) in (7b):

(7)  a.  Jane hit Fred.
     b.  Fred was hit by Jane.

If we translate (7a) as in (8a), the passive counterpart of the sentence in (7b) is translated in a straightforward way as (8b):

(8)  a.  $\text{Hit}(j, f)$
     b.  $\text{Hit'}(f, j)$

Grammatical constructions like the passive show that natural language makes active use of the semantic properties of lexical predicates.

An extended notion of converse relation can be used to describe the connection between three-place relations like *give to—receive from, sell to—borrow from*, where two of the arguments are switched:

(9)  a.  Anne gave an apple to Marc $\Leftrightarrow$ Marc received an apple from Anne
     b.  Bill sold a book to Sue $\Leftrightarrow$ Sue bought a book from Bill

In certain cases, however, it does not matter whether we take the arguments in the order $\langle x, y \rangle$ or $\langle y, x \rangle$. If Fred takes the same classes as Jane, then Jane obviously takes the same classes as Fred. Similarly, if Jane is Mary's roommate, then Mary is Jane's roommate:

(10) Mary is Jane's roommate $\Leftrightarrow$ Jane is Mary's roommate
     $\text{Roommate}(m, j) \Leftrightarrow \text{Roommate}(j, m)$

In section 2.1 above, we called such relations *symmetric*. Symmetric relations are a proper subset of the set of two-place relations we find in natural language. Formally, a relation is symmetric iff $R(x, y) \Leftrightarrow R(y, x)$. From the definition it is clear that symmetric relations are their own converse relations.

We can sometimes use the reciprocal pronoun *each other* as a grammatical means to express symmetry:

(11) a.  Sue and Bill like each other.
     b.  Marc and Jill gave each other a book.

Although the relation of liking and giving are not in general symmetric, the reciprocal pronoun indicates that the relation holds both ways in this particular case. However, the semantics of reciprocals is in general more complex, as illustrated by the example in (12):

(12) The girls are standing on each other

(12) does not mean that every girl is standing on every other girl, or that for every pair of girls $a$ and $b$ $a$ is standing on $b$ and $b$ is standing on $a$. So the strong interpretation of reciprocals in terms of symmetry is appropriate in certain contexts, but not in others. It would lead too far to discuss the semantics of reciprocals in more detail, but the interested reader is referred to Dalrymple et al. (1994) for more discussion.

Another property of relations is *reflexivity*. Formally, a relation $R$ is reflexive iff, for all $x$ to which the relation $R$ can be applied, it is true that $R(x, x)$. Examples of a reflexive relation are *be the same age as, be identical to, be at least as tall as*, as illustrated in (13):

(13)  a.  John is the same age as John.
      b.  Susan is identical to Susan.
      c.  Eve is at least as tall as Eve.

If we list the reflexive character of relations like *be the same age as* as a property in the lexicon, we can explain why the sentences in (13) qualify as tautologies. We find a grammaticalized version of reflexivity in many natural languages. We translate a sentence involving a reflexive pronoun such as *himself* or *herself* in such a way that the two arguments of the predicate refer to the same individual. For instance:

(14)  a.  Milly likes herself.
      b.  Like($m, m$)

We explicitly make the claim that, as far as Milly is concerned, the relation of liking is reflexive, that is, it accepts the same value in both arguments. The statement in (14) is informative because *like* is not by definition a reflexive relation, so it is not necessarily the case that every individual $x$ likes $x$. Reflexive pronouns can be considered as a grammaticalized way to reduce an $n$-place predicate to an $(n-1)$-place predicate such that two of the arguments of the $n$-place predicates are assigned the same semantic value.

Another property of relations we find in natural language is *transitivity*. A relation $R$ is transitive iff, for any $x, y, z$ such that $R(x, y)$ and $R(y, z)$ it is true that $R(x, z)$. Examples of transitive relations are *older than, be north of, be a sibling of*, etc:

(15)  a.  Jane is older than Fred. Fred is older than Sally. So Jane is older than Sally.
$((\text{Older}(j, f) \land \text{Older}(f, s)) \rightarrow \text{Older}(j, s))$

    b.  Copenhagen is north of Hamburg. Hamburg is north of Bonn. So Copenhagen is north of Bonn.
$((\text{North}(c, h) \land \text{North}(h, b)) \rightarrow \text{North}(c, b))$

    c.  Anne is a sibling of Olga. Olga is a sibling of Marc. So Anne is a sibling of Marc.
$((\text{Sibling-of}(a, o) \land \text{Sibling-of}(o, m)) \rightarrow \text{Sibling-of}(a, m))$

If Jane is older than Fred and Fred is older than Sally, then Jane is older than Sally. If Copenhagen is north of Hamburg and Hamburg is north of Bonn, Copenhagen is also north of Bonn. An example of a relation which looks similar, but which is not transitive is *father of*: if Paul is the father of Fred and Fred is the father of George, then Paul is not the father of George, but his grandfather. Another example of a non-transitive relation is *to know*: if Paul knows Fred and Fred knows George, then it does not follow that Paul knows George.

We can study many of the properties which are defined in the theory of relations in this way. The results play a role in structuring the information we have about relations in natural language. The way predicate logic is set up thus allows us to establish a link between lexical semantics and semantics at the sentence level.

## 4.2  Quantifiers

Terms like $s, j, f$, used in the examples above are *individual constants*: they denote specific individuals. They can be used to give the interpretation of proper names such as Socrates, Jane and Fred. They can*not* be used for a quantified expression like *every man* or *no student*.

Consider examples like (16):

(16)  a.  Every student failed the exam.
**wrong**: $\text{F}(e)$

    b.  No student failed the exam.
**wrong**: $\text{F}(n)$

(16a) does not ascribe the property of failing the exam to the individual called 'every student'. Similarly, (16b) does not ascribe this property to the empty set of students. Instead, (16a) means that if Jane, Jim and Paul constitute the set of students, then it is true for each one of them that he or she failed their own exam. And (16b) means that for none of the individual members of the set of students it is true that he or she failed their exam. Quantified NPs like *everybody, nobody* and *most students* are called non-referential NPs, because they do not refer to individuals. This does not mean that they do not have a denotation or that we cannot describe their semantic contribution in a precise way. We just need to introduce some additional machinery in order to do so.

## 4.2.1 Variable binding

In order to translate expressions like *every man* and *nobody* we have to use *variables* which can be bound by *quantifiers. Individual variables* such as $x, y, z$ create *open propositions*:

(17)  a.  Mortal$(x)$
      b.  Love$(x, y)$

Open propositions can be closed by prefixing an appropriate number of *quantifiers*. Predicate logic has two quantifiers, the existential quantifier $\exists$ and the universal quantifier $\forall$. Intuitively they stand for 'there is at least one' and 'for all', respectively. We will make their semantics more precise in a moment and concentrate on the syntax first. The syntax of quantificational statements is simple. The quantifier binds an individual variable $x, y, \ldots$, and we attach the quantifier with its variable to a proposition to turn it into a new proposition. The formal rule is as follows:

- Syntax of quantificational statements

    (i) If $\phi$ is a well-formed formula and $x$ is an individual variable, $\exists x \, \phi$ is a well-formed formula;

    (ii) If $\phi$ is a well-formed formula and $x$ is an individual variable, $\forall x \, \phi$ is a well-formed formula.

Prefixing the appropriate quantifier to the open proposition yields the following translations for the examples in (18):

(18)  a.  Everyone is mortal.
          $\forall x \, \text{Mortal}(x)$

      b.  Someone cried.
          $\exists x \, \text{Cry}(x)$

      c.  Everyone loves someone.
          (i)   $\forall x \, \exists y \, \text{Love}(x, y)$          or
          (ii)  $\exists y \, \forall x \, \text{Love}(x, y)$

Informally, the formula in (18a) reads 'for every individual $x$, it is true that $x$ is mortal'. (18b) claims that there is a person for whom it is true that she cries. (18c) involves two quantifiers that can be ordered in different ways. The different orders have different meanings. Intuitively, the two translations correspond to the following two claims. The first translation says that for every individual $x$ it is true that there is some individual $y$ such that $x$ loves $y$. There is no constraint saying that the two variables $x$ and $y$ have to refer to different individuals, so the first translation in (18c) comes out true in a context in which every individual $x$ loves him- or herself, but nobody else. The fact that the choice for the variable $y$ is dependent on the choice of $x$ implies that everyone can love someone else, but they could also love the same person. Note that for the second translation in (18c) to come true, there must be one specific person $y$ such that everyone loves $y$. Necessarily then, everyone loves the same person in (18c-ii).

Intuitively, the two translations in (18c) reflect different dependency relations. In (18c-i), the choice of $y$ is dependent on the choice of $x$, whereas in (18c-ii), the value of $y$ is fixed first, and the value of $x$ has to preserve that. We can make this idea of dependency more precise by defining the notion of the *scope* of a quantifier. If $x$ is a variable and $\phi$ is a formula to which a quantifier is attached to produce $\forall x\, \phi$ or $\exists x\, \phi$, then $\phi$ or any part of $\phi$ lies in the *scope* of that quantifier. Nothing excludes the possibility that $\phi$ already contains a quantifier. Thus the scope of one quantifier may be contained within the scope of another quantifier. This definition of scope makes (18c-i) a formula of type $\forall x\, \phi$, where the existential quantifier $\exists y$ is part of $\phi$, and is thus within the scope of the universal quantifier. (18c-ii) is of the form $\exists y\, \phi$, and the universal quantifier $\forall x$ is part of $\phi$, which brings it within the scope of the existential quantifier.

The notion of scope is also important to determine which variables are dependent for their interpretation on the quantifier $\forall$ or $\exists$. An occurrence of a variable $x$ is *bound* by a quantifier if it occurs in the scope of $\forall x$ or $\exists x$. If a quantifier operates on a complex formula, the brackets around the formula determine the scope of the quantifier. For instance, in (19a), both occurrences of the variable $x$ are bound by the universal quantifier, but in (19b), only the first one is:

(19)   a.   $\forall x\, (P(x) \wedge Q(x))$
        b.   $\forall x\, (P(x)) \wedge Q(x)$
        c.   $\forall x\, (P(x)) \wedge Q(y)$

Binding is thus a relation between a prefixed quantifier ranging over some variable $x$ and one or more occurrences of that variable $x$ in the scope of the quantifier. In order to avoid any confusion between the bound and the unbound occurrence of the variable $x$ in contexts like (19b), we adopt the general strategy of renaming variables whenever two occurrences of the same variable are not bound by the same quantifier. Renaming variables results in rewriting (19b) as its alphabetic variant (19c). The difference between bound and unbound variables in (19a) and (b) corresponds to the following contrast in a natural language like English:

(20)  a.  Every student sang and danced.
      b.  Every student sang and she danced.

The pronoun *she* in the second conjunct of (20b) cannot be dependent for its interpretation on the quantified NP *every student*. It should get its reference from somewhere else (presumably the larger linguistic context, or the utterance situation). In chapter 5 we will look at quantifier scope, binding and anaphora in more detail.

As usual, propositions can be combined by connectives. So now we can build complex propositions involving quantifiers, variables and connectives. This comes in useful in the translation of sentences like those in (21):

(21)  a.  Not everyone is happy.
          $\neg \forall x \, \text{Happy}(x)$          or
          $\exists x \neg \, \text{Happy}(x)$

      b.  Everyone was singing and dancing.
          $\forall x \, (\text{Sing}(x) \wedge \text{Dance}(x))$

      c.  No one smiled or laughed.
          $\neg \exists x (\text{Smile}(x) \vee \text{Laugh}(x))$          or
          $\forall x \neg (\text{Smile}(x) \vee \text{Laugh}(x))$

The fact that we propose two possible translations for (21a) and (c) suggests an intimate relationship between the existential and the universal quantifier. In fact, each of these quantifiers can be defined in terms of the other plus negation, as can be seen from the following logical equivalences:

- Quantifier Negation

   (i)   $\neg \forall x \, \phi(x) \Leftrightarrow \exists x \neg \, \phi(x)$
   (ii)  $\neg \exists x \, \phi(x) \Leftrightarrow \forall x \neg \, \phi(x)$
   (iii) $\forall x \, \phi(x) \Leftrightarrow \neg \exists x \neg \, \phi(x)$
   (iv)  $\exists x \, \phi(x) \Leftrightarrow \neg \forall x \neg \, \phi(x)$

Just as propositional logic can be defined in terms of negation plus one other connective, the quantificational system of predicate logic can be defined in terms of negation plus one quantifier. It is convenient to keep using both quantifiers, though, because it often allows us to simplify complex formulas.

We can appreciate the combination of quantifiers and connectives even better when we try to come up with a correct translation of natural language sentences such as (22). Note that this requires us to introduce a connective which describes the appropriate relation between the property denoted by the noun and the one denoted by the predicate:

(22)  a.  Every student is happy.
          $\forall x\,(\text{Student}(x) \rightarrow \text{Happy}(x))$
          **wrong**: $\forall x\,(\text{Student}(x) \wedge \text{Happy}(x))$

      b.  Some students danced.
          $\exists x\,(\text{Student}(x) \wedge \text{Dance}(x))$
          **wrong**: $\exists x\,(\text{Student}(x) \rightarrow \text{Dance}(x))$

      c.  No student complained.
          $\forall x\,(\text{Student}(x) \rightarrow \neg\,\text{Complain}(x))$          or
          $\neg\,\exists x\,(\text{Student}(x) \wedge \text{Complain}(x))$

      d.  Not every student was happy.
          $\neg\,\forall x\,(\text{Student}(x) \rightarrow \text{Happy}(x))$          or
          $\exists x\,(\text{Student}(x) \wedge \neg\,\text{Happy}(x))$

The examples in (22) illustrate that there is a natural connection between universal quantifiers and implication, and likewise between existential quantifiers and conjunction. (22a) means that if anyone has the student property, that individual must also have the happy property. We cannot relate the student and happy property in (22a) with conjunction, because this would require every individual in the universe of discourse in the model to be both a student and happy. Obviously, such a claim is too strong. Therefore we use a translation involving implication, which says that for every individual, if that individual is a student, then (s)he should also be happy. This is intuitively what the sentence expresses. Similarly, it would be inappropriate to use an implication in the translation of (22b). This may be somewhat harder to see, but essentially the use of implication would make a much weaker claim than what the sentence expresses. Remember that the truth conditions of implication specify that the formula comes out true when the antecedent is false. As a result, the use of implication in (22b) would mean that the sentence comes out true in a context in which there is any individual in the universe of discourse that is not a student, irrespective of whether there is anyone dancing. This is of course not what we want. Instead, we want to make the claim that there is at least one individual who has both the student property and the dancing property. This is expressed by the conjunction ∧. The two translations proposed for (22c) can be shown to be equivalent thanks to the Conditional law, the DeMorgan law, and the Quantifier negation law (see exercise 1).

Similar equivalences can be demonstrated for the two translations proposed for (22d). We conclude that it does not matter which particular formula one chooses for the translation of any natural language sentence, as long as they are members of the same equivalence class and specify the same truth conditions for the sentence. What counts is not the form of the predicate logical formula one provides for the sentence, but the truth conditions which that formula has, because they determine the interpretation of the natural language sentence in the model.

## 4.2.2  Semantics of quantificational structures

In this section we will define the formal interpretation of quantified sentences such as (23):

(23)  a.  Everyone is happy.
$\forall x$ Happy$(x)$

b.  Someone cried.
$\exists x$ Cry$(x)$

We argued that a quantifier like *everyone* or *no one* does not translate as an individual constant, because it does not refer to a specific entity in the universe of discourse. As a result, the interpretation of sentences involving quantifiers cannot be directly formulated in terms of predication. However, we can interpret the sentences in (23) as a straightforward extension of the predicate-argument structures discussed earlier if we realize that the quantifier requires us to generalize over the individual entities in the universe. Instead of just checking whether Chris is happy, we also need to check whether Fred is happy, and Jane, and Socrates, and Marc, etc. Intuitively, the truth of the quantified statement in (23a) requires that for all the individuals in our universe that we can substitute for $x$ in the sentence '$x$ is happy,' the outcome be 'true.' Suppose we find just one unhappy individual, say his name is Hans. Then the proposition 'Hans is happy' is false. Accordingly, we conclude that (23a) is false. For (23b) it is sufficient to find some individual or other in the universe we can substitute for $x$ and which makes the statement '$x$ cried' come out true in order for us to evaluate the statement 'someone cried' as true. In other words, (23b) is true if we can verify one of the propositions in the long disjunction 'Chris is happy or Fred is happy or Hans is happy or Jane is happy or ... '. It is only if we can find no individual $x$ who makes the formula '$x$ is happy' true that (23b) is falsified.

We formalize this intuitive idea of 'checking' the values that a variable $x$ can get by means of an *assignment function*. An assignment function is something like an interpretation function, but it is specifically designed to deal with the interpretation of variables, rather than constants. The role of an assignment function is to map the set of all variables in the language on the universe of discourse of the model. Different assignments denote different mapping relations. In order to get a better feeling for how assignment functions work, we will briefly look at how assignment functions can help us in the interpretation of pronouns. The interpretation of variables is much more 'variable' than the interpretation of constants, so variables are the appropriate translation equivalents of pronouns. Consider for instance (24a), which translates as (24b). The sentence means that Anne invited Bill in context (24c), and Carol invited Dave in context (24d):

(24)  a.   She invited him to the party.
      b.   Invite$(x, y)$
      c.   Anne$_i$ likes Bill$_j$, so she$_i$ invited him$_j$ to the party.
      d.   Carol$_i$ felt sorry for Dave$_j$, so she$_i$ invited him$_j$ to the party.

The contrast between (24c) and (d) is accounted for in terms of different assignment functions. In the context of (24c) 'Invite$(x, y)$' is interpreted with respect to the assignment $g$, which assigns Anne to $x$ and Bill to $y$: $g(x) = a$, $g(y) = b$. In the context of (24c), we need a different variable assignment $g'$ with respect to which we interpret the same proposition 'Invite$(x, y)$'. We assume that $g'$ assigns Carol to $x$ and Dave to $y$: $g'(x) = c$, and $g'(y) = d$. This approach preserves the intuition that there is only one proposition involved in both sentences. The referent of the pronoun is dependent on the referent of the antecedent NP it is coindexed with. If the antecedent is a proper name, the individual that it refers to will be the value that the assignment function gives for the variable.

We build the dependency on assignment functions into the general interpretation function. All expressions $\alpha$ are now interpreted with respect to a model $M$ and an assignment function $g$. This is written as: $[\![\alpha]\!]^{M,g}$.

Assignment functions play a role in the evaluation of quantified sentences, because quantifiers range over variables and check whether the statement holds for the different values a variable bound by a quantifier can get. Suppose that a proposition containing a quantifier is interpreted with respect to a certain variable assignment $g$. Then we must find out how we can define the truth value of a quantified formula $\exists x\,\phi$ or $\forall x\,\phi$ with respect to $g$. It is not enough to just look at the assignment $g$. The reason is that our initial assignment $g$ does not take into account the range of values a variable can get, but picks out just one of them. Suppose that our initial assignment $g$ assigned a certain value to $x$, say $g(x) = a$. This is then the only value $g$ assigns to $x$. Suppose now that $a$ makes $\phi$ true. Does this imply that the formula $\forall x\phi$ is true? Clearly not, because we don't know whether **all** individuals $x$ make $\phi$ true if we just know that $a$ does. Similarly, suppose $a$ does not make $\phi$ true. Does this mean that we have falsified the formula $\exists x\phi$? Of course not, because some other individual $b, c, \ldots$ in the universe of discourse might still make $\phi$ true. The point is that we don't know which other individuals $b, c, \ldots$ make $\phi$ true (or false) from looking only at the value $g$ assigns to $x$. If the intuitive idea underlying the interpretation of quantified statements is that we look at the range of possible values for $x$, we have no choice but to look at other assignment functions $g'$, $g''$, etc., which assign other values to $x$. In other words, quantificational statements require us to take into account not just the assignment $g$, but also the different individuals other assignment functions $g'$ assign to $x$. Fortunately, we don't need to look at all and any values assigned to all and any of the variables in the formula. The interpretation of a quantifier like $\exists x$ or $\forall x$ makes a claim about the values assigned to the variable $x$, but it does not say anything about other variables $y, z, \ldots$ The variables $y$ and $z$ are not bound by $\exists x$ or $\forall x$, so their value is irrelevant for the evaluation of the quantified statement. As a result, we can limit ourselves to alternative assignment functions $g'$, $g''$, etc., which differ from $g$ at most in the value they assign to $x$. This restriction is technically implemented by the introduction of assignment functions $g[x/c]$, where $g[x/e]$ refers to an assignment function $g'$ which differs from $g$ in that it assigns the individual $e$ to $x$, but assigns the same values as $g$ to all the other variables. All we need to do now is to check assignment functions $g', g'', g''', \ldots$ which assign $a, b, c \ldots$ to $x$, and this will take us through the range of individuals that can be the value of the variable $x$ in the universe of discourse $U$ of the model $M$. For the existential quantifier it is sufficient that there be some individual $e$ in the universe of discourse which makes $\phi$ true under some variable assignment $g[x/e]$ (this could even be $g$ itself!). For the universal quantifier it is required that every $e$ which can be assigned to $x$ under some variable assignment $g[x/e]$ make $\phi$ true. Formally:

- Truth conditions of quantified statements.
  For $g[x/e]$ a variable assignment which differs from $g$ at most in that it assigns the individual $e$ to $x$:

(i) $V_{M,g}(\forall x\, \phi) = 1$ iff $V_{M,g[x/e]}(\phi) = 1$ for all individuals $e$ in the universe of discourse $U$

(ii) $V_{M,g}(\exists x\, \phi) = 1$ iff $V_{M,g[x/e]}(\phi) = 1$ for at least one individual $e$ in the universe of discourse $U$

The combination of the two formulas with negation results in an interpretation of quantifiers such as *not everybody* and *nobody*. For instance $V_{M,g}(\neg\, \exists x\, \phi) = 1$ if and only if $V_{M,g}(\exists x\, \phi) = 0$. This will be the case if it is not possible to find an assignment function $g[x/e]$ which makes $\phi$ true for any individual $e$ in the universe of discourse $U$. The dependency on assignment functions reflects the non-referential character of quantified expressions.

The evaluation of propositions involving quantifiers embedded within the scope of other quantifiers follows the same rules. The expression is evaluated 'from the outside in.' This means that a formula like $\forall x\, \exists y$ Love$(x,y)$ is true if and only if every possible value of $x$ in the universe of discourse $U$ renders the expression $\exists y$ Love$(x,y)$ true. This implies that we have to find at least one value for $y$ which makes Love$(x,y)$ true, where $x$ has the value fixed by the assignment function in the previous step. In order to determine this, we let $x$ range over all the individuals in $U$, and for each value that $x$ can get, we hold that value fixed and check the truth value of $\exists y$ Love$(x,y)$ by again letting $y$ range over all the individuals in $U$. If we can find a second member of the pair standing in the love relation to the individual assigned to $x$, we say that the sentence is true.

It is useful to keep in mind that individual constants and predicate constants are still interpreted in terms of the interpretation function $I$, because we want their interpretation to be constant, no matter which value certain variables get assigned. Only individual variables are interpreted in terms of the assignment function $g$. The interpretation of any expression $\alpha$ is now formulated with respect to a model $M$ and an assignment function $g$: $[\![\alpha]\!]^{M,g}$:

- $[\![c]\!]^{M,g} = I(c)$ for $c$ an individual constant of $L$
  $[\![P]\!]^{M,g} = I(P)$ for $P$ a predicate constant of $L$
  $[\![x]\!]^{M,g} = g(x)$ for $x$ a variable of $L$

## 4.3  Inference patterns

The interpretation of quantificational sentences in predicate logic allows us to formulate the inference rules which account for the validity of the syllogism in (1). The inference rule we need for universally quantified sentences is universal instantiation:

(25) *Universal Instantiation*:

$$\frac{\forall x\, P(x)}{P(c)}$$

where $c$ is an arbitrarily chosen individual constant substituted for every free occurrence of $x$ in $P(x)$ of the premise and having as its semantic value an individual in the universe of discourse. The rule of universal instantiation plays a crucial role in the account of the syllogism in (1). This syllogism is repeated below with its translation in predicate logic:

(26)   a.   Every human is mortal.
             Socrates is a human.
             ───────────────
             Socrates is mortal.

       b.   $\forall x\, (\text{Human}(x) \rightarrow \text{Mortal}(x))$
            $\underline{\text{Human}(s)}$
            $\text{Mortal}(s)$

The syllogism is valid, because the step from the second premise to the conclusion is derived by universal instantiation from the first premise and the subsequent application of Modus Ponens. More precisely:

(27)   a.   $\forall x\, (\text{Human}(x) \rightarrow \text{Mortal}(x))$        Premise 1
       b.   $\text{Human}(s)$                                                    Premise 2
       c.   $\text{Human}(s) \rightarrow \text{Mortal}(s)$       from a. by Universal
            Instantiation
       d.   $\text{Mortal}(s)$      conclusion, from b. and c. by Modus Ponens

The fact that we can formulate inference rules which account for valid arguments such as the classical syllogisms illustrates the usefulness of predicate logic for the study of reasoning patterns expressed by natural language.

Parallel to the inference rule of universal instantiation, we have a rule of existential generalization, which is formulated as follows:

(28) *Existential Generalization*:

$$\frac{P(c)}{\exists x\, P(x)}$$

where $c$ is again an individual constant which has an individual in the universe of discourse as its semantic value. This inference rule allows us to explain an entailment relation we encountered in chapter 2, namely the inference from (29a) to (29b):

(29)  a.   Jane brought a cake.
      b.   Someone brought a cake.

The entailment is a straightforward instantiation of the rule of existential generalization.

## 4.4  Summary

The following provides a summary of the syntax and the semantics of a predicate logical language $L$. As expected, the interpretation procedure is fully compositional and recursive. As a result, the truth value of a proposition is fully determined by the semantic values of the composing elements and the way they are put together.

The syntax requires the definition of a vocabulary and of syntactic rules which generate well-formed formulas of $L$. The vocabulary consists of:

(i) individual constants: $j$, $m$, $s$, ... ;

(ii) individual variables: $x, y, z$ ... (also subscripted: $x_1, x_2, \ldots x_n$);

(iii) predicate constants: $P, Q, R$ ... , each with a fixed finite number of argument places;

(iv) a binary identity predicate $=$;

(v) the connectives of propositional logic: $\neg$, $\wedge$, $\vee$, $\rightarrow$, $\leftrightarrow$;

(vi) quantifiers $\exists$ and $\forall$;

(vii) brackets: (, ), (also square: [ and ])

The syntactic rules generate the set of well-formed formulas (wffs) of $L$ in the following way:

(i) If $t_1$ and $t_2$ are individual constants or variables then $t_1 = t_2$ is a wff;

(ii) If $P$ is an $n$-place predicate, and $t_1, t_2, \ldots t_n$ are individual constants or variables, then $P(t_1, t_2, \ldots t_n)$ is a wff;

(iii) If $\phi$ and $\psi$ are wffs, then $\neg\phi$, $(\phi \wedge \psi)$, $(\phi \vee \psi)$, $(\phi \rightarrow \psi)$, and $(\phi \leftrightarrow \psi)$ are wffs;

(iv) If $\phi$ is a wff, and $x$ is an individual variable, then $\forall x \, \phi$ and $\exists x \, \phi$ are wffs;

(v) Nothing else is a well-formed formula.

The first two rules generate the internal structure of what corresponds to the atomic propositions in propositional logic. The third clause produces the kind of complex propositions we are already familiar with from propositional logic. The fourth clause deals with quantificational statements. Note that any quantifier plus a variable $x$ can be prefixed to a formula $\phi$, even when $x$ does not occur in $\phi$. This implies that the syntax allows 'vacuous' quantification. Semantically, this move is innocent, although natural language seems to have rather strong prohibitions against vacuous quantification (consider for instance Kratzer 1995 for discussion). The fifth clause closes off the inductive definition.

Next we define the interpretation procedure for well-formed formulas of the language $L$. A model $M$ consists of a universe of discourse $U$ and an interpretation function $I$. The interpretation function $I$ is a function of the (individual and predicate) constants in $L$ onto the universe of discourse $U$. Furthermore, $g$ is an assignment function which maps variables into the universe of discourse $U$. The valuation function $V_{M,g}$, based on $M$ and $g$, is defined as follows:

(i)   If $t$ is an individual constant, then $[\![t]\!]^{M,g} = I(t)$

(ii)   If $t$ is an individual variable, then $[\![t]\!]^{M,g} = g(t)$

(iii)   If $X(t_1, \ldots, t_n)$ is an atomic statement, with $t_1, \ldots, t_n$ either individual constants or individual variables, then.
$V_{M,g}(X(t_1, \ldots, t_n)) = 1$ iff $\langle [\![t_1]\!]^{M,g}, \ldots, [\![t_n]\!]^{M,g} \rangle \in I(X)$

(iv)   $V_{M,g}(t_1 = t_2) = 1$ iff $[\![t_1]\!]^{M,g} = [\![t_2]\!]^{M,g}$

(v)   $V_{M,g}(\neg\phi) = 1$ iff $V_{M,g}(\phi) = 0$

(vi)   $V_{M,g}(\phi \wedge \psi) = 1$ iff $V_{M,g}(\phi) = 1$ and $V_{M,g}(\psi) = 1$

(vii)   $V_{M,g}(\phi \vee \psi) = 1$ iff $V_{M,g}(\phi) = 1$ or $V_{M,g}(\psi) = 1$

(viii)   $V_{M,g}(\phi \rightarrow \psi) = 1$ iff $V_{M,g}(\phi) = 0$ or $V_{M,g}(\psi) = 1$

(ix)   $V_{M,g}(\phi \leftrightarrow \psi) = 1$ iff $V_{M,g}(\phi) = V_{M,g}(\psi)$

(x)   $V_{M,g}(\forall x\phi) = 1$ iff $V_{M,g[x/e]}(\phi) = 1$
        for all individuals $e$ in $U$

(xi)   $V_{M,g}(\exists x\phi) = 1$ iff $V_{M,g[x/e]}(\phi) = 1$
        for some individual $e$ in $U$

## 4.5   Exercises

(1)! Consider the sentences in (i) and (ii):

(i)  Jill really likes Jack.

(ii)  Jack, Jill really likes.

What can you say about the difference in syntactic structure between (i) and (ii)? Translate the two sentences into first-order predicate logic. What can you say about the difference in meaning between (i) and (ii)?

(2) The sentence in (i) can be translated as in (ia) or (ib). The two formulas have the same truth conditions, so it does not matter which one we pick as the translation of the English sentence:

(i)  Not every student was happy.
   a.   $\neg \forall x \, (\text{Student}(x) \rightarrow \text{Happy}(x))$
   b.   $\exists x \, (\text{Student}(x) \land \neg \, \text{Happy}(x))$

Show that the combination of the Conditional law, the DeMorgan law, and the Quantifier negation law guarantees that this equivalence holds for all predicates $P$ and $Q$.

(3) Use the theory of relations to describe as many properties of the following predicates and pairs of predicates as you can. Motivate your answer by giving examples which show that the relevant properties hold of the predicates under consideration.

| | | | |
|---|---|---|---|
| a! | grandfather of | b. | have the same color as |
| c. | sit next to | d. | west of |
| e. | differ from | f. | earlier than |
| g. | be married to | h. | guest–host |
| i. | teacher–student | | |

(4) Explain the difference in semantic properties between:

   a.!  'ancestor of' and 'mother of'
   b.   'be older than' and 'be one year older than'
   c.   'sister of' and 'sibling of'
   d.   'be taller than' and 'be as tall as'

(5) Translate the following sentences into first-order predicate logic. Give the key to the translation.

(i)!  Fido likes someone.

(ii)!  People who live in New York love it.

(iii) Although no one made any noise, John was annoyed.

(iv) Everything is black or white.

(v) If someone is noisy, he annoys everybody.

(vi) No one answered every question.

(vii) All is well that ends well.

(6) Consider a model $M_2 = \langle U_2, I_2 \rangle$ such that:

- $U_2 = \{0, 1, 2, 3, 4, 5, 6, 7, 8, 9\}$
- $I_2(j) = 0$
- $I_2(m) = 9$
- $I_2(P) =$ the odd numbers in $U_2 = \{1, 3, 5, 7, 9\}$
- $I_2(Q) -$ the numbers in $U_2$ Bill Clinton uses in his lottery forms $= \{0, 1, 2, 3, 4, 5, 7, 8\}$
- $I_2(K) =$ the set of pairs $\langle x, y \rangle$ consisting of elements of $U_2$ such that $x$ is less than or equal to $y$
- $I_2(G) =$ the set of ordered triples $\langle x, y, z \rangle$ of elements of $U_2$ such that $x + y = z$
- Let $g_2(x_1) = 1$, $g_2(x_2) = 5$, $g_2(x_3) = 6$, and for all $n \geq 4$, $g_2(x_n) = 2$

6.1 Evaluate the following formulas in $M_2$ with respect to the assignment function $g_2$, showing the crucial steps:

(i)! $G(x_1, x_2, x_3)$

(ii)! $\forall x_1 \, G(x_1, j, x_1)$

(iii) $\forall x_2 \exists x_3 \, [G(x_1, x_2, x_3) \lor x_2 = m]$

6.2 What do the following formulas say in English, and what is their truth value in $M_2$ with respect to the assignment function $g_2$?

(iv)! $\forall x_1 \exists x_2 \, [K(x_1, x_2) \land \neg x_1 = x_2]$

(v) $\exists x_1 \, [Q(x_1) \land \neg P(x_1)] \land \exists x_1 \, [Q(x_1) \land P(x_1)]$

(vi) $\forall x_1 \, [[P(x_1) \land \neg x_1 = m] \rightarrow Q(x_1)]$

(vii) $\forall x_1 \, [Q(x_1) \rightarrow [P(x_1) \land \neg x_1 = m]]$

(viii) $\forall x_1 \, [\neg Q(x_1) \rightarrow [x_1 = m \lor \exists x_2 \, G(x_2, x_2, x_1)]]$

(ix) $\exists x_1 \, [G(x_1, x_1, x_1) \land \forall x_2 \, [[G(x_2, x_2, x_2) \leftrightarrow x_2 = x_1]]$

(x) $\forall x_1 \forall x_2 \forall x_3 [G(x_1, x_2, x_3) \rightarrow [K(x_2, x_3) \wedge \neg x_2 = x_3]]$

- 6.3 Assuming $M_2$ as a model, translate the following sentences of English in first-order predicate logic:

(xi)! Everything is odd or not odd.

(xii) For every $n$, the thing that yields $n$ when added to $n$ is 0.

(xiii) Everything is greater than or equal to itself.

(xiv) Every number Bill Clinton uses in his lottery forms is smaller than 9.

(xv) Bill Clinton uses no more than four odd numbers in his lottery forms.

(7) Determine whether the following natural language arguments are valid by checking the validity of their predicate-logical counterparts. In order to do so, translate the arguments into first-order predicate logic and give the key of your translation. The parts in brackets in (iii) provide background information and need not be translated. If the argument is valid, explain which rule(s) of inference show this (remember to use the inference rules from propositional logic if applicable!). If the argument is invalid, provide a counterexample (i.e. describe a situation which makes the premises true, but the conclusion false).

(i)! Everyone in the semantics class got an A for their exam. Jim did not get an A for his exam. Therefore, Jim is not in the semantics class.

(ii)! Some philosophers are absent-minded. Socrates is a philosopher. So Socrates is absent-minded.

(iii) (There are fifteen students in my class.) Every student passed their exam. Everyone who passed got an A or a B. Some students got an A. So some students got a B or lower.

(iv) Whoever forgives at least one person is a saint. There are no saints. So no one forgives anyone.

(v) Babies are illogical. Nobody who is despised can manage a crocodile. Illogical persons are despised. Therefore, babies cannot manage crocodiles.

# Chapter 5

# Scope and anaphora

Scope and scope ambiguities lead to a discussion about the treatment of purely semantic ambiguities in a theory of grammar. The notions of variable and variable binding provide a means to describe anaphoric pronouns in natural language. We also look at examples of anaphoric pronouns that are outside the scope of their binding operator and the problems this raises for the appropriateness of predicate logic as a tool for describing antecedent-anaphor relations in natural language.

## 5.1 Quantifier scope

First-order predicate logic has a number of interesting properties that make it suitable as a metalanguage for the analysis of natural language. For instance, first-order predicate logic generates an infinite number of well-formed formulas. This is because it has recursion: any well-formed formula can be extended by applying more connectives and/or quantifiers. The property of recursion is equally characteristic of natural language, as we have seen before. Moreover, first-order predicate logic is precise and fully compositional: we know exactly which well-formed formulas are generated by the syntax and which interpretation they get by the semantics. This means that we can use translations into predicate logic to disambiguate natural language expressions. An interesting example of this is the notion of scope. Earlier, we mentioned that in a formula of type $\forall x\, \phi$ or $\exists x\, \phi$, $\phi$ is the scope of the quantifier. We also say that $\phi$ and any part of $\phi$ are in the scope of the quantifier. Of course, other quantifiers can be embedded in $\phi$. If there is another quantifier in $\phi$, this quantifier is in the scope of $\forall x$ or $\exists x$ which has $\phi$ as its scope. The order of the prefixed quantifiers reflects their scope, so predicate logical formulas never display any scope ambiguities.

Some natural languages are like predicate logic in that the surface order of the quantifiers reflects their semantic scope. Mandarin Chinese is a good example (see May 1985, Aoun and Li 1993 and others for discussion). In languages like English, however, scope is more flexible, and less tied to surface syntactic structure. As a result, sentences are not always scopally unambiguous. Scope ambiguities arise when it is not possible to determine which quantifier has scope over another one from the syntax. As observed in chapters 2 and 4, we find scope ambiguities in sentences like (1):

(1)  a.  Someone accompanied everybody.
     b.  A mechanic inspected every plane.
     c.  No student read two books by Chomsky.

One way of spelling out the ambiguity is to translate the various readings of the natural language sentence into first-order predicate logic. Given that predicate logical formulas are always scopally unambiguous, the different readings of the sentence correspond to different translations. For instance, the two readings of (1a) get the following translations in predicate logic:

(2)       Someone accompanied everybody.
     a.  $\exists x\, \forall y\ \text{Accompany}(x,y)$
     b.  $\forall y\, \exists x\ \text{Accompany}(x,y)$

In (2a) the existential quantifier associated with the subject has wide scope over the universal quantifier associated with the direct object. In (2b) it is the universal quantifier which takes wide scope. The assignment of two different translations to the sentence adequately captures the ambiguity of the natural language example. Obviously, the two readings are not equivalent in first-order predicate logic. In this particular case there is an entailment relation between the two readings: whenever one specific person accompanies everybody, it is true that everybody is accompanied by someone. Accordingly, the predicate-logical formula (2a) entails (2b). There is no entailment relation between the two readings of (3), which translate as (3a) and (3b), respectively:

(3)     No one has seen a unicorn.
　　a.　$\neg \exists x, \exists y \, (\text{Unicorn}(y) \land \text{See}(x, y))$
　　b.　$\exists y \neg \exists x, (\text{Unicorn}(y) \land \text{See}(x, y))$

(3a) does not entail (3b), because one situation which makes (3) true under the wide scope reading for the subject spelled out in (3a) is a world in which unicorns do not exist. Such a claim is of course incompatible with the wide scope reading for the object represented in (3b). (3b) does not entail (3a) either. The fact that there is one mysterious unicorn no one has seen does not exclude the possibility that other unicorns have been sighted. The observation that the two readings are indeed independent means that we cannot treat scope ambiguities purely in terms of entailment relations.

In general, the laws of quantifier (in)dependence are as follows:

- Laws of quantifier (in)dependence

  (i) $\forall x \, \forall y \, \phi(x, y) \Leftrightarrow \forall y \, \forall x \, \phi(x, y)$

  (ii) $\exists x \, \exists y \, \phi(x, y) \Leftrightarrow \exists y \, \exists x \, \phi(x, y)$

  (iii) $\exists x \, \forall y \, \phi(x, y) \Rightarrow \forall y \, \exists x \, \phi(x, y)$

These laws show that a sequence of universal or existential quantifiers does not display scope ambiguities. Ambiguities arise if we mix different scope bearing operators. As (3) illustrates, the set of scope bearing operators includes quantifiers, but also a connective like negation. In section 5.3 below, we will see that other NPs such as interrogatives can also take scope, and in chapter 9, we will discuss scope ambiguities involving modals such as *must* and *can*. The examples discussed here show that it can be helpful to translate natural language examples into predicate logic in order to make the different readings explicit.

## 5.2 Deriving scope ambiguities

The discussion of (1)–(3) shows that it is easy to write out the two different interpretations a scopally ambiguous sentence gets by positing two different translations into first-order predicate logic. The question how we get from the linguistic form to these two formulas is another matter. This is less of a concern for the logician, but it is a linguist's task to organize the grammar of the language in such a way that scope ambiguities are derived in a systematic way. In a compositional approach to meaning, this means that we have to explain how the different readings of the natural language sentence come about as a result of the meanings of the different words and the way they are put together. There are different ways to go about this, and they reflect different insights about the syntax-semantics interface in the particular grammar formalism one adopts. In this section we will discuss three possible ways of deriving scope ambiguities in linguistic theory: quantifier raising, quantifying-in, and quantifier storage. A fourth way of dealing with scope ambiguities by using type-shifting is developed by Hendriks (1993), but a discussion of this method is beyond the scope of this book.

## 5.2.1 Quantifier raising

One way of accounting for scope ambiguities is to adopt a strategy which reduces any kind of semantic ambiguity to a difference in lexical or syntactic structure. Lexical ambiguities involve ambiguities in the lexical items being used. In chapter 2, this was illustrated with examples like *bank, pitcher, punch*. However, expressions like *someone, no one, everybody* do not have different lexical entries in the dictionary, and nothing suggests that they display lexical ambiguities. So scope ambiguities cannot be explained as lexical ambiguities. Syntactic ambiguities as in (4) clearly reflect a difference in syntactic structure, which is reflected in the bracketing of (4a) and (b):

(4)      intelligent students and faculty
   a.   [intelligent [students and faculty]]
   b.   [[intelligent students] and faculty]

However, there is no such structural, syntactic ambiguity in the English sentences in (5):

(5)   a.   Someone accompanied everybody.
      b.   A mechanic inspected every plane.
      c.   No student read two books by Chomsky.

We cannot provide different syntactic structures for these sentences in such a way that the bracketings bring out the different readings. For this reason, we earlier defined scope ambiguities as truly semantic ambiguities, which cannot be described by assigning different syntactic structures to the two readings. But if we adopt this position, the question arises how we can we maintain that there is a systematic relation between the way the syntactic structure is built up and the way the interpretation of the sentence is determined. For the predicate logical formulas, the different interpretations are reflected in the syntactic structure of the formulas. If we want to extend this syntactic approach to the natural language expressions, we can argue that for natural languages like English there is also a structural, syntactic difference which corresponds to the semantic ambiguity, but that this is represented at a level where it is not visible to the 'surface' syntactic structure of the sentence. This is the position adopted by generative grammar, developed by Chomsky (1977), May (1977, 1985), and others. In this grammatical formalism, all semantic ambiguities are taken to be essentially lexical or syntactic in nature. If we want to treat scope ambiguities as syntactic ambiguities, but preserve the distinction between scope ambiguities and ambiguities of the kind illustrated in (4), we need to add a syntactic level of representation where sentences involving quantifiers and other scope bearing operators can be disambiguated. In generative grammar, this level of syntactic representation is called 'Logical Form' or LF (May 1977, 1985). LF is a syntactic level of representation which functions as the input to semantic interpretation. The introduction of a level of logical form on top of already existing levels of DS and SS (suggesting 'deep' and 'surface' levels of syntactic representation) leads to the following schema for the organization of a generative grammar:

Figure 5.1: Relations between syntactic levels in generative grammar

The three syntactic levels of representation DS, SS and LF are related by so-called *transformations*. Tranformations are movement operations which move material from one position in the syntactic tree to some other position. The transformations from DS to SS take care of word order relations between active and passive sentences, affirmative and interrogative sentences, etc. SS corresponds to a level of representation that is more or less a syntactically labelled version of what we see when we see a sentence. SS is the input for both Phonological Form (PF) and Logical Form (LF), which implies that it maps both on the actual phonological realization and on the input level to semantic interpretation. The split between PF and LF suggests that any syntactic movement which relates SS to LF is invisible to PF. The split between PF and LF is crucial to account for ambiguities of the kind that we do not hear in the phonological realization of the sentence. Scope ambiguities are the most prominent examples of this type of ambiguity. The intuition that the ambiguity corresponding to 'competent women and men' is of a syntactic nature is now reflected in the observation that this ambiguity is present at all levels (DS, SS and LF): it leads to different bracketings at all three levels. The scope ambiguities of (5) are not present at SS or DS. This accounts for the intuition that these ambiguities reflect different interpretations rather than different 'deep' structures. However, scope ambiguities can be accounted for in the same structural way by claiming that they correspond to different syntactic structures at the level of LF. Given the split between LF and PF, this explains why scope ambiguities do not get different phonological realizations.

The question is now how we obtain the two different LF representations for the two readings of a sentence like (5a). As already mentioned, the different levels of syntactic representation in a generative grammar are related by transformations which move material around in the tree. Moved constituents leave a *trace* behind in the position where they came from. The existence of the trace guarantees that moved constituents are interpreted in relation to their original position. The movement we need in order to account for scope ambiguities is called *Quantifier Raising* (compare May 1977, 1985). Quantifier Raising is an operation which maps the one SS representation of (5a) onto two different LF structures by moving the quantifiers present in the sentence to the front and leaving traces in their original positions. The result is a syntactic representation quite similar to a predicate logical formula with fronted quantifiers and traces in the original position of the NP. If there is more than one quantifier in the sentence, the quantifiers are moved one at a time. The order in which the quantifiers are moved is crucial, for it leads to different frontings of the quantifier, which is what accounts for the different readings of the sentence:

(6)     Someone accompanied everybody.
   a.   $[_S$ someone$_i$ $[_S$ everybody$_j$ $[_S e_i$ accompanied $e_j]]]$
   b.   $[_S$ everybody$_j$ $[_S$ someone$_i$ $[_S e_i$ accompanied $e_j]]]$

LF is assumed to be a syntactic structure which serves as the input to semantic interpretation. The two structures in (6) are mapped in a straightforward way onto the first-order formulas in (2a) and (2b) above. The fronted quantifiers translate into $\exists$ and $\forall$. The traces are interpreted as the variables bound by the quantifier.

The treatment of scope ambiguities shows that the generative view of grammar adopts an *interpretive semantics*. The adoption of an interpretive semantics means that syntactic construction takes place prior to semantic interpretation. In other words, the syntactic structure is built up first, and it is not until after we have performed all the necessary operations on this syntactic structure that we start interpreting the tree we have constructed.

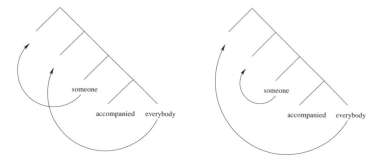

Figure 5.2: Quantifier Raising

An important result of this setup of the grammar it that much of the semantic work is in fact done in the syntax. This feature of the grammar comes out best if we consider the treatment of strongly semantically motivated ambiguities such as scope ambiguities. Such ambiguities are represented as structural ambiguities (although at a level where we cannot see it), much in the way of 'intelligent students and faculty.' Once we have disambiguated the syntactic structure, we can immediately map it onto the semantic representation. In this view, all non-lexical ambiguities are accounted for in terms of different syntactic trees at some level of representation. Because of the emphasis on syntactic structure, we can also speak of a *configurational* view of interpretation.

## 5.2.2 Quantifying-in

The interpretive semantics adopted by generative grammar is not the only way in which one can view the relation between syntax and semantics. A radically different way of relating syntax and semantics is to say that the semantic interpretation is not built on top of a complete syntactic structure, but that syntactic structure and semantic interpretation are built up in parallel. This basically means that every syntactic rule corresponds to a semantic rule, and both structure and interpretation are built up in parallel. We call this a *derivational* theory of interpretation, because it is is based on a *rule-to-rule* hypothesis of meaning. This approach to the relation between syntax and semantics is adopted by Montague grammar. This approach to grammar is named after the logical semanticist Richard Montague, who outlined the program in a series of papers written in the late sixties, the most important ones of which are collected in Montague (1974).

The fundamental difference between an interpretive and a derivational semantics can be illustrated with a simple sentence without quantifiers such as (7):

(7)   John loves Mary.

In a generative grammar, we would build up the syntactic structure for the sentence and then map it onto LF. Given that there are no quantifiers involved in the sentence, Quantifier Raising does not apply, and the sentence will be interpreted as describing a *love* relation between John and Mary. In a derivational theory of meaning, we have to decide how to combine the different components both syntactically and semantically. The syntactic rules typically combine no more than two expressions at a time, so the semantic rules follow this. For a transitive sentence like (7), this implies that the verb combines with its arguments one at a time. There are two ways in which we can think of (7) as being put together at the last stage of a constructive derivation: we can combine 'John' with 'love Mary' or 'Mary' with 'John loves'. We can represent these two ways as in (8a) and (8b):

(8)      John loves Mary.
    a.   John + —— love Mary
    b.   John loves —— + Mary

The blanks show where the remaining parts of the sentences are to be inserted. In each case, we have a noun phrase plus something else. In both cases the something else is a sentence that is missing a noun phrase, but the informal representations in (8) show that the noun phrase can be missing in different places. According to the rule-to-rule hypothesis, we expect the open sentence to have a meaning of its own. If we know how to interpret the open sentence, and we know how to combine it with the noun phrase denotation, we can build up both the syntax and the semantics of the sentence as a whole. Intuitively, we want to interpret the sentence with a blank as a property or a set, independently of the question whether it is the first or the second NP which is still missing from the sentence. This leads to the following paraphrases of the final stage of construction of the meaning of the sentence:

(9)      John loves Mary.
    a.   The property of loving Mary is a property of John
    b.   The property of being loved by John is a property of Mary

Fortunately, we know how to interpret predicates in an extensional, model-theoretic framework. The two-place predicate denotes a set of pairs (10a). We can derive two different sets from the relation *love*, by filling in one of the argument positions of the two-place predicate (10b, c):

(10)  a.  $[\![\,\text{Love}\,]\!] = \{\langle x, y\rangle\mid \text{Love}(x, y)\}$
    b.  $[\![\,\text{Love Mary}\,]\!] = \{x \mid \text{Love}(x, m)\}$
    c.  $[\![\,\text{Being loved by John}\,]\!] = \{y \mid \text{Love}(j, y)\}$
    d.  $[\![\,\text{John is such that he loves Mary}\,]\!] = 1$ iff
        $j \in \{x \mid \text{Love}(x, m)\}$
    e.  $[\![\,\text{Mary is such that she is being loved by John}\,]\!] = 1$ iff
        $m \in \{y \mid \text{Love}(j, y)\}$
    f.  $[\![\,\text{John loves Mary}\,]\!] = [\![\,\text{Love(j, m)}\,]\!] = 1$ iff
        $\langle j, m\rangle \in \{\langle x, y\rangle\mid \text{Love}(x, y)\}$

Fixing one or the other of the arguments of the love relation gives us the two sets in (10b) and (c). Filling in the remaining argument in both cases and interpreting predication as set-membership leads to the claims (10d) and (e). In both cases, the truth conditions amount to those given in (10f). So truth-conditionally speaking, there is no difference between the two derivations. All we can say is that they present different perspectives on the situation: the derivation in (10d) talks about John, and the one in (10e) ascribes a property to Mary.

Although the two derivations sketched here are semantically equivalent, linguists are biased towards the first case. The derivation reflects a way of building up the predicate-argument structure in which the predicate combines with its arguments one at a time. This corresponds quite closely to trees that respect binary branching. We think of the part 'loves Mary' as one constituent and of 'John loves' not as one constituent, because the VP can be recovered as a node in the tree, but the combination of the subject with just the verb cannot. In order to respect the way the syntactic tree is built up, but preserve the possibility of deriving two different properties from the relation *love*, we can use indexed pronouns as in the tree in figure 5.3.

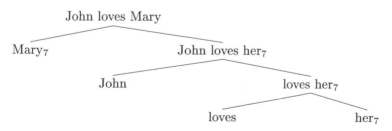

Figure 5.3: Quantifying-in

The indexed pronoun stands for a free variable, which creates an open proposition. At the final stage of the construction we identify the free variable with the constant $m$ standing for Mary. This is reflected in the syntactic operation of coindexing the proper name Mary with the pronoun $her_7$. The identification of the free variable with the semantic value of the proper name turns the open proposition into a closed proposition. The derivation illustrated in figure 5.3 is called *quantifying-in*.

As long as we restrict ourselves to sentences that involve proper names, we may wonder whether we really want to complicate the derivation along these lines. After all, the different ways of putting together the noun phrases and the predicate do not yield a difference in truth conditions: in both cases the derivation leads to a formula of type Love($j, m$) (compare 10f). One of the properties of Montague Grammar is that derivational ambiguities of this kind are freely allowed, because they are not like configurational ambiguities. The reason is that intermediate stages of the derivation in Montague grammar are not like levels of representation as in generative grammar, but reflect different ways of building the structural tree of the sentence. Spurious derivational ambiguities are then similar to the existence of different, but logically equivalent translations in a logical language like predicate logic. It is not until different derivations yield different meanings that the procedure of quantifying-in becomes semantically interesting. In examples like (11), the two different ways of putting the quantificational noun phrases together with the predicate lead to different scope configurations of the two quantifiers:

(11)    Someone accompanied everybody.
   a.   Someone + —— accompanied everybody
   b.   Someone accompanied —— + everybody

We can paraphrase these two interpretations in English as follows:

(12)    Someone accompanied everybody.
   a.   The property of accompanying everybody is a property of someone.
   b.   The property of being accompanied by someone is a property of everybody.

As before, we can spell out these interpretations in set-theoretic notation:

(13)  a.  $[\![ \text{Accompany} ]\!] = \{\langle x, y \rangle | \text{ Accompany}(x,y)\}$
      b.  $[\![ \text{Accompany everybody} ]\!] = \{x \,|\, \forall y \text{ Accompany}(x,y)\}$
      c.  $[\![ \text{Being accompanied by somebody} ]\!] =$
          $\{y \,|\, \exists x \text{ Acompany}(x,y)\}$
      d.  $[\![ \text{Someone is such that (s)he accompanies everybody} ]\!]$
          $= 1$ iff $\exists x \forall y \text{ Accompany}(x,y)$
      e.  $[\![ \text{Everyone is such that (s)he is being accompanied by}$
          $\text{somebody} ]\!] = 1$ iff $\forall y \exists x \text{ Accompany}(x,y)$

Combining the other quantificational NP with the interpretations given in (13b) and (c) will no longer lead to one reading, but to two different interpretations. These interpretations differ in just the way we discussed above. So now the ambiguity is not based any longer on properties of a particular configuration, but on two different ways of deriving the sentence.

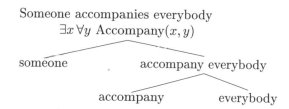

Figure 5.4: Wide-scope existential

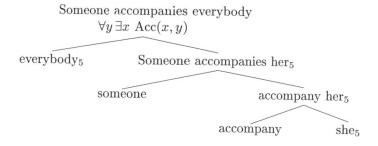

Figure 5.5: Narrow-scope existential

At the final stage of the construction in figure 5.5, the indexed pronoun is identified with the variable bound by the universal quantifier. This has the effect of giving the object wide scope over the subject. The derivation in figure 5.5 illustrates the true semantic force of quantifying-in as a mechanism which allows us to derive wide scope readings of more deeply embedded NPs without assuming a structural ambiguity at any level of representation. The rule-to-rule hypothesis is typical for a Montague grammar style of analysis.

## 5.2.3 Quantifier storage

A third possible way of deriving scope ambiguities has been developed by Cooper (1975, 1983) and is known as *quantifier storage* or *Cooper storage*. Cooper storage can be viewed as an elegant generalization of quantifying-in. Note that both Quantifier Raising and Quantifying-in lead to differences in syntactic structure in order to account for purely semantic ambiguities. In Montague grammar this is less of a problem, because the ambiguity is *derivational* and not *configurational*, but the semantic ambiguity is still present in the syntax one way or the other. The main motivation for Cooper's storage approach is built on the intuition that if scope ambiguities are truly semantic in nature then there is no reason to give more than one syntactic structure or derivation for sentences like 'Someone loves everybody.' Cooper storage involves a technique of semantic representation in which scope ambiguities are obtained without special syntactic rules. If we think of the structural description as a tree and the compositional semantics as working from the bottom of the tree to the top, the storage technique involves putting an NP interpretation 'on ice' for a while until you have interpreted enough of the tree to represent the scope you want to give to the NP (Cooper 1983: 55). Technically, this is achieved by complicating the interpretation procedure. In addition to the regular NP-denotation and other translations of simple and complex expressions we have a *store*, which is a (possibly empty) list of ordered pairs consisting of an NP-denotation together with an indexed variable. At certain points (in particular when interpreting quantified expressions) we do not simply assign a denotation to that part of the tree, but a denotation together with a store. The store remains empty if we wish to obtain readings of sentences that do not involve wide scope quantification for objects etc. If we wish to build up wide scope readings for objects and other expressions that are syntactically lower in the tree than expressions we want the NP to take scope over, the indexed NP remains in the store. It is carried along each time we interpret a larger part of the tree, until we reach the structure over which we want the NP to have scope. At that point we may take the NP-interpretation out of storage and quantify it in, so that the indexed variable disappears and is replaced by the regular NP-denotation. We introduce a general constraint on the interpretation of sentences which says that we only have an adequate interpretation of the tree if the store is empty, either because no NP was ever stored or because those that were in store have all been quantified in. Cooper implements the technique of quantifier storage in a Montague grammar. A version of quantifier storage is also found in HPSG. Pollard and Sag (1994) use a feature [ QSTORE ] which can be discharged at various places in the tree. The place where the feature is discharged determines the scope of the relevant quantifier.

We do not have the logical tools at this point to spell out either quantifying-in or Cooper storage in formal detail here, but the different approaches illustrate the general discussion on where to represent scope ambiguities: in the syntax or the semantics. It is hard to decide which approach is 'better.' If you implement them carefully and take into account the tricky details and difficult cases, the different approaches yield more or less the same results. It depends mainly on the particular framework you want to work in whether you choose to complicate the syntactic rules or the semantic interpretation to derive scope ambiguities.

In recent years, linguists have aimed at the development of more fine-grained theories of scope that take into account the scopal variability of different quantificational NPs. Liu (1990) observes that although sentences like (14a) and (b) are scopally ambiguous, whereas (14c) and (d) are not:

(14)  a.  A student accompanied every visitor
       b.  Most students read two books by Chomsky
       c.  A student accompanied few visitors
       d.  Most students read no book by Chomsky

The two readings of (14a) and (b) correlate with the wide or narrow scope the object takes with respect to the subject. (14c) and (c) do not have a reading in which the object takes wide scope over the subject. Liu concludes that 'negative' quantifiers (or more precisely: monotone decreasing quantifiers in the sense defined in chapter 8 below) in object position only take narrow scope with respect to the subject. A general rule of quantifier raising, quantifying-in or Cooper storage would generate too many readings. Therefore, various theories have been advanced that do away with general mechanisms generating scope ambiguities in favor of analyses which group quantificational expressions into classes with a specific scopal behavior. Recent proposals adopting syntactic, semantic and/or pragmatic approaches to scope include Abusch (1994), Farkas (1997), Beghelli and Stowell (1997), Szabolcsi (1997) and Büring (1997).

## 5.3    Other scope bearing expressions

### 5.3.1    Scope in questions

Scope ambiguities arise with quantifiers and negation, but also with other natural language operators, for instance interrogative NPs. Interrogatives are often referred to as *wh*-expressions, because interrogative expressions in English typically start with *wh-*, compare *who, which, what, where*, etc. A question like (15) allows three kinds of answers:

(15)      Which woman does every man love?
    a.    Mary
    b.    John loves Mary, Bill loves Suzy, ...
    c.    his mother

These different answers can be related to a scope ambiguity between *which woman* and *every man* in the question. If we read (15) with wide scope for the *wh*-expressions we obtain the interpretation in (16a):

(16)    a.    Which woman is such that every man loves her?
    b.    For every man, which woman does he love?

(15a) is an appropriate answer to (16a): Mary is the woman loved by every man. (15a) is an *individual answer* to the question. If we give the quantifier wide scope over the *wh*-expression, we obtain the question in (16b): for each man we want to know who is the woman that man loves. An appropriate answer to this question can be (15b), in which we give a list of pairs such that the first member of the pair is a man who loves the second member of the pair, which is a woman. The list 'John loves Mary, Bill loves Suzy, George loves Ann, ... ' is one possible set of pairs which stand in the love relation. We call (15b) a *pair-list answer* to the question (the terminology is from Groenendijk and Stokhof 1984). Quantifying-in can be extended to account for scope ambiguities with *wh*-expressions as shown by Groenendijk and Stokhof (1984). The wide scope reading for the quantified NP is obtained by quantifying it into the question as in (17b):

(17)      Which woman does every man love?
    a.    Which woman + —— does every man love
    b.    Which woman does —— love + every man

The interpretation of the two derivations can be paraphrased as in (18):

(18)    a.    Who is the woman such that every man loves that woman?
    b.    For every man $x$, which woman $y$ does $x$ love?

The regular derivation of the question in (17a) requires an individual answer: Mary is such that she is loved by every man. If we quantify the NP into the question in (17b), this leads to a question which is appropriately answered by giving a pair-list answer. This provides a list of pairs in which every man $x$ is paired up with the woman $y$ loved by $x$. The answer in (15c) is called a *functional answer*, because it involves a functional expression, in this case the mother-of function. The answer is such that there is one function, but for every man $x$ the outcome will be a different woman, namely the output of the function mother-of-$x$ for that $x$. The answers in (15b) and (15c) are clearly related: a list of pairs corresponds to the extension of a function, because functions are a special kind of two-place relations. Remember that a function attributes a unique value to the entity it applies to. The function therefore denotes a set of pairs relating the argument and its value. The relevance of this connection for the interpretation of questions is discussed by Chierchia (1993). Notwithstanding the close connection between functions and sets of pairs, it is important to keep the pair-list answers and the functional answers apart, because not all quantifiers allow both pair-list and functional answers. Compare (15) and (19):

(19)     Which woman does no man love?
  a.     Mary
  b.     #John loves Mary, Bill loves Suzy, ...
  c.     his mother in law

Negative quantifiers like *no man* allow a wide scope reading for the *wh*-expressions, which triggers an individual answer. They do not, however, allow a wide scope reading for the quantified NP, and the pair-list answer is blocked accordingly. (19b) is not ungrammatical, but it is incoherent in the context at hand. The inappropriateness of the answer is indicated by the #-sign. The contrast between (15) and (19) shows that pair-list readings do not obey the same restrictions as functional readings. Functional readings require a special treatment, but we won't go into the details of their analysis here and limit ourselves to the scope ambiguities related to the individual and pair-list answers. Note that the reading on which a negative quantifier like *no man* takes wide scope over the *wh*-expression is blocked for semantic reasons. It doesn't make sense to ask 'For no man $x$, which woman does $x$ love'. This effectively amounts to not asking a question. If we would give the quantified NP wide scope, a reading would result on which the interrogative can be answered by saying nothing at all. In natural language, such semantic anomalies are typically avoided.

## 5.3.2 Split constructions

The extension of scope relations to *wh*-expressions opens up an entire new domain of linguistic research. It turns out that certain interrogative constructions are sensitive to the scopal properties of the quantified NP involved. An example is the *combien*-split construction in French. This is a construction which allows the *wh*-expression *combien* ('how many') to go up front, while the rest of the (object) NP stays behind (Obenauer 1983, 1994). Given that movement of the *wh*-expression is optional, there are two ways to ask the question 'How many books have you read?':

(20)   a.   Combien de livres as-tu lus?
             How many of books have you read

        b.   Combien as-tu lu de livres?
             How many have you read of books

There are no differences in meaning between (20a) and (b), but of course pronouns are like proper names in that they do not display scope effects. If we look at split constructions involving quantified NPs, we observe that universal quantifiers allow splitting (21), whereas negative quantifiers do not (22):

(21)   a.   Combien de livres ont-ils tous lus?
             How many of books have they all read

        b.   Combien ont-ils tous lu de livres?
             How many have they all read of books

(22)   a.   Combien de livres est-ce qu'aucun étudiant n'a lus?
             How many of books WH-PART no student NEG has read

        b.   *Combien est-ce qu'aucun étudiant n'a lu de livres?
             How many WH-PART no student NEG has read of books

It is hard to develop a purely syntactic account of these data, because the only difference between the sentences in (21) and (22) involves the nature of the quantificational NP that intervenes between the *wh*-expression and the part of the NP that is left behind. Accordingly, we find more semantically oriented analyses in the literature. One observation which has been made is that the quantified NP in the split construction has to take wide scope with respect to the *wh*-expression (de Swart 1992). We can see this if we compare the split and the non-split versions of (21). We observe that (21a) is ambiguous, but (21b) is not. That is, (21a) can either ask how many books there are such that they have been read by everyone, or it can ask for everyone, how many books they have read. Thus the non-split version allows the universal quantifier to take either wide or narrow scope with respect to the *wh*-expression, which leads to scope ambiguities. The split version (21b) is unambiguous: only the wide scope interpretation for the universal quantifier is allowed, and the sentence asks for everyone, how many books they have read. If split constructions in general force the quantified NP to take wide scope over the *wh*-expression, we can explain why negative quantifiers are blocked in this construction. After all, we know that there are semantic reasons why negative quantifiers never take scope over a *wh*-expression: this amounts to asking no question at all (see above). If this explanation is on the right track, it also shows that there are limits to the autonomy of syntax: we appeal to semantic properties of the NP involved in order to rule out examples like (22b) as ungrammatical. The study of scope ambiguities is thus relevant from a logical as well as a cross-linguistic point of view.

## 5.4  Anaphora

### 5.4.1  Deictic, referential and bound variable interpretations

In chapter 1, we distinguished between deictic and anaphoric interpretations of pronouns. Pronouns like *I* and *you* are essentially deictic in that their interpretation is crucially dependent on the context of utterance: we need to know who is the speaker and who the addressee of a certain utterance in order to determine the referent of first and second person pronouns. Third person pronouns optionally get a deictic interpretation. This use of *he, she, they* is illustrated in (23):

(23) (Jane pointing to Bill): "He is the one I saw on the night of the party"

In the absence of a pointing gesture, the referent of the pronoun is usually determined by the linguistic context. We called this an anaphoric interpretation of the pronoun. Anaphoric pronouns which are dependent for their interpretation on proper names or other referential expressions can be handled by translating them in terms of the same individual constant. Consider (24):

(24)  a.  Milly$_i$ likes herself$_i$.
         Like$(m, m)$

      b.  If Milly$_i$ likes Fred$_j$, she$_i$ will invite him$_j$.
         (Like$(m, f)$ → Invite$(m, f)$)

      c.  Milly$_i$ and Fred$_j$ like each other$_{i,j}$.
         (Like$(m, f)$ ∧ Like$(f, m)$)

This means that at least some of the instances of the anaphor-antecedent relation can be treated by interpreting *coindexing* in the syntax as *coreferentiality* in the semantics.

For anaphoric pronouns dependent on quantificational expressions, the situation is more complex, because the coindexing between the pronoun and the quantificational NP cannot be interpreted in terms of coreferentiality:

(25)  a.  Everyone$_i$ hates himself$_i$.
      b.  Everyone$_i$ likes his$_i$ mother.
      c.  Everyone$_i$ thinks he$_i$ is brilliant.

Intuitively, sentences like (25) require that the value of the pronoun covaries with the quantifier. If the universe of discourse consists of John, Mary and Socrates, for example, then (25a) means that John hates John, Mary hates Mary, and Socrates hates Socrates. Similarly, for (25c), John thinks that John is brilliant, Mary thinks that Mary is brilliant and Socrates thinks that Socrates is brilliant. We can account for the interpretation of coindexing as binding in these cases, by translating the pronoun as another instance of the variable the quantifier ranges over. Moreover, it is interpreted as lying in the scope of the quantifier, which allows us to establish a relation of binding between the quantifier and the pronoun. Remember that if $x$ is a variable and $\phi$ is a formula to which a quantifier is attached to produce $\forall x\, \phi$ or $\exists x\, \phi$, then $\phi$ or any part of $\phi$ lies in the scope of that quantifier. An occurrence of a variable $x$ is bound if it occurs in the scope of $\forall x$ or $\exists x$. Binding is thus a relation between a prefixed quantifier and an occurrence of a variable in its scope. The predicate-logical notion of binding provides the analytical tools to handle anaphoric relations in which the pronoun is dependent on a quantificational NP:

(26)  a.  Everyone$_i$ hates himself$_i$.
         $\forall x\, \text{Hate}(x, x)$

      b.  Everyone$_i$ likes his$_i$ mother.
         $\forall x\, \exists y\, (\text{Mother-of}(y, x) \wedge \forall z\, (\text{Mother-of}(z, x) \rightarrow [z = y]) \wedge$
         $\text{Like}(x, y))$

      c.  Everyone$_i$ thinks he$_i$ is brilliant.
         $\forall x\, (x \text{ thinks that } x \text{ is brilliant})$

(26a) is a straightforward extension of (24a) to the quantificational case. We can take the representation of the possessive in (26b) to involve a uniqueness condition, so that every individual has exactly one mother, who (s)he likes. The structure of (26c) is a bit more complex. As we will see in chapter 9, we can interpret embedding verbs like *to think* as a relation between individuals and propositions. We have no way of formally representing such relations in first-order logic, which is why the representation in (26c) remains informal. But intuitively, the binding relation we see here is the same as in (26a) or (b). The bound variable interpretation of (26c) can be paraphrased as: 'for every individual $x$, it is true that $x$ thinks that $x$ is brilliant'. The coindexing of the pronoun with the quantified NP implies that the referent of the pronoun is dependent on the choice of the individual for the variable bound by the quantifier.

### 5.4.2 Quantification and anaphora in complex constructions

When quantifiers are deeply embedded in the formula, it can be useful to move them all up front, so that we can see more easily what the scope of each quantifier is. In conjunctions and disjunctions, we are always allowed to move the quantifier up front, as long as we respect the overall binding configuration. For instance, a formula $(\phi \wedge \exists x \psi)$ is equivalent to $\exists x \, (\phi \wedge \psi)$ provided $x$ is not free in $\phi$. Movement of the quantifier in conditionals is regulated by the following laws:

- Laws of quantifier movement (conditionals)

  (i) $(\phi \rightarrow \forall x \, \psi(x)) \Leftrightarrow \forall x \, (\phi \rightarrow \psi(x))$
     provided $x$ is not free in $\phi$

  (ii) $(\phi \rightarrow \exists x \, \psi(x)) \Leftrightarrow \exists x \, (\phi \rightarrow \psi(x))$
     provided $x$ is not free in $\phi$

  (iii) $(\forall x \, \phi(x) \rightarrow \psi) \Leftrightarrow \exists x (\phi(x) \rightarrow \psi))$
     provided $x$ is not free in $\psi$

  (iv) $(\exists x \, \phi(x) \rightarrow \psi) \Leftrightarrow \forall x (\phi(x) \rightarrow \psi))$
     provided $x$ is not free in $\psi$

The most striking fact here is that a universal quantifier in the antecedent of a conditional switches to an existential quantifier that takes wide scope over the conditional as a whole, and an existential quantifier switches to a universal quantifier. The validity of the quantifier laws (iii) and (iv) for natural language is illustrated with the equivalence between the pairs of sentences in (27a) and (27b) respectively:

(27)  a.  If every problem set counts, Sue fails the exam. ⇔
          There is an object such that if it is a problem set and it
          counts, Sue fails the exam.

      b.  If a storm hits the coast, there is a lot of damage. ⇔
          For every object, it is the case that if it it a storm that hits
          the coast, there is a lot of damage.

The equivalencies illustrated in (27) follow from the semantics of the
conditional, the quantifiers, and the laws of quantifier movement for conjunction or disjunction (see exercise 1).

Note that all the laws specify that the variable bound by the moved
quantifier is not to be free in the part of the formula which the unmoved
quantifier did not take scope over, but the moved quantifier does. The
conditions on variables not being free in the relevant parts are necessary to
avoid undesirable binding of variables. We can illustrate this with natural
language examples and their translations in predicate logic. For instance:

(28)  a.  She likes Stanford, and everyone is happy $\not\Leftrightarrow$
          Everyone likes Stanford and is happy
          $(\text{Like}(x, s) \land \forall x\, \text{Happy}(x)) \not\Leftrightarrow \forall x\, (\text{Like}(x, s) \land \text{Happy}(x))$

      b.  She bikes to school or everyone takes the bus $\not\Leftrightarrow$
          Everyone bikes to school or takes the bus
          $\text{Bike}(x) \lor \forall x\, \text{Take-bus}(x) \not\Leftrightarrow \forall x\, (\text{Bike}(x) \lor \text{Take-bus}(x))$

Similar observations can be made with respect to conditional constructions:

(29)  a.  *If she$_i$ likes Stanford, everyone$_i$ is happy $\not\Leftrightarrow$
          Everyone who likes Stanford is happy

      b.  $(\text{Like}(x, s) \rightarrow \forall x\, \text{Happy}(x)) \not\Leftrightarrow$
          $\forall x\, (\text{Like}(x, s) \rightarrow \text{Happy}(x))$

We can explain the ungrammaticality of (29a) with the binding relation
as indicated by the indices as a violation of law (i) above. A violation of
law (iii) rules out (30a):

(30)  a.  *If everyone$_i$ likes Stanford, she$_i$ is happy $\not\Leftrightarrow$
          There is a person who is happy if she likes Stanford

      b.  $(\forall x\, \text{Like}(x, s) \rightarrow \text{Happy}(x)) \not\Leftrightarrow$
          $\exists x\, (\text{Like}(x, s) \rightarrow \text{Happy}(x))$

Unfortunately, these laws for quantifier movement in conditionals also rule out grammatical sentences of English, such as:

(31)  a.  If a student$_i$ likes Stanford, she$_i$ is happy $\Leftrightarrow$
          Every student who likes Stanford is happy

  b.  $(\exists x\,(\text{Student}(x) \wedge \text{Like}(x,s)) \rightarrow \text{Happy}(x)) \nLeftrightarrow$
      $\forall x\,(\text{Student}(x) \wedge \text{Like}(x,s)) \rightarrow \text{Happy}(x))$

The fact that (31a) means what it does is not predicted by first-order predicate logic. As the formula in (31b) shows, the indicated binding relation is a violation of law (iv) above. The variable $x$ is in fact free in the consequent of the conditional when the existential quantifier is embedded in the antecedent, but it gets bound if we rewrite this with a wide scope universal quantifier. However, the natural language sentence seems to get the bound variable interpretation all right, and the universally quantified formula in (31b) is in fact the correct translation of the sentence in (31a).

Although we can come up with adequate translations for sentences like (31a), the laws which govern scope and anaphoric relations in first-order predicate logic do not model the meaning of natural language constructions involving indefinite NPs correctly. The sentences in (30) and (31) raise problems for the linguist who is trying to use predicate logic as an analytical tool for the analysis of natural language, because the laws of quantifier movement in predicate logic do not distinguish between universal and existential quantifiers. As a result, the logic does not predict that the binding relation in (31a) is allowed, whereas the one in (30a) is not. We will discuss this issue in more detail in chapter 6. In chapter 7, we will take a more systematic look at the limits of first-order logic.

## 5.5  Exercises

(1)! Show that $(\exists x\,\phi(x) \rightarrow \psi)$ is equivalent to $\forall x(\phi(x) \rightarrow \psi)$, provided $x$ is not free in $\psi$, using the standard properties of the conditional, the quantifiers, and the laws on quantifier movement for conjunction (or disjunction).

(2)! Assume that (i) is ambiguous (it isn't for all speakers, but assume it is for you). Translate the two readings into first-order predicate logic. Show that the two interpretations are independent and there is no entailment relation between them. (You can do this by setting up a situation in which one formula comes out true and the other one false, and vice versa).

(i) No linguists admire no linguists.

(3)! In standard English, a sentence like (i) is interpreted in terms of double negation. In AAVE (=African American Vernacular English) (i) is rather interpreted as (ii). Some Romance languages like French and Spanish allow an interpretation of double negation in terms of either (i) or (ii), but with a strong preference for the (ii) interpretation. This is here illustrated with the French sentence (iii):

  (i) No one saw nothing.

  (ii) No one saw anything.

  (iii) Personne n'a rien vu.                             [French]
       Nobody NEG has nothing seen

Give the translations of (i)–(iii) in predicate logic. Suggest a compositional analysis of negative quantifiers in the different languages which explains these data.

(4) Translate the following sentences into predicate logic and give the key to the translation. Indicate whether the pronoun is interpreted as coreferential with its antecedent or whether there is a binding relation involved.

  (i)! Fido is a dog, and Bill loves him.

  (ii)! No one loves himself, unless it is John.

  (iii) Someone owns a car but rides his bike as well.

  (iv) John has a cat, and he takes good care of it.

  (v) If someone does not love New York, he does not know it.

  (vi) Someone who is noisy annoys everyone but himself.

(5) Sentences like (i)—(iv) allow different translations depending on the relative scope of the quantifiers with respect to each other. Give the predicate-logical formulas for all the possible scope readings and determine for each formula which of the other formulas it entails.

  (i)! A professor gave every student a book.

  (ii) No professor gave a student two books.

  (iii) Some delegate from every city attended two meetings.

  (iv) No student knows every linguist who wrote a book on semantics.

(6) Translate the following sentences into first-order predicate logic. (Subscripts are used to indicate the intended pronoun-antecedent relations).

(i)! John$_i$ loves his$_i$ wife.

(ii) John$_i$ loves his$_i$ wife's youngest sister.

(iii) No executive$_i$ admires the person who shines his$_i$ shoes.

(iv) Only Satan$_i$ pities himself$_i$.

(v) All but one poet$_i$ hates himself$_i$.

(7) Sentences like (i)–(iii) are ambiguous, depending on the interpretation of the pronoun. Give translations of the different readings in first-order predicate logic (assume that the missing VP in (i) and (iii) is somehow 'copied' in the second conjunct). Explain how the ambiguity comes about in the natural language sentence.

(i)! John loves his cat, and so does Bill.

(ii) Only Satan hates his mother.

(iii) John likes his teachers, and Bill does too, but his mother doesn't.

(8) Consider the following examples of the (Dutch) construction which is known as the 'wat voor' split:

(i)   a. Wat voor boeken heb je gelezen?                    [Dutch]
         What for books have you read
      b. Wat heb je voor boeken gelezen?
         What have you for books read

(ii)  a. Wat voor boeken heeft iedereen gelezen?
         What for books has everybody read
      b. Wat heeft iedereen voor boeken gelezen?
         What has everybody for books read

(iii) a. Wat voor boeken heeft niemand gelezen?
         What for books has nobody read
      b. *Wat heeft niemand voor boeken gelezen?
         What has nobody for books read

(ia) has the same meaning as (ib). (iia) is ambiguous, depending on the relative scope of the wh-phrase and the quantifier. (iib) is unambiguous: it only has the reading on which the universal quantifier has wide scope over the wh-phrase. (iiia) is also unambiguous: is only has the reading in which the wh-phrase has wide scope over the quantifier. (iiib) is ungrammatical.

Answer the following questions about these data:

8.1 Give (quasi) logical forms of the two readings of (iia) in which you translate the *who*-expression as a variable-binding operator WH(x). Give similar (quasi) logical forms of (iib) and (iiia).

8.2 Give a tentative explanation for the ungrammaticality of (iiib).

Consider the following possible answers to the questions in (i)–(iii):

(iv) Detective stories.

(v) Jane read detective stories, Fred read poetry, and Julie read biographies.

Which questions in (i)-(iii) can be appropriately answered by which of these answers?

# Chapter 6

# Discourse and donkey anaphora

Many syntactic and semantic theories focus on the structure and meaning of sentences. But communication typically involves a sequence of sentences which hang together in a certain way. This means that we have to look beyond the meaning of individual sentences and determine the way they are pieced together to make a coherent discourse. In recent years, a number of linguistic theories have been developed which take the discourse as their primary syntactic and semantic unit. They are often referred to as 'dynamic theories of meaning'. The similarities and differences between various approaches to discourse are illustrated by the way they treat problems of reference and anaphora. Questions which arise are: How are discourse anaphora licensed? How do we find the antecedent of an anaphor? The answers given to these questions reflect the different perspectives adopted in the study of natural language in human communication.

# 6.1 Discourse as the basic unit of interpretation

## 6.1.1 Discourse anaphora

We know that *phonemes* are the minimal distinctive phonological units of a language. We distinguish *bin* from *pin*, so *b* and *p* are distinctive sounds. Phonemes as such carry no meaning. *Morphemes* are defined as the minimal meaningful units of a language, where morphemes consist of strings of one or more phonemes. For instance, we have *performer* and *performance*. Both involve the root *perform* (which is itself a meaningful unit), but they differ in the derivative morpheme they attach to the stem. As a result, the former refers to the agent of the action, and the latter refers to the action itself. Words can be combined to build structually complex expressions such as constituents and sentences. It is beyond the scope of morphology to study the structure of such larger units; this is done in syntax. Most syntactic theories take the *sentence* as the basic unit for the study of the structure of language. The central notion here is *grammaticality*. For instance, generative grammar wants the syntax to generate all and only the well-formed sentences of a language.

As pointed out in chapter 2, there is an interesting historical development in semantics from the study of words to the study of larger structural units like phrases and sentences. Most formal semantic theories developed in the 1960's and 1970's are strongly rooted in some syntactic theory or other, and take the sentence as their basic unit. Most of these theories try to build up complex meanings 'bottom up' from the lexical meanings. This is reflected in the well-known principle of the compositionality of meaning: the meaning of the whole is a function of the meaning of the parts and the way they are put together.

Discourse analysis has always played an important role in pragmatics and text linguistics. However, it was not until the 1980's that discourse became a hot issue in the more formal approaches to semantics that we are discussing in this textbook. This new interest arose from certain puzzles in the interpretation of anaphoric relations at the discourse level. Examples like (1), where a referential expression licenses an anaphoric pronoun in the second sentence, constitute the easy cases:

(1)   a.   Susan$_i$ came in. She$_i$ wanted to schedule a meeting.
           Come($s$) ∧ Schedule($x$)
           Come($s$) ∧ Schedule($s$)
       b.   The head of the department$_i$ came in. She$_i$ wanted to schedule a meeting.

We assume that sentence sequencing is interpreted as conjunction of the two propositions. Following the standard conventions in linguistics we adopted in chapter 1, we give the pronoun the same subscript as its antecedent. Coindexing is a syntactic device which allows us to study the constraints on particular antecedent-anaphor relations. Usually, the coindexing chosen is not the only one available. We could point to someone else as the referent of *she* in the second sentence of (1a) or (1b). We will come back to the issue of choosing the right index in section 6.4 below. For the moment, we assume that we somehow 'know' how to get the index which determines the intended interpretation of the pronoun in the given context. In (1), coindexing in the syntax corresponds with *coreference* in the semantics. Proper names and definite descriptions are referential expressions which point to and pick out a specific individual in the universe of discourse. As argued in chapter 4, proper names translate as *individual constants* in first order predicate logic. Pronouns translate as *individual variables*. The interpretation of an individual variable is dependent on the assignment function $g$.

We assume that coindexing in the syntax gives us instructions about the identification of the pronoun. If the pronoun *she* in (1a), denoting the variable $x$, is coindexed with a proper name denoting the constant $s$, we take this to mean that the value assigned to the variable $x$ is $s$. That is: $g(x) = s$. So the coindexing constrains the assignment function in such a way that the appropriate value of the pronoun is the individual referred to in the first sentence. For pronouns dependent on quantificational expressions, the situation is more complex. Quantificational NPs do not point to a specific individual in the universe of discourse the way proper names refer to them, so we cannot translate them in terms of individual constants. In order to translate expressions like *every student* and *nobody* we have to use *variables* which can be bound by *quantifiers*.

In chapter 5, we exploited the predicate-logical notion of binding to handle anaphoric relations in which the pronoun is dependent on a quantificational NP in constructions like (2):

(2)   a.   Everyone$_i$ hates himself$_i$.
           $\forall x$ Hate$(x, x)$

The bound variable interpretation of (2) is possible because the reflexive pronoun translates as a variable $x$ that is in the scope of the universal quantifier $\forall$.

Given that the co-indexing between quantificational expressions and anaphora is interpreted in terms of a binding relation, we expect quantificational NPs not to license anaphoric pronouns in a later sentence. Such pronouns cannot be bound by the quantifier, because its scope ends at the sentence boundary. The prediction that anaphoric relations between pronouns and quantificational antecedents are not licensed across the sentence boundary is borne out by the comparison of the well-formed complex sentences in (3) and the unfelicitous discourses in (4):

(3)    a.    Every student$_i$ worried she$_i$ might fail the test.
        b.    No student$_i$ thought she$_i$ had passed the exam.

(4)    a.    Every student$_i$ came in. #She$_i$ wanted to schedule a meeting.
$$(\forall x\,(\mathrm{Student}(x) \rightarrow \mathrm{Come}(x)) \wedge \mathrm{Schedule}(x))$$
        b.    No student$_i$ came to the meeting. #She$_i$ needed to prepare for class.
$$(\neg\,\exists x\,(\mathrm{Student}(x) \wedge \mathrm{Come}(x)) \wedge \mathrm{Prepare}(x))$$

The pronoun *she* in (3a) and (b) is in the scope of a universal or negative universal quantifier, and the coindexing indicates that we interpret it as a bound variable. That is, the referent of the pronoun is dependent on the choice of the individual for the variable. So every student $x$ worries that $x$ might fail the test, and for no student $x$ it is true that $x$ thought $x$ had passed the exam. The examples in (4) are different. Of course the second sentences of (4a) and (b) are not ungrammatical in the syntactic sense of being ill-formed. But coindexing the pronoun with the quantified NP does not lead to a coherent interpretation. We cannot interpret the coindexing relation as coreference, because the quantified NP is not a referential expression. No bound variable interpretation is available, because the pronoun is outside the scope of the quantifier. The variable $x$ in the second conjunct of (4a) and (b) is thus a free variable, the value of which is dependent on the assignment function. The pronoun *she* can therefore refer to any salient (female) individual in the larger context or situation, but we cannot give the pronoun an interpretation on which it is dependent on the quantifier. This is exactly what first-order predicate logic predicts on the basis of the standard definitions of scope and binding. So far then, the interpretation of anaphoric pronouns at the discourse level can be derived in a straightforward way from the semantic properties of the antecedent.

However, there are certain cases which do not quite fit this pattern. These involve discourse anaphora which have indefinite NPs as their antecedent, as in (6), which are to be compared to the bound variable cases in (5):

(5)    a.    A student$_i$ thought she$_i$ had passed the exam.
        b.    Some students$_i$ worried they$_i$ might fail the test.

(6)   a.   A student$_i$ came in. She$_i$ wanted to schedule a meeting.
           $[\exists x \,[\text{Student}(x) \wedge \text{Come}(x)] \wedge \text{Schedule}(x)]$
      b.   Bill owns some sheep. George vaccinates them.
           $[\exists x \,[\text{Sheep}(x) \wedge \text{Own}(\text{bill},x)] \wedge \text{Vaccinate}(\text{george},x)]$

The indefinite NPs *a student* and *some sheep* are not referential expressions like proper names or definite NPs, so we cannot interpret the coindexing in (6) as coreference. The pronouns *it* and *them* are bound by the existential quantifier in (5), but not in (6), because the scope of the quantifier ends at the sentence boundary. This means that the variable $x$ is outside the scope of the existential quantifier $\exists$, and remains unbound. $x$ is thus a free variable, the value of which is dependent on the assignment function. Basically, this means $x$ could refer to any salient individual in the context. But typically, we do not interpret the second sentence of (6a) to claim some salient female individual wanted to schedule a meeting, or that George vaccinates just anything that happens to be around. We want the pronouns *she* and *them* to pick up the referent introduced in the first sentence of each discourse. Accordingly, they refer to the student who just came in and the group of sheep owned by Bill, respectively.

One potential analysis of the anaphoric relations in (6) is a reduction to cases which can be treated at the sentence level. This would avoid the introduction of special discourse machinery, and therefore it would be the most conservative approach. A straightforward proposal along these lines would be to treat sentence sequencing as VP-conjunction. This would make (7a) equivalent to (7b):

(7)   a.   A student$_i$ called me. She$_i$ asked about the exam.
      b.   A student$_i$ called me and (she$_i$) asked about the exam.

This approach works for the particular case discussed here, but it does not extend to other examples. For instance, (8a) and (b) are not equivalent:

(8)   a.   Exactly one student$_i$ called me. She$_i$ asked about the exam.
      b.   Exactly one student$_i$ called me and asked about the exam.

(8b) claims that there is exactly one student who satisfies both the property of calling, and the property of asking. (8b) comes out true in a context in which several students called me, but only one of them asked about the exam. However, (8a) comes out false in that context, as the first sentence excludes the possibility of more than one student calling.

Intuitively, the discourse anaphorical relations in (5) and (6) do not involve a reduction to the sentence-level, but an incremental interpretation in which the second sentence is interpreted in the context set up by the interpretation of the first sentence. This has led many researchers to establish a distinction between 'real' individuals (i.e. individuals that exist in the universe of discourse of the model) and so-called *discourse referents* (Karttunen 1976). Discourse referents are introduced as the discourse unfolds, and they are 'stand-ins' for real individuals in the representation of the discourse. If we assume that the indefinite NPs in 5) and (6) introduce new discourse referents, we intuitively set up an anchor for further anaphoric reference. An important implication of this idea is that the phenomenon of discourse anaphora illustrated in (5) and (6) requires a semantic theory which goes beyond the sentence level and takes the discourse as its basic unit. This has nothing to do with syntax: grammaticality judgments really apply to sentences, and we cannot contrast well-formed versus ill-formed discourses in the same way. Hobbs (1979) argues that the role played by grammaticality within sentences compares to the role coherence plays beyond sentence boundaries. So semantics starts to live a life of its own at the discourse level. This does not mean that discourse semantics is no longer part of the theory of grammar. Rather, we have to view the grammar as a modular system in which each module chooses its own basic unit. Morphology is one level up from phonology, because it looks at meaningful strings of phonemes, rather than individual phonemes. Syntax in its turn takes us beyond morphology, because it looks at the way words combine to build structural units. Along these lines, we need not be surprised that the semantics of discourse takes us one level up from syntax by looking at coherent sequences of sentences. So we can adopt a perspective on discourse which does not differ much in approach from the kind of formal syntax and semantics we are familiar with.

Once we agree that we need to be able to talk about meaning beyond the sentence level, the question arises how we can build a semantic theory that takes discourse as the basic unit of interpretation. The interest in discourse anaphora has made semantics a lot more 'dynamic' or 'procedural'. This has led to a whole new set of research questions (see Muskens, van Benthem and Visser 1997 for a general overview). For the cases of reference to individuals, the main question is how an incremental, partial theory of discourse meaning handles anaphoric relations as in (6)–(8). This question can be phrased as: how can we design a logic which explains why indefinite NPs can license discourse anaphora, and other quantifiers cannot (compare 4). Given that this phenomenon has been characterized as the property to establish anaphoric relations beyond the (traditional) scope of the quantifier, it is not surprising that discourse anaphora should be studied in connection with other contexts in which this property manifests itself.

## 6.1.2 Donkey anaphora

The splitting between indefinite NPs and other quantifiers also occurs in conditional and quantificational constructions. Compare the following sentences:

(9)   a.   *If every student$_i$ likes Copenhagen, she$_i$ is happy.

        b.   If a student$_i$ likes Copenhagen, she$_i$ is happy.

(10)   a.   *Every student who read every paper$_i$ on semantics liked it$_i$.

        b.   Every student who read a paper$_i$ on semantics liked it$_i$.

The representations of (9a) and (10a), given in (11a) and (b) respectively, show that the pronoun translates as a free variable. The coindexing thus marks an illegitimate binding relation, which explains why (9a) and (10a) are ill-formed:

(11)   a.   $((\forall x\,(\text{Student}(x) \to \text{Like}(x,c))) \to \text{Happy}(x))$

        b.   $((\forall x\,\forall y\,((\text{Student}(x) \wedge \text{Paper}(y)) \to \text{Read}(x,y))) \to \text{Like}(x,y))$

The variable $x$ in Happy$(x)$ is not bound by the universal quantifier $\forall x$ in (11a); the formula could just as well have been written Happy$(y)$. The same thing is true for the variable $y$ in Like$(x,y)$ in (11b), which is not bound by the universal quantifiers either; this formula could just as well have been written *Like*$(x,w)$. The general rules of predicate logic correctly rule out these examples as illegitimate binding beyond the scope of the quantifier.

However, if we adopt the rules governing scope and binding relations that predicate logic provides, we cannot explain the felicitous anaphorical relations in (9b) and (10b). After all, the representations these sentences lead to in (12a) and (12b) involve anaphoric pronouns outside the scope of the quantifier:

(12)   a.   $((\exists x\,(\text{Student}(x) \wedge \text{Like}(x,c))) \to \text{Happy}(x))$

        b.   $((\exists x\,\exists y\,(\text{Student}(x) \wedge \text{Paper}(y) \wedge \text{Read}(x,y))) \to \text{Like}(x,y))$

The quantificational structure of (12a) and (b) is not any different from the one we gave in (11a) and (b). As far as the predicate-logical formulas are concerned, the relevant variables $x$ and $y$ remain free. If anaphoric relations in natural language are constrained by the predicate-logical rules of scope and binding, we would expect the coindexing in (9b) and (10b) to be illegitimate. However, it is not.

The problem is not that it is difficult to formulate an appropriate translation for the sentences in (9b) and (10b). The representations in (13) are well-formed formulas in first-order predicate logic, and they do a fine job of capturing the meaning of the natural language sentence:

(13)   a.   $(\forall x \, (\text{Student}(x) \wedge \text{Like}(x, c)) \rightarrow \text{Happy}(x))$
       b.   $(\forall x \, \forall y \, (\text{Student}(x) \wedge \text{Paper}(y) \wedge \text{Read}(x, y)) \rightarrow \text{Like}(x, y))$

The problem with the representations under (13) is that they do not seem to fit our general aim of developing a compositional theory of meaning. Note in particular that the indefinite NP which shows up in the antecedent of a conditional in (11b) and in the relative clause of a universally quantified NP in (12b) is translated in (13) in terms of a wide scope universal quantifier. However, universal quantifiers are not normally taken to be the meaning of an indefinite NP. So we seem to have a dilemma: we can compositionally derive the formulas in (12), but they do not give us the desired binding relation. The formulas in (13) give us the desired interpretation, but we do not know how to derive them in a compositional way. This raises the question whether standard first-order predicate logic is the appropriate meta-language to use in the interpretation of natural language.

It has been pointed out that the translation of a narrow scope indefinite NP as a wide scope universal quantifier is not impossible, in view of the laws of quantifier movement of first-order predicate logic introduced in chapter 5 above. For easy reference, the laws are reproduced here:

- Laws of quantifier movement

  (i)   $(\phi \rightarrow \forall x \, \psi(x)) \Leftrightarrow \forall x \, (\phi \rightarrow \psi(x))$
        provided $x$ is not free in $\phi$

  (ii)  $(\phi \rightarrow \exists x \, \psi(x)) \Leftrightarrow \exists x \, (\phi \rightarrow \psi(x))$
        provided $x$ is not free in $\phi$

  (iii) $(\forall x \, \phi(x) \rightarrow \psi) \Leftrightarrow \exists x (\phi(x) \rightarrow \psi)$
        provided $x$ is not free in $\psi$

  (iv)  $(\exists x \, \phi(x) \rightarrow \psi) \Leftrightarrow \forall x (\phi(x) \rightarrow \psi)$
        provided $x$ is not free in $\psi$

The relevant clause for our discussion is (iv). This clause allows a narrow scope existential quantifier in the antecedent of a conditional to translate as a universal quantifier taking wide scope over the conditional as a whole. This suggests that (12) and (13) are in fact very close in meaning.

However, they are not equivalent because clause (iv) stipulates that the variable $x$ should not be free in the consequent of the conditional. As a result of this additional condition, we cannot simply rewrite (12) as (13), because the variable $x$ which is free in (12) is bound in (13). Egli (1979) argues that the constraint on the variable remaining free is just ignored in these cases. Unfortunately, any attempt in the direction of relaxing the scope constraints of first-order logic is bound to fail, because such an approach cannot explain why we do worry about the variable remaining free in examples like (9a) and (10a). In these cases, the intended anaphoric link is unavailable, and the laws on quantifier movement capture this correctly. An additional problem for an explanation along the lines of Egli (1979) is that the laws on quantifier movement only regulate the behavior of first-order quantifiers. This means that we cannot account for similar sentences involving a determiner like *most*:

(14) Most students who read a paper$_i$ on semantics liked it$_i$.

First-order predicate logic does not tell us how to make the interpretation of the pronoun dependent on the quantified NP, because it does not give an interpretation of the binding quantifier in the first place (see chapter 7 for more discussion of the limits of first-order predicate logic).

The problem raised by conditional sentences like (9) and (10) is called the problem of 'donkey' anaphora. The phenomenon was named after the original examples discussed by Geach (1962), which involved farmers and donkeys:

(15)  a.   If a farmer$_i$ owns a donkey$_j$ he$_i$ beats it$_j$.
      b.   Every farmer$_i$ who owns a donkey$_j$ beats it$_j$.

The problems raised by discourse and donkey anaphora are related, because both depend on a special relation between an indefinite NP and an anaphoric pronoun outside the regular scope domain of the NP. In principle, there are three different lines along which we can try to approach the problem of discourse and donkey anaphora. The first option is to say that there is something special about the anaphoric pronoun in these cases. It cannot be interpreted in terms of regular coreference or binding, but it gets some other interpretation. This solution is explored in the e-type approach. A second line of explanation is to say that there is something special about the indefinite NP. If it does not behave as a regular quantifier, maybe we should not translate it as an existential quantifier. This has given rise to theories like File Change semantics and Discourse Representation Theory. These theories interpret the indefinite NPs as variables and use a mechanism of unselective binding to allow them to be bound by other quantifiers

in the sentence or the discourse. The third possibility is to somehow extend
the scope domain of the indefinite NP. This solution is adopted in Dynamic
Predicate Logic, which develops a notion of dynamic binding. In the following sections, we will first briefly discuss the general aim of a dynamic
theory (section 6.2), and then study the three types of analyses developed
to deal with discourse and donkey anaphora (section 6.3).

## 6.2 General aims of dynamic semantics

The traditional view held by logicians and philosophers of language is that
meaning is connected to denotations in a model (for proper names, predicates and so forth) and truth conditions (for sentences). Chierchia (1995)
calls this the "view of meaning as content", because it takes the primary
task of semantics to be that of identifying the informational *content* of
expressions. This is a rather static view of meaning. Linguists are quite
aware that truth-conditional issues are not all there is to language. We all
know that we do not only assert sentences, we also ask for information.
And we can do many other things with words (promise, threaten, baptize,
etc.). There is a serious tradition in linguistics studying questions (and
answers) (e.g. Hamblin 1973, Karttunen 1977, Groenendijk and Stokhof
1984), and other speech acts in such a way that they are compatible with
the truth-theoretical approach to assertions. This means that there is a
constant interaction between the domains that are traditionally referred
to as semantics and pragmatics. The phenomenon of discourse anaphora
is typically relevant to the semantics-pragmatics borderline. At the same
time, it is of interest for researchers concerned with language processing.
In a language processing view, the meaning of an expression is regarded as
an instruction to the hearer to 'construct' (part of) a representation. This
view fits in well with the intuitive way in which we interpret discourse:
we do not wait until the very end of the entire discourse before we start
interpreting it. The idea of *incremental interpretation* is that we interpret
one sentence at a time and look at each sentence as an extension of the
information built up by the context so far. A dynamic theory of natural
language meaning is thus formulated in terms of 'updating'. The picture of
the situation we have changes as we add more information, so the context
is updated with the information contributed by the sentence.

The dynamic view of the meaning of discourse has important consequences for our view of semantics. First, updating involves an interpretation of sentence sequencing which corresponds with an asymmetric version
of conjunction. In classical first-order logic, $p \wedge q$ is equivalent to $q \wedge p$.
But in natural language, (16a) is a coherent discourse under the intended

interpretation indicated by co-indexing, but (16b) is not:

(16)   a.    A student$_i$ came in. She$_i$ wanted to schedule a meeting.
        b.    #She$_i$ wanted to schedule a meeting. A student$_i$ came in.

The infelicity of (16b) suggests that sentence sequencing in natural language is not symmetric. Instead, we want to interpret the second sentence as an update of the first one. That is, we restrict the interpretation of the second sentence to contexts which make the first sentence true.

Second, an incremental theory of discourse is necessarily a *partial* theory of meaning. Sentence-based semantics typically works with complete models and favors a holistic interpretation. In a static approach, one cannot really talk about 'old' and 'new' information. As a result, a static approach does not capture the intuition that indefinite NPs introduce a 'new' referent into the discourse, which is available from then for anaphoric reference. The only way in which we can update the context with the information contributed by the sentence is to adopt a partial theory of meaning which allows our universe of discourse to grow, and the picture we have of the situation to change as we add more information.

Last but not least, the dynamic view implies that meaning becomes procedural: it is a relation between input and output conditions. If we assume that input and output conditions are formalized as information states, we can say that the semantic value of a sentence is a function from information states to information states. Chierchia (1995) refers to this as the "view of meaning as context change" and talks about the "dynamics of meaning". Note that the dynamic view does not replace the static view, but extends it to account for certain phenomena at the discourse level. Note further that dynamic semantics does not do away with the semantics-pragmatics distinction altogether. Although dynamic semantics deals with certain phenomena which were traditionally taken to be part of pragmatics, there is still an important role for pragmatics to play in an overall theory of discourse (as we will see in section 6.4 below).

# 6.3   Anaphoric relations in sentence and discourse

In this section we discuss the three possible approaches to handling anaphora that occur outside the scope of their binder: the e-type approach to anaphoric pronouns, unselective binding of variables introduced by indefinite NPs, and dynamic existential quantifiers for the interpretation of indefinite NPs.

## 6.3.1 E-type anaphora

In the late '70's, Evans developed a way to account for anaphoric pronouns that are outside the scope of their binding operator by giving the pronoun a special interpretation (see the collected work in Evans 1985). According to Evans, pronouns outside the scope of their binding operator are not *bound* by the quantifier. In order to account for the observation that discourse and donkey anaphora are dependent on an indefinite NP, he claims that these pronouns reconstruct their descriptive content on the basis of the antecedent NP. Besides coreferentiality and binding, we thus have a third way of interpreting coindexing in the syntax.

The so-called e-type anaphor is nothing but a disguised description. Usually, the descriptive content of the e-type anaphor consists in the conjunction of the common noun and the predicate. For instance:

(17)  a.  A student came in. She had a question about the exam.
          she = *the* student who came in
      b.  Bill owns some sheep and Max vaccinates them.
          them = *the* sheep Bill owns

The e-type approach extends to the quantificational cases in (18):

(18)  a.  If a student likes Copenhagen, she is happy.
          she = for every case we examine, *the* student in question
          who likes Copenhagen
      b.  Every student who read a paper on semantics liked it.
          it = for every student, *the* paper she read

If the e-type approach is generally available as an interpretation mechanism, the question arises how much freedom the pronoun has in reconstructing its descriptive content. Cooper (1979) suggests that reconstruction is dependent on a contextually salient function. If we would interpret this broadly, we should be able to reconstruct the descriptive context of an e-type pronoun from any salient expression picking out a unique referent in the context. However, examples like (19) and (20) show that the available interpretations are constrained by the syntax:

(19)  a.  Bill owns a cat. Max takes care of it.
      b.  Bill is a cat-owner. # Max takes care of it.

(20)  a.  Everyone who owns a cat takes good care of it.
      b.  *Every cat-owner takes good care of it.

We may assume that the function which maps cat-owners to the cat they own is salient in (19) and (20), because we are talking about cats and owners. Although this function can be used to reconstruct the descriptive content of the e-type pronoun in (19a) and (20a), it is unable to license the pronoun *it* in (19b) and (20b). The data in (19) and (20) suggest that an e-type pronoun needs to be licensed by a 'real' antecedent, given by an indefinite NP for instance. The general conclusion is that the pronoun reconstructs its descriptive content on the basis of an NP, rather than on the basis of a contextually available function. These observations make it clear that the relation between the pronoun and its antecedent is tighter than what a liberal view of the e-type analysis predicts. This is not to say that we cannot tighten up the relation between the pronoun and its antecedent in an e-type analysis. But such restrictions have to be formulated on top of the interpretation procedure, for they do not follow naturally from the e-type analysis itself.

Another question that the e-type approach raises concerns the presuppositions of uniqueness associated with definite descriptions. According to Russell (1905), definite descriptions get the interpretation in (21):

(21) $\exists x\,(P(x) \wedge \forall y\,(P(y) \to y = x))$

Under this interpretation, there is an object $x$ which has a certain property $P$ and no other object has this property. If we adopt this interpretation for e-type pronouns, we expect everyone in (19) and (20) to own (and take care of) just one cat, everyone in (18b) to read (and like) exactly one paper on semantics, etc. Heim (1982) points out that uniqueness presuppositions in the context of donkey sentences mean that in examples like (19b) and (20a), we would have to assume that we quantify over people who read exactly one paper on semantics, or who own exactly one cat. This seems like a counterintuitive requirement. In interpreting sentences like (19b) or (20a), we do not want to exclude from our domain of quantification people who own more than one cat or who read more than one paper on semantics. Heim argues that it is generally not appropriate to associate uniqueness presuppositions with donkey anaphora. Examples like (22) support her view that this would be undesirable:

(22) Everyone who buys a sage plant in this store gets eight others along with it.

The sentence makes it explicit that sage plants are sold in bunches of nine. Given that every buyer gets nine sage plants, it is impossible to interpret *it* as the unique sage plant for every buyer. None of the plants in the bunch has any characteristic properties which allow it to be picked out with a singular description. Given that the sentence is felicitous, something must be wrong with the interpretation of the pronoun as a definite description that carries a presupposition of uniqueness.

Heim (1982) rejects the e-type analysis because the uniqueness condition on definite descriptions is incompatible with the interpretation of donkey anaphora in sentences like (22). More recently, it has been argued that the 'sage plant examples' do not provide a convincing counterargument against the e-type analysis of discourse and donkey anaphora. The problem of (22) is not so much the interpretation of the pronoun as a hidden description, but the interpretation of the description as carrying a presupposition of uniqueness. We can envisage a slightly different interpretation of definite descriptions that does not have these problems. Independently of the e-type analysis, Neale (1990) proposes to interpret definite descriptions as numberless descriptions. If we adopt this proposal, we can have e-type pronouns which do not carry uniqueness presuppositions. A revival of the e-type approach in work by Heim (1990), van der Does (1994), Lappin and Francez (1994), and others shows that quite sophisticated analyses of donkey sentences can be developed based on this strategy.

The e-type analysis illustrates an approach to discourse donkey anaphora which tries to account for the observations made in section 6.1 by changing the interpretation of the anaphoric pronoun. A second solution which has been developed leaves the interpretation of the pronoun intact, but changes the interpretation of the indefinite NP. This approach to the problem of discourse and donkey anaphora is exemplified by File Change Semantics and Discourse Representation Theory.

## 6.3.2  Unselective binding

As an alternative to the e-type approach, Heim (1982) developed File Change semantics, and Kamp (1981) and Kamp and Reyle (1993) developed Discourse Representation Theory (DRT).[1] DRT assumes a separate level of representation for the discourse. There is no direct relation between linguistic expressions and their interpretation in a model, but there is an intermediate level of semantic representation, which provides a partial model reflecting the information conveyed by the discourse so far. This intermediate level is like a mental, or cognitive, representation of the text, which is not dispensable (as is the intermediate level of representation in classical theories of meaning such as Montague Grammar). This is a much

---

[1]The presentation follows Kamp's 'box' notation rather than Heim's files. My introduction to DRT is very intuitive and informal. For more details and a complete formulation of construction rules and embedding conditions, I refer to Kamp and Reyle (1993).

debated feature of DRT, but we will not go into it here. Note that the intermediate level of representation is written in a language of 'boxes'. The boxes are called Discourse Representation Structures (DRSs). The theory is set up in such a way that we formulate *construction rules* which take natural language expressions as input and have boxes as output. The boxes contain *discourse referents*, which are 'stand-ins' for the individuals introduced by the text. This allows us to have only partial information about the properties of these individuals: all we know about them is what we know about the discourse referents. What we know about discourse referents is specified in DRS *conditions*. DRT adopts the perspective of the hearer, rather than the speaker: the focus is on processing rather than generating language. The boxes are interpreted via *embedding conditions*. The embedding conditions map the boxes into the model. A discourse is true if the box which is constructed for it can be embedded into the model. That is, the model has to contain individuals that instantiate the discourse referents, and all the DRS conditions have to be verified. The embedding conditions are the counterpart to truth conditions in classical first-order logic.

The introduction of discourse referents and conditions is one of the things that are regulated by construction rules. The typical role of indefinite NPs is to introduce new discourse referents into the DRS. Consider the discourse in (23):

(23) A student$_i$ called Jane. She$_i$ asked about the exam.

The indefinite NP in the first sentence introduces an individual which has the property of being a student. The verb phrase adds that this individual has the property of calling Jane. The proper name introduces a discourse referent and a condition that the referent bears the name *Jane*. The transitive verb introduces a two-place relation that holds between discourse referents. The representation of the first sentence of (23) is spelled out in figure 6.1.

$$\boxed{\begin{array}{c} x \quad y \\[4pt] \text{Student}(x) \\ \text{Jane}(y) \\ \text{Call}(x,y) \end{array}}$$

Figure 6.1: A student called Jane

The discourse referents of the DRS are listed in the top row of the box. They are followed by conditions describing the properties of the discourse referents. The DRS is true if and only if we can find an embedding function $f$ which assigns individual values to all the discourse referents in such a way that the individual has the properties described by the conditions in the DRS. This implies that there has to exist some student who called Jane. The existential force of the indefinite NP is located in the embedding function, for there is no quantifier present in the DRS. The main difference between the interpretation of proper names and indefinite NPs is that a proper name picks out the unique (intended) bearer of the name, whereas indefinite NPs accept any individual which satisfies the conditions in question. As a result, proper names usually pick out one specific embedding function, whereas for indefinite NPs there may be many embedding functions which make the sentence come out true. This supports the view that discourse referents are only stand-ins for real individuals.

The incremental interpretation of the discourse means that the second sentence adds more discourse referents and more conditions to the same DRS. Thus we extend the interpretation built up so far. The construction rule for the pronoun involves finding an appropriate antecedent for it, by linking it to an accessible discourse referent in the DRS under construction. The pronoun *she* is coindexed with the indefinite NP *a student*. This triggers a construction rule which tries to identify the discourse referent $u$ with some appropriate and accessible antecedent. An appropriate antecedent for the pronoun is the discourse referent $x$ introduced for the indefinite NP. This discourse referent is accessible, because it occurs in the same box. Given that we are able to find an appropriate and accessible antecedent for the pronoun, identification of the two discourse referents is allowed. The next step is that the construction rule introduces the condition $u = x$ into the DRS. The predicate of the second sentence adds a further condition on the discourse referent introduced by the indefinite NP in the first sentence. The interpretation of the two sentence discourse is spelled out in figure 6.2.

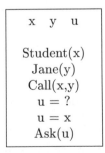

Figure 6.2: A student$_i$ called Jane. She$_i$ asked about the exam.

The interpretation of indefinite NPs in DRT focuses on their role of introducing new discourse referents into the DRS. Real quantificational NPs such as *every student* also introduce new discourse referents, but DRT treats these quantifiers in a rather different way. The interpretation of universal and other quantifiers invokes a box-splitting construction rule, which introduces two sub boxes related by the connective ⇒. The construction rule for universal NPs puts the restriction on the quantifier in the left subordinate box and the scope of the quantifier in the right subordinate box. Consider the DRS constructed for the first sentence of (24) in 6.3.

(24) Every student called Jane. She asked a question about the exam.

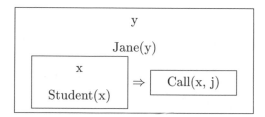

Figure 6.3: Every student called Jane.

The verification procedure for ⇒ requires every embedding function which verifies the left embedded box to extend to a function which verifies the right embedded box. The interpretation of ⇒ is thus very similar to the interpretation of the conditional in propositional logic (compare chapter 3). In the case of figure 6.3, this interpretation requires every individual which satisfies the property of being a student (and can thus function as the value for the discourse referent $x$) to have the property of calling Jane. The similarity with first-order predicate logical formulas makes it possible to grasp this at an intuitive level.

Note that the discourse referent introduced by the NP is not present in the top box, because the quantificational NP cannot be directly mapped onto some specific individual in the universe of discourse. The result of this construction is that a discourse referent is introduced in a subordinate box. In this position it is *inaccessible* for anaphoric pronouns in subsequent sentences that add further information at the level of the main box. If we extend the DRS in figure 6.3 with the interpretation of the second sentence of (24), we end up with the DRS in Figure 6.4.

The pronoun *she* introduces a discourse referent $u$ in the top box, just like in figure 6.2 above. The pronoun needs to find an antecedent, so $u$ tries to identify with some accessible discourse referent in the DRS. The referent $y$ is available in the top box, but the identification of $u$ with $y$ does not

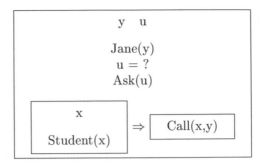

Figure 6.4: Every student$_i$ called Jane. She$_i$ asked a question about the exam.

yield a coherent interpretation of the discourse: we expect a caller to have a question, not the person being called. The coindexing of the pronoun with the quantificational NP indicates that the intended antecedent for *she* is the quantified NP *every student*. However, the discourse referent $x$ introduced by the quantified NP is not accessible, because it is contained in a subordinate box. In DRT, accessibility requires the antecedent to be in a box 'as high as' or 'higher than' the discourse referent for the pronoun. This translates as a condition on the structure of embedded boxes. Accessible antecedents are in the same box, in a box to the left, or in a box which embeds the one that contains the discourse referent for the pronoun.[2] The result is a DRS for which we cannot give a coherent interpretation with the pronoun taking the quantified NP as its antecedent.

The DRSs in figures 6.2 and 6.4 show that indefinite NPs and quantified NPs are treated in essentially different ways. The construction rules these expressions trigger make indefinite NPs, but not quantified NPs suitable antecedents for discourse anaphora. The next step is to consider what happens if we embed an indefinite NP under a universal quantifier, as in (25), where the anaphor is a donkey pronoun. In DRT, (25) gets the representation in Figure 6.5.

(25) Every student who read a paper$_i$ on semantics liked it$_i$

As pointed out in relation to figure 6.4, we assume that discourse referents introduced in boxes to the left and up of the anaphor provide accessible antecedents for the anaphoric pronoun. The pronoun *it* is coindexed with *a paper*. The coindexing relation reflects a dependency relation of the anaphor on the indefinite NP. Observe that the intended antecedent $y$ of

---

[2]This is reminiscent of c-command relations in a tree-like structure. Compare chapter 2 for a discussion of configurational constraints on anaphora.

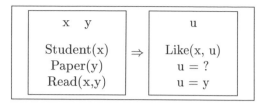

Figure 6.5: Every student who read a paper$_i$ on semantics liked it$_i$.

the pronoun *it* is in the box to the left of the one which contains $u$. According to the rules on accessibility, this means that $y$ is accessible to $u$. Thus we can interpret *it* as being dependent for its interpretation on the indefinite NP *a paper*.

Note, however, that the indefinite NP *a paper* is embedded under a universal quantifier. Remember that the connective $\Rightarrow$ is defined in such a way that for all embedding functions which make the left box true it should be possible to extend them to one which makes the right box true. Because the embedding function assigns individuals to all the discourse referents in the left box, this formulation amounts to universal quantification over all the discourse referents in the left box. The identification of $u$ with $y$ brings the pronoun under the scope of the universal quantifier, and the donkey anaphor is interpreted as a regular bound pronoun. Given the universal force of the binder, the meaning of the sentence can be paraphrased as 'for every student $x$, and every paper $y$ that $x$ read, $x$ liked $y$'.

The interpretation of $\Rightarrow$ reflects an important difference between DRT and classical first-order logic. In standard first-order logic, all quantification is selective. That is, the universal or existential quantifier in a formula $\forall x\, \phi$ or $\exists x\, \phi$ binds only the variable $x$, and not any other variable around in the formula $\phi$. The connective $\Rightarrow$, however, binds all the variables standing for discourse referents in the left subordinate box. This amounts to assuming *unselective* quantification over all the variables in the restriction of the quantifier. It is the combination of the interpretation of indefinite NPs as introducing variables with the concept of unselective binding which allows File Change Semantics and DRT to provide a unified analysis of both discourse and donkey anaphora.

Summing up, we observe that DRT has a number of interesting characteristics. It takes discourses rather than sentences as its basic semantic unit. It reflects the idea that discourse is interpreted incrementally and involves partial models. DRSs are partial models of the discourse built up so far, and they are fully interpretable at every stage of the discourse.

The result is a compositional interpretation of discourse anaphora.[3] The advantages of the Kamp/Heim approach to indefinites are clear. First, we do not need a third way of interpreting coindexing in the syntax: we can make do with the classical mechanisms of coreferentiality and binding. The second main achievement is a principled explanation of the difference in behavior between quantified NPs such as *every student* and *no student* on the one hand, and indefinite NPs on the other hand. The explanation is that quantified NPs are real quantifiers, which introduce binding operators. Indefinite NPs do not have any quantificational force of their own; they just translate as free variables. Furthermore, the Kamp/Heim approach to indefinites and the method of unselective binding have been successfully applied to a wide variety of linguistic problems. Examples include a treatment of plural discourse anaphora (Kamp and Reyle 1993) and of temporal anaphora (Kamp and Rohrer 1983, Partee 1984, Hinrichs 1986, Kamp and Reyle 1993), an account of generic and partitive interpretations of bare plurals and singular indefinites (Diesing 1992, Kratzer 1995, Krifka et al. 1995), and an analysis of presuppositions (van der Sandt 1992, Beaver 1997).

Notwithstanding the success of the framework, the DRT approach to anaphora also faces some serious problems. Crucially, the interpretation of donkey pronouns involves the assumption that indefinites always take over the quantificational force of their binder. This does not always yield the correct interpretation. Consider an example like (26) :

(26) Most students who own a cat take good care of it.
$\text{Most}_{x,y} ((\text{Student}(x) \wedge \text{Cat}(y) \wedge \text{Own}(x,y))(Care(x,y)))$

The interpretation of *most* as an unselective quantifier that binds both the student and the cat variable results in an interpretation in which the sentence quantifies over *pairs* of students and cats and claims that for most of these pairs, it is true that the student takes good care of the cat. But suppose we have a situation in which there are 10 students, 9 of which own one cat each, and they take good care of it. The 10th student owns 15 cats, and neglects them. The DRT analysis of the sentence yields the truth-value false, because most pairs of a student and a cat are such that the student does not take good care of the cat. Intuitively, however, we would consider the sentence to be true in the given context. After all, most students are such that they take good care of the cat they own. These observations suggest that a sentence like (26) expresses quantification over cat-owning students rather than over pairs of a student and a cat. This problem

---

[3] Actually, the compositionality of DRT is a much debated issue. We will take it for granted that it is at least possible to give a compositional version of DRT.

arises with all quantifiers which have more than existential, but less than universal force, such as *most, many* and *few*. Because the problem has to do with proportions, it is called the *proportion problem*. The proportion problem spreads through the whole system, because unselective binding is a central property of DRT. For instance, we can come up with variants of the proportion problem which involve temporal anaphora (see Partee 1984 and de Swart 1991 for discussion). We can devise solutions to the proportion problem within DRT, but it is clear that the existence of the problem as such sheds doubt on the question whether we really want to treat natural language determiners as unselective quantifiers (see Kadmon 1987, Heim 1990, Chierchia 1992 for further discussion).

DRT proposes a radical difference between indefinite NPs and real quantificational NPs. This distinction explains the difference in licensing of discourse anaphora between NPs like *a student* and *every student*. Several people have observed that this means that we lose the nice, uniform analysis of NPs that has been developed within Montague Grammar and which we exploit in generalized quantifier theory (see chapter 8 below). This also relates to certain empirical problems. It has been observed that the difference between *a* and *every, no* is gradual, rather than absolute. That is to say, in certain cases these quantifiers also allow binding beyond the scope of the operator, as shown by the examples in (27) (from Fodor and Sag 1982 and Roberts 1989 respectively):

(27)    a.    Each student in the syntax class was accused of cheating on the exam, and he was reprimanded by the dean.

        b.    Either there is no bathroom in this house, or it is in a funny place.

(27a) means that every student who cheated was reprimanded by the dean and (27b) means that the bathroom is in a funny place if there is one. In standard DRT it is hard to account for these cases. In (27a) the anaphoric pronoun is dependent on a real quantificational NP, and not on an indefinite NP which does not have any quantificational force of its own. The negation operator in (27b) is supposed to close off the binding domain of the indefinite NP, which should therefore be inaccessible to the pronoun in the right disjunct. If we take these examples seriously, we seem to need a more general approach to binding beyond the scope of the operator. Within DRT, we find several proposals. For instance, Roberts (1989, 1996) explores the use of domain restrictions on quantificational and modal operators to account for cases like (27a) and Krahmer and Muskens (1995) give a revised definition of negation in DRT which handles examples like (27b). But the problems have also inspired researchers to develop radically different approaches to discourse and donkey anaphora. In order to bridge the gap between indefinite NPs and other quantificational NPs, alternative analyses have been developed which propose an extension of the binding domain of certain quantifiers (in particular, existential ones), but not others. The proposals for dynamic binding follow ideas developed by Groenendijk and Stokhof (1990, 1991). This brings us to the third type of solution to the problems raised by the phenomena of discourse and donkey anaphora, namely a change of the concept of binding domain of a quantifier.

### 6.3.3  Dynamic binding

In the literature, we find several systems which try to combine the traditional interpretation of indefinite NPs in terms of existential quantifiers and the idea that indefinite NPs introduce a discourse referent that can be picked up by an anaphoric pronoun in subsequent sentences or in the consequent of a conditional. This provides new analyses of discourse and donkey anaphora. Examples of such combined dynamic systems are Barwise (1987), Schubert and Pelletier (1989) and Groenendijk and Stokhof (1991). These systems can be viewed as dynamic extensions of first order predicate logic.[4] We will concentrate here on the dynamic predicate logic (DPL) developed by Groenendijk and Stokhof.

The starting point for DPL is the view that the utterance of a sentence brings the hearer from a certain state of information to another one. As long as we restrict ourselves to information about individuals that are in our domain of discourse, we can identify an information state with an assignment of objects to variables. Context change is then the change from an input assignment to an output assignment. Accordingly, the interpretation of a formula in DPL is a set of ordered pairs of assignments, the set of its possible 'input-output' pairs. For instance, (28a) is interpreted as in (28b):

(28)  a.  $\exists x\, P(x)$
      b.  $[\![\exists x\, P(x)]\!] = \{\langle g, h\rangle \mid h[x]g \land h(x) \in F(P)\}$

$h[x]g$ means that assignment $h$ differs from $g$ at most with respect to the value it assigns to $x$. $F$ is the interpretation function which assigns

---

[4]Groenendijk and Stokhof (1990) develop a dynamic extension of Montague grammar, which is based on a higher-order type-theoretical logic. Given that this book does not introduce the full machinery of Montague grammar, a presentation of dynamic Montague grammar is outside the scope of our discussion. For an excellent introduction to Montague grammar, the reader is referred to Dowty, Wall and Peters (1981) or Gamut (1991), volume 2.

individuals to individual constants and sets of n-tuples of individuals to n-place predicates. All assignments $h$ that are in the interpretation of $P(x)$ are taken to be possible outputs with $g$ as input.

In order to treat discourse anaphora, we need to combine the dynamic interpretation of indefinite NPs with an analysis of sentence sequencing. In DPL, sentence sequencing is represented as dynamic conjunction. The definition is in (29):

(29) $[\![\phi \wedge \psi]\!] = \{\langle g, h \rangle \mid \exists k : \langle g, k \rangle \in [\![\phi]\!] \wedge \langle k, h \rangle \in [\![\psi]\!]\}$

According to this definition, the interpretation of $\phi \wedge \psi$ with input $g$ may result in output $h$ if and only if there is some $k$ such that interpreting $\phi$ in $g$ may lead to $k$, and interpreting $\psi$ in $k$ gets us from $k$ to $h$. The fact that the second conjunct is interpreted with respect to the assignment which results after interpreting the first conjunct means that we have an incremental interpretation. That is, the second sentence is interpreted in the context which results after processing the first sentence.

Suppose now that $\phi$ contains an existential quantifier. In that case, the output of processing the first conjunct means that we have a variable assignment which assigns a certain object to the variable $x$ bound by the existential quantifier. Given that this is the input assignment for the second conjunct, any occurrence of $x$ in the second conjunct will be taken to refer to that same object. Because of its power to pass on variable bindings from the left conjunct to the right one, conjunction is called an internally dynamic connective. And because of its capacity to keep passing on bindings to conjuncts yet to come, it functions as an externally dynamic connective as well.

The combined dynamic treatment of the existential quantifier and conjunction solves the problem of discourse anaphora in sequences like (30):

(30) A student$_i$ called Jane. She$_i$ asked a question about the exam.

The pronoun and the indefinite NP bear the same index, which means that they use the same variable in their interpretation. The output assignment of the first sentence fixes the value assigned to the variable $x$ bound by the existential quantifier. Given that this is the input assignment for the second sentence, the value of $x$ is passed on to the next sentence. An occurrence of the same variable in the second sentence is not in the scope of the existential quantifier in the ordinary sense. However, the dynamic interpretation of conjunction implies that it is bound by the quantifier with the same force as an occurrence of the same variable in the first sentence.

Implication is another internally dynamic connective. With respect to a certain input assignment, the antecedent of an implication results in a set of assignments that verify the antecedent. For the implication as a whole, it is required that each of these verifying assignments be a possible input for the consequent. This is reflected in the following interpretation of implication:

(31) $[\![\phi \rightarrow \psi]\!] = \{\langle g, h \rangle \mid h = g \wedge \forall k : \langle h, k \rangle \in [\![\phi]\!] \Rightarrow \exists j : \langle k, j \rangle \in [\![\psi]\!]\}$

Suppose that the antecedent contains an indefinite NP which translates in terms of a dynamic existential quantifier binding a variable $x$. Suppose further that the consequent contains a pronoun which is coindexed with the indefinite NP, so that it introduces an occurrence of the same variable $x$. In that case, the quantification over output assignments of the antecedent guarantees that the value assigned to $x$ is passed on to the consequent. This guarantees the right anaphoric bindings in donkey sentences like (32a) and (32b):

(32)   a.   If a farmer$_i$ owns a donkey$_j$ he$_i$ beats it$_j$.
       b.   Every farmer who owns a donkey$_i$ beats it$_i$.

The binding effect of the existential quantifier occurring in the antecedent extends to occurrences of the corresponding variable in the consequent. Universal quantification over the output assignments of the antecedent indirectly gives the indefinite NP universal force. In this way, DPL yields the same interpretation for donkey sentences as Kamp (1981) and Heim (1982) obtain by interpreting indefinites as variables.

In accordance with standard assumptions, implication, negation and the universal quantifier are taken to be externally static. This takes care of the illegitimate binding relations in examples like (4) above, repeated here as (33):

(33)   a.   Every student$_i$ came in. #She$_i$ wanted to schedule a meeting.
            $(\forall x \, (\text{Student}(x) \rightarrow \text{Come}(x)) \wedge \text{Schedule}(x))$
       b.   No student$_i$ came to the meeting. #She$_i$ needed to prepare for class.
            $(\neg \exists x \, (\text{Student}(x) \wedge \text{Come}(x)) \wedge \text{Prepare}(x))$

However, Groenendijk and Stokhof (1990) show that the static definition of these operations can be related to their dynamic counterpart in a systematic way. An externally dynamic universal quantifier and a dynamic variant of negation are needed to deal with examples like (26) above, and repeated here as (34):

(34)  a.  Each student in the syntax class was accused of cheating on the exam, and he was reprimanded by the dean.
      b.  Either there is no bathroom in this house, or it is in a funny place.

It would lead too far to work out Groenendijk and Stokhof's analysis of these examples in detail, but the basic idea is simple. Unlike the unselective binding approach, the dynamic framework treats indefinite NPs like *a student* and quantificational NPs like *every book* essentially as the same type of expression. The binding effects we know from discourse and donkey anaphora fall out of extensions of the scope domain of the quantifier. This makes it relatively easy to extend the externally dynamic treatment of existential quantification to negation and universal quantification. The main advantage of the dynamic framework is thus that we stay close to traditional predicate logic and provide a unified treatment of indefinite and quantificational NPs. Such a unified treatment is the basis of the theory of generalized quantifiers we will discuss in chapter 8 below.

Given that the difference between indefinite NPs and other quantified NPs is not absolute, but only relative (universal quantifiers and negation are usually static, but have dynamic definitions as well), it is possible to extend the treatment of discourse and donkey anaphora to other quantifiers. Chierchia (1992) shows that we can extend Groenendijk and Stokhof's definition to generalized quantifier interpretations of determiners like *most*. He shows that in his system the proportion problem does not arise, because determiners only bind the variable of the 'head noun'. Thus in cases like (28) above, we automatically get quantification over cat-owning students, rather than over pairs of students and cats. Chierchia (1992, 1995) further argues that we need to combine dynamic logic with an e-type approach in order to get the various donkey sentences their correct interpretations. More generally, the developments within the e-type approach, DRT and dynamic logic are such that they converge into one general dynamic analysis. There are more and more 'mixed' systems, which combine the insights of both DRT and dynamic logic (see for instance Muskens 1995).

## 6.4   Anaphora resolution

Not everyone looks at discourse the way we have done so far. The "structural" or "formal" paradigm we have been discussing looks at the structure of language as a code and tries to write a grammar for it. The analysis of the code is prior to the analysis of the use and concepts such as the speech community or speech acts. But many researchers look at discourse from the point of view of language use, and the function of language in communication. This is often called the "functional" paradigm. The functional paradigm looks at the structure of speech as an act or an event, and studies different ways of speaking. The focus is on the relation between code and use, which leads to the study of stylistic or social functions, speech styles, etc. Along these lines, sociolinguists claim that the analysis of language use cannot be independent of the purposes and the functions of language in human life. This ultimately leads to critical language scholarship, that is, the study of language, power and ideology. But there are less extreme positions within the functionalist paradigm. Examples include conversational analysis, which makes a detailed analysis of actual examples of (mostly spoken) conversation or dialogue with considerable attention paid to turn-taking, side-tracking and return to main story line, etc. This helps us determine the strategies by which people achieve communication in interaction. Variation analysis studies speech styles, vernacular versus formal speech, African-American Vernacular, gender related varieties, etc. The information structuring approach is concerned with topic-comment relations and background-focus articulation. This diversity shows that discourse analysis conceived in the broad sense uses a notion of context which involves the entire social and cultural setting (speech community, social and cultural identity). One of the sources for more discussion is Schiffrin (1994). In this section, we will look at discourse from a functional perspective, but limit the discussion to purely linguistic issues. We will reconsider some of the data introduced earlier in this chapter and focus on the question of how we determine the antecedent of a discourse anaphor.

So far we have forced the pronoun to take up a certain interpretation by coindexing it with the NP we intended to be its antecedent. Discourses in real life do not normally come with subscripts, so the question arises how we know where to put them. As we have emphasized throughout this chapter, coindexing is a syntactic device which reflects the outcome of a process of anaphora resolution. Many linguists are interested in the possibility of certain coindexing relations being acceptable in the grammar of a language. In that case, the intended coindexing is simply posited. From the point of view of the hearer in a real-life exchange, determining the intended antecedent of a pronoun is a real processing issue. A better understanding of human processing is not the only motivation to study anaphora resolution. If we want to model the strategies of speaker and hearer in a natural language understanding system, we are interested in finding out where the indices come from for computational reasons as well. One of the reasons why it is hard to develop a good theory of natural language processing is that anaphora resolution is not a fully compositional process. In section 6.3.2 above, we argued that the pronoun wants to unify with an appropriate and accessible antecedent. Usually we can determine which antecedents are accessible to certain pronouns in a compositional procedure. However, different factors come into play to determine which of the accessible antecedents provides the actual interpretation of the pronoun. These factors are not always tied to the syntactic construction, which makes it impossible to defend a fully compositional analysis of discourse anaphora. However, we can formulate a number of interpretation strategies which make interesting predictions about the actual choice of the antecedent.

Let us first illustrate that we cannot reduce anaphora resolution to a purely grammatical phenomenon. For some cases grammar is indeed all we need, even if there is more than one accessible antecedent for the pronoun. Consider the following example, taken from Kameyama (1996):

(35) John hit Bill. *He* hit *him* back.

The discourse referents introduced for *John* and *Bill* are accessible antecedents for the two pronouns *he* and *him*. However, hearers typically interpret the second sentence of (35) as conveying the information that Bill hit John. According to Kameyama, this is a result of the presupposition introduced by the lexical item *back*. *Back* presupposes that a similar event has already occurred, but the distribution of roles in that previous event is exactly the reverse of the one in the current event. Thus an '$x$ hit $y$ back' event presupposes that a '$y$ hit $x$' event has previously occurred. The presupposed event is spelled out in the first sentence of (35). This means that the names of $x$ and $y$ are fixed. The reversal of the argument roles implies that the second sentence unambiguously describes an event of Bill hitting John.

(35) nicely shows that purely linguistic information can fully determine anaphora resolution. However, in most other cases in which linguistic information plays a role, it is either as a default inference, or in combination with some other source of information. As an example of a default inference, Kameyama (1995) mentions grammatical parallelism. Consider the discourse in (36):

(36) John hit Bill. *He* doesn't like *him*.

In Kameyama's experiment, more hearers interpreted the second sentence as claiming that John does not like Bill, than that Bill does not like John. What seems to determine the interpretation of (36) is a general preference for grammatical parallelism. This leads the subject and object pronoun in the second sentence to relate to the subject and object NP of the first sentence, respectively. The comparison with (35) shows that this is just a default inference rule, which can easily be overruled by the contribution of a lexical item such as *back*.

Lexical information can also give rise to weaker, defeasible inferences, which leads to a preferred interpretation. The following example is taken from Webber (1991):

(37)   a.   Segal, however, had his own problems with women. He had been trying to keep his marriage of seven years from falling apart. When *that* became impossible ...

         b.   Segal, however, had his own problems with women. He had been trying to keep his marriage of seven years from falling apart. When *that* became inevitable ...

The first two sentences of these discourses are identical. The second sentence introduces a complex verb construction. The adjectives *impossible* and *inevitable* are related to different parts of that complex action. When someone tries to avoid something bad from happening, but 'that' was impossible, one infers that the person failed, and what was impossible was to avoid the bad thing from happening. So the *that* in (37a) relates to Segal's keeping his marriage from falling apart. When someone tries to avoid something and one hears 'that' was inevitable, one infers that the person failed, and what was inevitable was the bad thing happening. So *that* in (37b) relates to Segal's marriage of seven years falling apart. The semantic information contributed by the two adjectives guides the interpretation procedure by generating certain inferences. Note that it is easy to spell out how the adjectives affect the resolution of the pronoun *that* at an intuitive level on the basis of a specific example. It is less obvious to phrase the inference rules in such a way that they automatically generate the correct interpretation in every context. The interaction between lexical information and discourse interpretation is an important object of study in computational semantics. For more discussion, see Asher (1993), Asher and Lascarides (1995), Nunberg (1995), etc.

The situation is further complicated by the fact that lexical information often has the character of a default inference, which can be overruled by more specific information. This is illustrated by the following example, taken from Vermeulen (1994):

(38)   a.   The brick was thrown against the window. *It* broke.

         b.   John was surprised by the strength of the window. The brick was thrown against the window. *It* broke.

If we hear or read (38a) as a complete text, then the resolution process seems to favor a link between *it* and *the window*. Note that this procedure cannot just rely on the syntax of the input text: syntactically there is no reason why *it* should be the window, rather than the brick. Grammatical parallelism would even favor this resolution. However, grammatical parallelism is overruled by lexical information. We may assume that lexical semantics provides us with information about the fragility of objects. From this, we know that windows typically have a higher value on the scale of fragility than bricks. This will lead us to conclude that in (38a), it is more likely that the window broke than the brick. (38b) shows that this is a default inference which can be destroyed in a richer context. (38b) specifically claims that the window is exceptionally strong. World knowledge about a particular situation overrules the default information provided by lexical semantics. As a result the window gets a lower value on the scale of fragility in this context. Its value may drop even lower than the value of the brick, which opens up the possibility that we interpret the brick as the breaking object in (38b). This example shows that the default inference that grammatical parallelism gives rise to is weaker than the one lexical meaning generates. However, both default inferences can be overruled by knowledge of the particular situation at hand, even if this seems to require some effort in the form of a richer context.

Aside from linguistic information, other types of information contribute to the resolution of the anaphor. We will briefly discuss two of them: topic-focus articulation and textual coherence relations. Especially cases in which lexical or grammatical information interacts with and reinforces these other sources of information, the combination (almost) fully determines the referent of the pronoun.

According to Reinhart (1982), the topic of a sentence is pragmatically defined as what the sentence is about, and the comment is what we predicate of the topic. It is quite generally assumed that topics make good antecedents for pronouns, because their referents are maximally salient at the point in the discourse at which the pronoun is used (e.g. Lambrecht 1994). The observation that the mother is the topic of the discourse helps explain why it is harder to continue the text in (39a) with (39b) than with (39c):

(39)  a.  The mother picked up the baby. She had been ironing all afternoon. She was very tired.
      b.  *It* had been crying all day.
      c.  The baby had been crying all day.

Both the mother and the baby are introduced in the first sentence of (39a). The discourse continues talking about the mother, so she is the topic of the subsequent sentences. The baby is moved into the background, and a definite NP (39c), rather than a pronoun (39b) is appropriate to reactivate the referent and bring it back into the foreground. Fox (1987) provides numerous examples which show that distance is not the only reason why the use of a definite NP to refer to the baby is preferred over the use of a pronoun. The organization of the sentence and the discourse in terms of old and new, prominent and less prominent information provides a hierarchical structure that anaphora resolution appeals to.

Although subjects are generally taken to be default topics, Reinhart (1982) argues that this preference is much stronger in passive sentences than in active ones. Consider the pair of examples in (40):

(40)   a.   When *she* entered the room, Lili was greeted by Lucie.
        b.   When *she* entered the room, Lucie greeted Lili.

In (40a), the cataphoric (forward looking) pronoun *she* must be interpreted as referring to Lili, whereas in (40b), it can refer to either Lucie or Lili. Given that the only difference between the two sentences is the choice between an active or a passive construction of the main clause, this grammatical contrast must somehow be related to the resolution of the anaphor. According to Reinhart, passive sentences grammaticalize topichood. Reinhart's observations suggest that there are connections between a pragmatic phenomenon like topichood and a grammatical phenomenon like subjecthood. Vallduví (1994) discusses a wide range of constructions in which information structuring and grammar interact.

Information structure is more generally dependent on the coherent interpretation of the discourse. Hobbs (1979) argues that we need to develop a theory of coherence relations (also called discourse or rhetorical relations), which give structure to a discourse. Phenomena such as anaphora resolution then come about as a side effect of the coherence relations between sentences in the discourse. Consider Hobbs' examples (41a) and (b):

(41)   a.   John can open Bill's safe. He knows the combination.
        b.   Bill is worried because his safe can be opened by John. He knows the combination.

Grammatical parallelism allows us to resolve *he* in the second sentence of (41a) as referring to John. But that strategy would not work for (41b). Hobbs argues that the relevant coherence relation in (41b) is Elaboration, and that a combination of that relation with some general knowledge and a unification approach allows us to resolve the anaphor as referring to John. The relation of Elaboration is defined as follows:

(42)   $S_1$ is an Elaboration of $S_0$ if a proposition $P$ follows from the assertions of both $S_0$ and $S_1$ (but $S_1$ contains a property of one of the elements of $P$ that is not in $S_0$).

Hobbs develops the following argumentation to resolve the anaphor in (42b). Suppose we have in our store of commonly possessed world knowledge the axioms in (43) and the rule of plausible inference in (44):

(43)   a.   $Can(x, state) \rightarrow Know(x, Cause(Do(x, a), state))$.
          If $x$ can bring about a state, then there is an action $a$ such that $x$ knows that $x$ doing $a$ will cause the state to hold.
       b.   $(Combination(x, y) \wedge Person(z)) \rightarrow Cause(Dial(z, x, y), Open(y))$
          If $x$ is the combination of $y$ and $z$ is a person, then $z$ dialing $x$ on $y$ will cause $y$ to be open.

(44)   $Know(x, p)$ and $p \rightarrow q > Know(x, q)$
       One is normally able to draw the commonly known implications of what one knows (but of course not always; $>$ captures the notion of default inference as opposed to the strict inference $\rightarrow$).

The Elaboration relation in (41b) is recognized as follows. From the assertion of "John can open the safe", we can infer by axiom (43a) that John knows some action that he can perform to cause the safe to be open, that is:

(45)   $Know(john, Cause(Do(john, a), Open(safe)))$

The second sentence of (42b) asserts that 'he' knows the combination. Axiom (43b) in combination with the inference rule in (44) allows us to conclude from this that 'he' knows that dialing the combination of some object causes it to open:

(46)   $Know(he, Cause(Dial(z, comb, y), Open(y)))$

If we assume that there is a coherence relation between the two sentences, we can match (45) and (46). If we identify 'he' with John, $z$ with John, and $y$ with the safe, the definition of Elaboration in (42) is satisfied. The Elaboration lies in the greater specificity regarding the action John would perform to open the safe: he might use his knowledge of the combination to do this. The example illustrates that Hobbs' rules use a mixture of linguistic and non-linguistic knowledge to infer coherence relations. Much current research in computational semantics focuses on the mechanisms that underlie the interaction of these different sources of knowledge in actual discourse.

We conclude that the interpretation of discourse and donkey anaphora provides an interesting example of the kind of problems that arise when we start looking at meaning at the discourse level. On the one hand, we see that the traditional formal semantic approach that we have discussed in previous chapters needs to be extended in order to deal with the dynamic binding phenomena induced by indefinite NPs. On the other hand, we observe that interpretation strategies that have been developed in text linguistics and pragmatics prove helpful in the search for the appropriate antecedent for a discourse anaphor. The examples of anaphora resolution which have been discussed in this section and in section 1.3 illustrate that the formal and functional approaches to discourse complement each other in interesting ways.

## 6.5  Exercises

(1) ! Translate the following examples into first-order predicate logic.

   (i) Everyone who has a four year old child sends it to school.

   (ii) Everyone who has a quarter puts it in the parking meter.

   (ii) No one who has a son in high school lends him the car on a week night.

Do the translations you propose yield correct truth conditions in cases in which people have more than one four year old child/quarter/son in high school? Give a possible explanation for the differences/similarities you find, and suggest a solution for the problems you find.

(2) The unselective binding approach treats both determiners like *every, most* and adverbs like *always, usually* as unselective binders. This approach correctly assigns the same interpretation to the sentences in (i) and (ii):

   (i) Every student who likes semantics gets a good grade.

   (ii) A student who likes semantics always gets a good grade.

   2.1 Spell out the interpretation of (i) and (ii) along the lines of the unselective binding approach. Provide translations of these interpretations into (standard) first-order predicate logic and show that they are indeed equivalent.

Not all sentences of the form in (i) and (ii) turn out to be equivalent. Compare (i) and (ii) with (iii) and (iv):

(iii) Every student who came to the party liked it.

(iv) ??A student who came to the party always liked it.

2.2 It has been argued that the contrast between (iii) and (iv) has to do with the object of quantification. Determiners bind individual variables, whereas adverbs of quantification may bind individual variables, but also need to bind some temporal variable. Use this argument to explain why (iv) is infelicitous, whereas (iii) is perfectly all right.

More differences between determiners and adverbs of quantification are illustrated by conditionals which contain two indefinites in their antecedent. We observe that the meaning of (v) is rendered by quantification over the subject as in (vi). The meaning of (vii) on the other hand is better captured in terms of quantification over the object as in (viii):

(v) If a student has a pet, he usually takes good care of it.

(vi) Most students who has a pet takes good care of it.

(vii) If a drummer lives in an apartment complex, it is usually half empty.

(viii) Most apartment complexes in which a drummer lives are half empty.

It has been argued that syntax determines what determiners quantify over (namely, the variable introduced by the head noun), whereas adverbs of quantification are syntactically more flexible. They are sensitive to the topic-focus structure of the conditional and quantify over the variable that is introduced by the topic of the *if*-clause.

2.3 Use this argumentation to determine the quantificational structure of the examples in (v)–(viii). In particular, spell out which variable is bound by the quantifier, and explain how we determine this. Reflect on the consequences of the differences you observe between determiners and adverbs of quantification for the unselective binding theory. Does the e-type approach or the dynamic binding framework fare better with these examples? Motivate your answer by sketching the analysis of the examples in (v)–(viii) in these frameworks.

(3) Consider the following two discourses:

(i) [ Every dog]$_i$ came in. It$_i$ lay down under the table.

(ii) [ Every player]$_i$ chooses a pawn. He$_i$ puts it on square one.

In which context is the intended anaphoric relationship easier to get? It has been suggested that the notion of 'script' or 'stereotypical' story or behavior can account for this difference. Use this notion to explain why the discourses in (i) and (ii) have different possibilities of anaphoric relations. Give an example of a context in which the intended anaphoric relationship, which you found bad in the above example, is actually felicitous.

(4) As pointed out in section 6.4 above, Fox (1987) argues that distance between the pronoun and its antecedent in a discourse is not crucial in the process of anaphora resolution. The contrast between (i) and (ii) illustrates this:[5]

(i) A: Well, I have to go. I have to do a lot of studying. And Hillary said she'd call me if she was going to go to the library with me. But I don't think she will. Anyway, I'm going to have these papers xeroxed and I'll come back in a little bit.

B: Okay, say hi to Hillary for me.

A: Okay, I will.

(ii) A: My mother wanted to know how your grandmother is doing.

B: I don't know, I guess she is all right. She went to the hospital again today.

A: Mm–hm?

B: I guess today was the days she's supposed to find out if she goes in there for an operation or not.

A: Mm hm.

B: So I don't know, she wasn't home by the time when I left for school today. Well, my aunt went with her anyway this time. My mother didn't go.

A: Mm hm.

B: But I don't know, she will probably have to go in soon, though.

In (i), the last reference to Hillary is only three lines away from the most recent mention, and no other accessible female discourse referent is available in the discourse. Even so, the use of a full NP rather than a pronoun is appropriate. In (ii), the pronoun *she* in the last utterance refers unambiguously to the grandmother, who is

---

[5]The examples are from Fox (1987), but written out as regular sentences, rather than the transcriptions of real conversations Fox provides. For the issue at hand, this is irrelevant.

introduced in the first utterance. However, the nearest female referent is B's mother, and another female referent (B's aunt) is mentioned as well. This means that the nearest accessible discourse referent is not the intended referent. According to Fox, discourse structure rather than distance between the anaphor and its antecedent determines whether a referent can be picked up with a pronoun or needs to be identified with a full NP. Use your knowledge about topic/focus structure and discourse relations to give a description of the discourse structure of (i) and (ii) which explains the observations made here.

# Chapter 7

# Limits of first-order predicate logic

Besides connectives and quantifiers, first-order predicate logic contains just two kinds of symbols: individual expressions (constants/variables) and predicate constants. We need a system which has more types in order to account for modifiers, higher-order predicates and higher-order quantifiers. Moreover, we observe that a purely extensional theory of meaning cannot account for certain intensional expressions we find in natural language.

## 7.1  Not enough types

Besides connectives and quantifiers, first-order predicate logic contains just two kinds of symbols. There are individual expressions which come in two kinds: individual constants and individual variables. Both refer to entities in a given universe of discourse (although in different ways). And there are predicate constants, expressions which refer to sets of entities (or sets of $n$-tuples of entities). This means that in predicate logic one can say things about the properties entities have and the relations they bear to other entities. But in natural language we can talk about much more than those kinds of things, which suggests that we need a richer set of types of expressions. Consider:

(1)  a.  Susan is healthy.
     b.  Swimming is healthy.
     c.  John has all the properties of Santa Claus.
     d.  Red has something in common with green.

(1a) predicates 'being healthy' of Susan. We can represent this as Healthy($s$) in (2a):

(2)  a.  Healthy($s$)
     b.  Healthy(Swim)
     c.  $\forall P\,(P(s) \rightarrow P(j))$
     d.  $\exists \mathcal{P}\,(\mathcal{P}(\text{Red}) \wedge \mathcal{P}(\text{Green})\,)$

(1b) shows that we can also predicate a property of a property: the act of swimming is a healthy activity. But something like Healthy(Swim) in (2b) is not a well-formed formula in first-order predicate logic: we can only predicate things of individuals (either constants or variables). A similar problem arises in (1c), which expresses quantification over properties rather than over individuals. We would want to represent this as something like (2c). But we cannot do this in first-order predicate logic, because we only have predicate constants and no predicate variables. (1d) is even worse, because it goes another level up. We are quantifying over properties of properties: there is a property which is common to both red and green (which are properties themselves). So the formula in (2d) is another level up from (2c), because it quantifies over properties of properties.

Similar problems arise in the interpretation of natural language modifiers. Compare the interpretation of the adjectives in (3a) and (3b):

(3)  a.  There was a red book on the table.
     b.  There was a small elephant in the zoo.

We can translate (3a) as in (4a), but (3b) cannot be taken to mean what (4b) expresses:

(4)  a.  $\exists x\,(\text{Book}(x) \wedge \text{Red}(x) \wedge \text{On-the-table}(x))$
     b.  $\exists x\,(\text{Elephant}(x) \wedge \text{Small}(x) \wedge \text{In-the-zoo}(x))$

There is a crucial difference between 'absolute' adjectives like *red* in (3a) and 'relative' adjectives like *small* in (3b). Absolute adjectives describe properties of individuals independently of the contribution of the head noun. Relative adjectives are dependent on the noun they modify. The set of red books is a subset of the set of books, which we can find by taking the intersection of the set of books and the set of red objects.

In the same way, the set of small elephants is a subset of the set of elephants. But unlike in the case of 'red books' we cannot construe this set from the intersection of the set of elephants and the set of small objects. After all, a small elephant is still a rather big object. Relative adjectives do not describe properties of individuals independently of the contribution of the head noun. The essence of a modifier is to be dependent for its interpretation on the expression it modifies. This is something we cannot represent in standard first-order predicate logic, so we cannot translate (3b) into this language.

Similar problems arise with adverbs like *slowly* in sentences like (5):

(5) Milly swam slowly.

(5) does not mean that Milly swam and that she was slow. Maybe Milly is a swimming champion nobody can keep up with when she is in good shape, and she might still swim twice as fast as I do when she is swimming slowly compared to what she usually does. This suggests that the adverb *slowly* does not describe a property of individuals, but a way of performing an activity like swimming. Accordingly, it needs to be interpreted as a modifier of the verb phrase rather than as a predicate over individuals.

Just as in the case of predicates, we can always go another level up. That is, we do not just need modifiers of predicates, we also need modifiers of modifiers:

(6)  a.  There was a very small elephant in the zoo.
     b.  Milly swam terribly slowly.

Clearly, *very* and *terribly* are not predicates over individuals, they are not even modifying the common noun or the verb, they are intensifiers and indicate the degree to which the individual is *small* or performs an activity *slowly*.

The examples in (1), (3), (5) and (6) indicate that we have to enrich our logic with more types, so that we can interpret properties of properties, quantification over properties, modification of properties, modification of modifiers, etc. One way to solve these problems is to move to a higher-order theory. The predicate logic we have used so far is called first-order, because we only have variables which stand for individuals, and we only have predication over individuals. If we introduce variables for predicates and allow predication over predicates, we move to a *second-order* logic. In such a theory, formulas like (2b) are well-formed. Note that in order to capture examples like (1d) we would need to move to a third-order logic, where we have not only second-order predicate constants, but also variables over properties of properties, such as $\mathcal{P}$. Semantics has borrowed a number of insights from the mathematical *theory of types* to work out a hihgher-order logic based on a richer set of types of expressions which comes closer to the kind of diversity we find in natural language. The reader is referred to Dowty, Wall and Peters (1981) or Gamut (1991, volume 2) for an introduction to higher-order logic and type theory. In this book, we will limit ourselves to one example of a higher-order expression, namely the (second-order) notion of a generalized quantifier as a relation between sets (see chapter 8). The motivation for the introduction of such generalized quantifiers is given in sections 7.2 and 7.3 below.

Not all problems related to the interpretation of modifiers are solved if we base our semantic theory on a higher-order logic. A further complication that the semantics of modifiers brings in concerns the interpretation of sentences like (7):

(7)  a.   A former student of the department wrote a book on se-
          mantics.
     b.   The alleged killer was seen in San Jose.

We cannot capture the meaning of adjectives like *former* or *alleged* by claiming that the set of formcr students of the department is a subset of the set of students of the department, because the contribution of *former* is exactly to say that the person is no longer a student. Along similar lines, it would be incorrect to describe the set of alleged killers as a subset of the set of killers, because the person in question might very well turn out not to have committed any crime at all. This shows that the extension of the modified NP cannot be derived from the extension of the original NP. Instead, we should derive the property of being a former student from the property of being a student, and the property of being an alleged killer from the property of being a killer. This implies that the semantics of adjectives (and adverbs like *formerly, allegedly*) cannot be handled by an extensional theory of interpretation, and we need to bring a notion of *intensionality* into our semantics. The issue of intensionality will be addressed in chapter 9.

## 7.2   Not enough quantifiers

When dealing with natural language, one does not only want to represent logical quantifiers such as $\exists$ and $\forall$, but basically *all* quantifiers of natural language. The quantifiers $\forall$ and $\exists$ can do a lot of work, but cannot account for all natural language quantifiers. Their force comes from the fact that we can combine them with other quantifiers and connectives. For instance, we can combine existential and universal quantifiers with negation to produce *no, not all* as in (8a) and (b):

(8)  a.  No students laughed.
$\neg\exists x\,(\mathrm{Student}(x) \wedge \mathrm{Laugh}(x))$

b.  Not every student laughed.
$\neg\forall x\,(\mathrm{Student}(x) \rightarrow \mathrm{Laugh}(x))$

c.  At least two students laughed.
$\exists x\,\exists y\,(x \neq y \wedge \mathrm{Student}(x) \wedge \mathrm{Student}(y) \wedge \mathrm{Laugh}(x) \wedge \mathrm{Laugh}(y))$

d.  The chair of the committee laughed.
$\exists x\,(\mathrm{Chair}(x) \wedge \forall y\,(\mathrm{Chair}(y) \rightarrow [y = x]) \wedge \mathrm{Laugh}(x))$

We can create formulas like (8c) to represent numerals such as *at least two*. We can even find a way to capture definite descriptions. The translation in (8d) in terms of a combination of existential quantification and a uniqueness condition was developed by Russell (1905). Note that we already made use of the Russellian interpretation of definite descriptions in our analysis of the possessive determiner in chapter 5 (example 26b). The translation in (8d) also illustrates a more general difference between proper names and definite descriptions. Both can be used to pick out a certain individual, but unlike proper names, definite descriptions have a descriptive content which characterizes the individual as having a certain property. This difference will play an important role in intensional theories of meaning (see chapter 9).

But there are limits to what we can do to translate quantificational expressions from natural language into predicate logic. Problems arise with the interpretation of *most*, for instance. We cannot represent the meaning of *most* in terms of $\forall$ and/or $\exists$. Let us see what happens if we try. It is clear that *most* cannot be interpreted in terms of a combination of $\exists$, $\forall$, and negation, for 'most' is more than 'some' but less than 'all'. Moreover, it involves a proportional meaning component which is missing from combinations like 'not all' or 'some not'. One reasonable thing we could envisage doing if no combination of existing quantifiers and connectives can describe the meaning of *most* is to extend first-order predicate logic with a new quantifier $M$ (for 'most') and assign it the following truth conditions:

(9)  $Mx\,Px$ is true iff for most individuals $x$ in the universe of discourse U it is true that $x$ has the property $P$.

If we adopt this definition of the quantifier $M$ and try to translate a sentence like (10) using $M$, we need to relate the two predicates by means of a connective. The following translations result when we try conjunction (as with the existential quantifier) and implication (as with the universal quantifier):

(10)  a.  Most children laughed.
      b.  $Mx\,(\mathrm{Child}(x) \wedge \mathrm{Laugh}(x))$
      c.  $Mx\,(\mathrm{Child}(x) \rightarrow \mathrm{Laugh}(x))$

(10a) says that most individuals are such that they are children and they laugh. This cannot be correct: a model containing more adults than children would immediately rule out the sentence as false. (10b) also goes wrong in such a context. Suppose we have a context in which there are 20 adults, all of whom laugh, and 5 children, none of whom laughs. (10b) is true in such a model: for most individuals the conditional comes out true because the antecedent is falsified. Again, this contradicts our intuitions. We can try other (combinations of) connectives, but these do not work either.

All these translations yield the wrong truth conditions, because the meaning of *most children* cannot be calculated from the meaning of 'most individuals $x$'. We do not directly quantify over individuals, but we quantify over the individuals that satisfy the property of being a child, and take a proportion of that set. This implies that the interpretation of *most* has to take into account the set of individuals denoted by the noun. As Barwise and Cooper (1981) put it: the determiner essentially "lives on" the denotation of the noun. It is not possible to capture this dependency relation in first-order predicate logic, because the interpretation for the quantifiers $\forall$ and $\exists$ in terms of the assignment function $g$ is built on the idea of checking the application of the formula to all or some individuals in the universe of discourse (compare chapter 4). The interpretation of a natural-language quantifier like *most* is not just dependent on the universe of discourse, but on some subset within the universe. The observation that the interpretation of *most* is to be defined relative to a set of individuals leads to the conclusion that it is impossible to account for this quantificational expression in a first-order theory which only allows quantification over individuals. If we want to account for the semantics of proportional quantifiers like *most* in terms of their translation into some logical language, we have to move to a second-order theory.

## 7.3   Compositionality

We observed that first-order predicate logic is a good starting point for the analysis of natural language, because it has recursion and a fully compositional interpretation. Although this is certainly true, we should realize that compositionality is maintained at the expense of the syntax of natural language. That is to say, the logic itself has a fully compositional interpretation procedure, but there is no compositional translation process which allows us to recover parts of the syntactic structure of the natural language sentence in the logical formula used as its translation. This is particularly problematic for a derivational theory of interpretation such as the one used in Montague grammar, because the rule-to-rule hypothesis of meaning claims that at every stage of the syntactic derivation we have a semantic interpretation for the part of the tree already built up. In fact, the trees we gave in section 5.2.2 show that we do not have a translation associated with any part of the tree, except for the propositional level. As pointed out in that section, we have clear intuitions about what the parts of the sentence mean, and we can come up with model-theoretic interpretations for parts of the tree, but first-order logic does not provide us with adequate translations of these parts, because the syntax of first-order predicate logic bears no relation to the syntax of natural language. The problem is thus that we cannot really implement a derivational theory of grammar if we do not know how to translate the parts of a syntactic tree. This point can be illustrated with any expression which forms a syntactic constituent and for which we want to provide an interpretation. For instance, two-place predicates in predicate logic have the structure in (11c):

(11)  a.   Milly loves Fred.
      b.   $Love(m, f)$
      c.   $[_S$ Milly $[_{VP}$ loves Fred$]]$

The predicate-logical formula in (11b) has a 'flat' syntactic structure: both arguments are on a par. However, in the syntax of English, there is an asymmetry between subject and object. The object and the verb combine into a VP, which then combines with the subject to build a sentence, as in (11c). Of course, the precise syntactic structure we end up with depends on the choice of our syntactic framework. In this book, we try to make as few syntactic assumptions as we can, in order to make our semantic theory as general as possible. However, we do take it for granted that most syntactic theories of English introduce some asymmetry between the subject and the object and have the transitive verb and the object NP form a constituent. If we want to build a compositional interpretation which reflects the embedded syntactic structure in (11c), we need to have an interpretation procedure which reflects constituent structure. That is, we have to have access to the interpretation of the VP at the intermediate level of construction. Intuitively, this shouldn't be too hard: the interpretation of the VP *loves Fred* is a property, just like a one-place predicate like *laugh*.

However, nothing like a VP can be found in the predicate-logical representation in (11b). There is no correspondence between the structural description of the natural language sentence and the translation into first-order predicate logic: the sentence is translated as a whole. This is clearly not in accordance with the rule-to-rule hypothesis, nor with the principle of compositionality of meaning, which requires that we derive the meaning of the natural language sentence from the meanings of its parts and the way they are put together.

There are other examples in which we would like to have an interpretation procedure which respects constituent structure. As Barwise and Cooper (1981) emphasize, there is no uniform analysis of NPs in predicate logic. This becomes clear if we compare the following sentences:

(12)  a.  Jim laughed.
          $\text{Laugh}(j)$

      b.  Every student laughed.
          $\forall x\,(\text{Student}(x) \rightarrow \text{Laugh}(x))$

      c.  Some students laughed.
          $\exists x\,(\text{Student}(x) \wedge \text{Laugh}(x))$

      d.  Most students laughed.
          (there is no first-order translation for d)

The syntactic structure of the sentences under (12) is essentially the same: they are all $[_S\ \text{NP VP}\ ]$ constructions. But this is not reflected in the predicate logical formula. The notion of NP as a constituent in the tree is recoverable from (12a), but not from (12b) and (c). In these predicate-logical formulas there is no part of the formula which represents the meaning of the NP as such. (12d) cannot even be translated into first-order logic, but of course we want this sentence to get a compositional interpretation which reflects the same syntactic construction as the other three sentences. The conclusion we draw from these examples is that if we want the syntax and semantics of natural language to run in parallel, we need to have a semantic notion of what an NP is, just as we have a syntactic notion of what an NP is.

In sum, the problems of first-order predicate logic are that we do not have enough types, not enough quantifiers and not enough compositionality. Therefore, we crucially need higher-order levels of interpretation. As an example of what the introduction of second-order interpretations can achieve, we will focus on the interpretation of quantifiers like *most* and NPs more generally in chapter 8. The issue of the intensional nature of modifiers like *former* and *alleged* will be taken up in chapter 9.

# 7.4 Exercises

(1) Consider the sentences in (i)–(x):

- (i) ! Mary has a false passport.
- (ii) ! Eighty percent of the students passed.
- (iii) At least two, but less than five students failed.
- (iv) Cooking is fun.
- (v) Not everyone cooked his own dinner.
- (vi) Less than half of the students know each other.
- (vii) Phil wore a beautiful shirt.
- (viii) Harry bought two fake diamonds.
- (ix) Few diamonds, if any, are real.
- (x) Eve writes very well.
- (xi) German white wines are sweet.

For those sentences among (i)–(xi) which can be interpreted in first-order logic, give a translation of the sentence into this language. Give the key to the variables you use. If one or more of the sentences in (i)–(xi) cannot be interpreted in first-order logic, explain why. Indicate what kind of a logical language we need in order to capture the meaning of the sentence.

# Chapter 8

# Generalized Quantifier theory

In this chapter, we discuss the interpretation of NPs and determiners in terms of generalized quantifier theory. We further discuss semantic properties of determiners and NPs, which play a role in the explanation of such phenomena as existential constructions, conjunction/disjunction reduction, partitives, and negative polarity items.

## 8.1   NPs and determiners

In the previous chapter, we pointed out that expressions like *Socrates*, *every student* and *most linguists* are syntactically characterized as NPs. If we treat the NP as a syntactic unit, a compositional theory of meaning requires that it also be a semantic unit. The question then arises what kind of denotation we can associate with NPs. In our introduction to first-order predicate logic, we argued that we can combine predicates and arguments by predication. If we combine a one-place predicate like *snore* and a proper name like *Jane* as in (1), we predicate the property of snoring of Jane, and translate the sentence as in (1a):

(1)        Jane snores.
    a.    $\text{Snore}(j)$
    b.    $[\![\,\text{Snore}(j)\,]\!] = 1$ iff $[\![\,j\,]\!] \in [\![\,\text{Snore}\,]\!]$
    c.    $[\![\,\text{Snore}\,]\!] = \{x \in U \mid \text{Snore}(x)\}$

We interpret the predication relation in (1a) as set-membership and claim that the individual referred to by the constant $j$ has to be a member of the interpretation of the predicate in order for the sentence to be true (1b). Given that the one-place predicate refers to a set of individuals, this can be further spelled out as in (1c). But if we have a higher-order logic in which we can predicate things of properties and relations, we could also have defined the predicate-argument structure the other way around, as in (2a):

(2)        Jane snores.
    a.    Jane(Snore)
    b.    $[\![\,\text{Jane(Snore)}\,]\!] = 1$ iff $[\![\,\text{Snore}\,]\!] \in [\![\,\text{Jane}\,]\!]$
    c.    $[\![\,\text{Jane}\,]\!] = \{X \subseteq U \mid j \in X\}$

If we take the predicate *to snore* to be an argument of the subject *Jane*, we are switching the predication relations around, and therefore the set-membership relation. Instead of checking whether Jane is a member of the denotation of *to snore*, (2a) claims that the property of snoring is one of the properties Jane has. In (2b) we formalize this as the requirement that the denotation of the VP be a member of the denotation of the proper name *Jane* in order for the sentence to be true. Of course the formula in (2a) is ill-formed in a first-order logic, so we have to use a second-order logic. In order to interpret the second-order formula in (2a), we cannot translate the proper name *Jane* as an individual constant, for properties cannot be related to individuals by set-membership relations. However, we can preserve the interpretation of predication as set-membership if we give the proper name *Jane* a translation in terms of sets of properties. After all, a property can be a member of a set of properties. Intuitively, the switch from individual constants to sets of properties is related to different perspectives on the individual. So far, we have looked at proper names as referential expressions: they point to a specific individual in the universe of discourse of the model. But we can also think of individuals as characterized by the properties they have. Suppose we know Jane as a person who has brown hair, who plays soccer, who likes black coffee, and who snores. Then the name *Jane* immediately gives rise to the picture of this individual having all these properties. This is what corresponds to the translation of the proper name *Jane* not as an individual constant, but as a bundle of properties (the properties that Jane has). Given that properties are extensionally interpreted as sets of individuals, we claim that the denotation of *Jane* in (2b) is a set of sets, namely the set of all those sets $X$ such that $j$ is a member of $X$. This is spelled out in (2c), and it is reflected in figure 8.1.

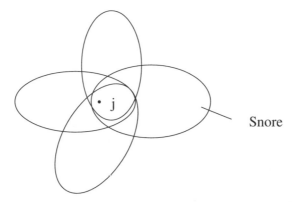

Figure 8.1: Jane snores

The introduction of a set of sets is the standard translation of NPs in Montague grammar (cf. Montague 1973). Sets of sets are outside the scope of a first-order logic, so when we discussed predicate logic, we could not raise the possibility of such an interpretation. But once we have made higher-order interpretations available in our semantic theory, we can easily introduce (2c) along with (1c), because they are fully equivalent. This means that if we combine a proper name with a VP, we can choose to make the NP the semantic argument of the VP, or the VP the semantic argument of the NP. It does not matter which predicate-argument structure we adopt for the sentence, for the two options lead to different, but equivalent translations. The translations are equivalent, because they lead to the same model-theoretic interpretation which requires the individual Jane to be a member of the set of snoring individuals in order for the sentence to be true. We conclude from this that the introduction of a second-order interpretation does not contribute anything to the interpretation of proper names, but it does not do any harm either. For quantificational NPs, the situation is different, and it is here that we see the main advantage of the interpretation of NPs as sets of sets.

In chapter 4, we argued that first-order logic cannot treat quantificational NPs such as *every student* in the same way as proper nouns, because these expressions are non-referential in the sense that they do not refer to particular individuals in the domain. As a result, (3b) cannot be the correct translation of (3):

(3)      Every student danced.
   a.   [$_{NP}$ every student [$_{VP}$ danced ]]
   b.   **wrong**: Dance(every student)
   c.   $\forall x$ (Student($x$) $\rightarrow$ Dance($x$))

The translation of (3) in first-order predicate logic is given in (3c), and it provides the correct truth conditions for the sentence. However, as pointed out in chapter 7, the drawback of this translation is that we lose the insight that the NP and VP are related via a predication relation. Although there are syntactic units representing both the NP and the VP in (3a), these syntactic constituents are not treated as semantic constituents in the translation (3c). We can restore compositionality if we assume that the predicate-argument structure is not as in (3b), but as in (4b):

(4)      Every student danced.
   a.   [$_{NP}$ every student [$_{VP}$ danced ]]
   b.   Every student(danced)
   c.   [[ every student(danced) ]] = 1 iff
        [[ Dance ]] $\in$ [[ every student ]]
   d.   $\{x \in U \mid \text{Dance}(x)\} \in \{X \subseteq U \mid [[ \text{Student} ]] \subseteq X\}$

In (4b), the NP is the predicate, and the VP its argument. This translation is the exact mirror image of the syntactic structure of the sentence given in (4a). If we interpret predication in terms of set-membership as before, a representation like (4b) leads us to say that the sentence is true if and only if the set of individuals denoted by the VP is a member of the interpretation of the NP as in (4c). In a second-order logic, the assumption that the NP denotes a set of properties allows us to interpret this statement in such a way that the property described by the VP is a member of the set of properties denoted by the NP. The intuition is that an NP like *every student* denotes the set of properties every student has. In the context of (4), the establishment of a predication relation means that dancing is one of the properties every student has. Other properties in the set denoted by *every student* may be *to be intelligent, to prepare for exams, to like the arts*, etc. In order to support the claim that *to dance* is a property of every student, we have to make sure that the set of dancers is a member of the set of sets which are a superset of the student set (4d). This interpretation is reflected in the Venn diagram in figure 8.2.

We can easily extend this interpretation model to other quantificational NPs. For instance the NP *some students* denotes the set of properties that some students have. In the extensional view of properties as sets of individuals, this corresponds to the set of individuals that have a non-empty

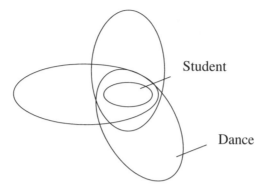

Figure 8.2: Every student danced

intersection with the set of students. This leads to the Venn diagram in figure 8.3. A sentence like (5) is true if and only if the property of laughing is a member of the set of properties some students have:

(5) Some students laughed.

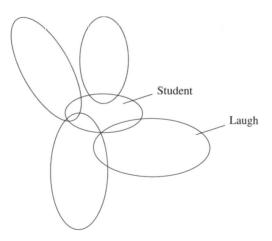

Figure 8.3: Some students laughed

The approach also generalizes to NPs that cannot be translated in first-order predicate logic, such as *most cats*:

(6) Most cats have green eyes.

A sentence like (6) is true if and only if the intersection of the set of cats with the set of individuals that have green eyes contains more than half of the total number of individuals that make up the set of cats.

The translation of NPs in terms of sets of sets corresponds with the mathematical notion of a *generalized quantifier*. Accordingly, the study of the properties of expressions that denote families of sets is referred to as Generalized Quantifier theory. As mentioned earlier, an interpretation of NPs as denoting generalized quantifiers (sets of sets) is built into Montague grammar. Barwise and Cooper (1981) apply the insights of the mathematical theory of generalized quantifiers to natural language and work out the semantic properties of NPs in this framework. Their starting point is that a sentence of the form $[_S$ NP VP$]$ is true iff the denotation of the VP is a member of the generalized quantifier, that is, the family of sets denoted by the NP. We write $A$ as the denotation of the common noun: $A = [\![ \, \text{N} \, ]\!]$, and $\mid A \mid$ for the cardinality of the set $A$. The truth conditions for various NPs can now be formulated as follows:

(7)  a.          $[\![\text{Jane}]\!] = \{X \subseteq U \mid j \in X\}$
     b.          $[\![\text{all N}]\!] = \{X \subseteq U \mid A \subseteq X\}$
     c.          $[\![\text{some N}]\!] = \{X \subseteq U \mid X \cap A \neq \emptyset\}$
     d.          $[\![\text{no N}]\!] = \{X \subseteq U \mid X \cap A = \emptyset\}$
     e. $[\![(\text{at least two}) \text{ N}]\!] = \{X \subseteq U \mid\mid X \cap A \mid \geq 2\}$
     f.          $[\![\text{most N}]\!] = \{X \subseteq U \mid\mid X \cap A \mid > 1/2 \mid A \mid\}$ or
                 $\{X \subseteq U \mid\mid X \cap A \mid > \mid X - A \mid\}$

A second-order interpretation of determiners as denoting relations between sets solves the problems related to the interpretation of quantifiers like *most*. The examples show that the translation of NPs as sets of properties is a fruitful way to develop a compositional interpretation of NPs and to generalize over NPs of different kinds (proper names, quantificational NPs definable in first-order logic, quantificational NPs not definable in first-order logic).

Barwise and Cooper (1981) emphasize that it is the NP which corresponds to the generalized quantifier, not the determiner. But if we want to extract the contribution of the determiner from the formulas in (7), we can try to 'unpack' the definitions. As Barwise and Cooper point out, determiners are functions that map common noun denotations onto generalized quantifiers. The generalized quantifier in turn takes the VP as its argument to build a proposition. This is illustrated for (4) with the tree-like representation in figure 8.4.

We call this the *functional* perspective on generalized quantifiers, because it mirrors the syntactic structure of the sentence as closely as possible.

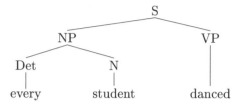

Figure 8.4: functional perspective on generalized quantifiers

However, 'undoing' in a sense the effects of hierarchical structure and taking a set-theoretic perspective, we can view the denotation of a determiner as a binary relation between sets of individuals. This *relational* perspective on determiners is not in conflict with the *functional* view. Remember that two-place predicates like *to love, to hit,* etc. denote sets of individuals. There is an asymmetry between subjects and objects, because the predicate combines with its arguments one at a time (the object first, and then the subject). But any two-place predicate denotes a relation between individuals. In the same way, a determiner is interpreted as a two-place predicate, but a second-order one. There is an asymmetry between the common noun and the VP, because the determiner combines first with the common noun and then with the VP. However, any determiner denotes a set of pairs of sets, namely those sets which stand to each other in the relation denoted by the determiner. The semantic difference between the different determiners of a natural language like English resides in the specific relation they denote. For instance *every* denotes the subset relation, *some* the relation of non-empty intersection, *no* the relation of empty intersection, etc.

The relational perspective is adopted in the work of Zwarts (1983) and van Benthem (1986). As mentioned above, in Barwise and Cooper's terminology, it is NPs that correspond to generalized quantifiers, not determiners. However, researchers who are working in the relational perspective often talk loosely about determiners as generalized quantifiers. As long as the context makes it clear what type of denotation is intended by the term 'generalized quantifier', this is rather innocent. Here are some examples of how determiners are interpreted in the relational perspective:

(8)   a.      $[\![\text{ All } (A, B) ]\!] = 1$ iff $A \subseteq B$
    b.      $[\![\text{ Some } (A, B) ]\!] = 1$ iff $A \cap B \neq \emptyset$
    c.      $[\![\text{ No } (A, B) ]\!] = 1$ iff $A \cap B = \emptyset$
    d.   $[\![\text{ At least five } (A, B) ]\!] = 1$ iff $| A \cap B | \geq 5$
    e.      $[\![\text{ Most } (A, B) ]\!] = 1$ iff $| A \cap B | > | A - B |$
    f.      $[\![\text{ Many } (A, B) ]\!] = 1$ iff $| A \cap B | \geq m$
    g.      $[\![\text{ Many } (A, B) ]\!] = 1$ iff $| A \cap B | > m/n | A |$

The variables $m$ and $n$ in (8) stand for natural numbers used to calculate the relations between the sets. These numbers are generally context-dependent and assumed to be known to the language users in a given situation. Determiners like *many* and *few* can have either a cardinal or a proportional interpretation, as illustrated in (9):

(9)  a.  There are many smart students in the semantics class.
     b.  Many students in the semantics class are really smart.

(9a) means that the number of smart students in the semantics class is rather high. This is captured by the cardinal interpretation of *many* in (8f). (9b) claims that among the students of the semantics class, many of them are really smart. Given that we now calculate the number of smart students with respect to the set of students in the semantics class as a whole, we have a proportional interpretation, which is captured by (8g). Note that (9a) but not (9b) is compatible with the number of students in the semantics class being small. The difference between cardinal and proportional interpretations is reflected in the different truth conditions of (8f) and (8g). They illustrate one advantage of the relational, set-theoretic perspective, namely the fact that it allows us to focus on the properties of the determiner, rather than the NP as a whole. The set-theoretical insight that determiners denote relations between sets of individuals allows us to apply methods from the theory of relations to the semantics of natural language determiners. There are two types of properties of determiners that are interesting to study in this perspective. On the one hand, we want to find out what properties natural language determiner denotations have in common and how to define these characteristics in the general theory of relations (section 8.2). On the other hand, we want to see if there are semantic properties which characterize certain subclasses of determiners, and investigate the role these properties play in accounting for the distribution of generalized quantifiers in various contexts (section 8.3).

## 8.2  Constraints on determiner denotations

The reason that *most* cannot be represented in first-order logic is that the determiner is essentially dependent on the interpretation of the head noun. The well-known quantifiers $\forall$ and $\exists$ from first-order logic range over the entire domain of discourse and cannot provide an interpretation for such determiners as *most*. However, the interpretation of determiners as (second-order) relations between sets allows a unified interpretation of all natural language determiners, because this approach takes into account the contribution of the common noun. As Barwise and Cooper (1981) put it, natural language determiners "live on" the denotation of the common noun. Another way of putting is to say that determiners in natural language tend to be *conservative*. Consider (3) again, repeated here as (10):

(10) Every student danced.

The evaluation of (10) requires us to check for each student whether or not (s)he has the dancing property. We are not concerned with dancing individuals outside the set of students, for they do not have an impact on the truth value of (10). The determiner *every* is 'left leaning' in the sense that we look first at the set of individuals that belong to the common noun denotation, and determine which of those satisfy the VP-denotation. We do not take into consideration individuals that have the property denoted by the VP, but that are not in the denotation of the common noun. Formally, conservativity is defined as follows:

- Conservativity
  For all $A, B \subseteq U$: $Q_U(A, B) \Leftrightarrow Q_U(A, A \cap B)$

The conservativity of natural language determiners is reflected in the equivalence between pairs of sentences like the ones in (11):

(11)  a.  All children sing $\Leftrightarrow$ All children are children that sing
      b.  Most children sing $\Leftrightarrow$ Most children are children that sing
      c.  No children sing $\Leftrightarrow$ No children are children that sing

Not all natural language determiners are conservative. Notable exceptions are *only* and certain interpretations of *many* (cf. Westerståhl 1985, de Hoop and Solà 1996, Herburger 1997):

(12)  a.  Only babies cry $\not\Leftrightarrow$ Only babies are babies that cry
      b.  Many Scandinavians have won the Nobel Prize $\not\Leftrightarrow$
          Many Scandinavians are Scandinavians who have won the Nobel Prize
      c.  Many incompetent cooks applied $\not\Leftrightarrow$
          Many incompetent cooks are cooks that applied

Instead of 'left leaning' determiners, we seem to have 'right leaning' determiners in these cases: (12a) is equivalent to 'The only crying individuals are crying babies' and (12b) reads as: 'Many individuals who won the Nobel Prize are Scandinavians who won the Nobel Prize'. To a certain degree, one can argue that these cases are exceptional. *Many* has conservative interpretations besides the non-conservative one illustrated in (12b), so maybe this is just a special use of the determiner. Furthermore, it has been argued that *only* is not in fact a determiner, because it can also modify NPs as in *only John* or *only some babies* and even VPs as in 'John only swims'. Therefore, the property of Conservativity is considered to be a (nearly) universal property of natural language quantifiers.

Another property which is a quasi-universal characteristic of natural language quantifiers is *Extension*. Extension states the principle of context neutrality. It guarantees that the determiner has the same structure in every model. Extension is formulated as closure under growth of the universe of discourse:

- Extension
  For all $A, B \subseteq U$: if $Q_U(A, B)$ and $U \subseteq U'$ then $Q_{U'}(A, B)$

This means that a quantifier which has a certain meaning as a relation between two sets $A$ and $B$ will not change its meaning if the universe becomes bigger without affecting the size of the sets $A$ and $B$. An example of a non-extensional quantifier is provided by certain uses of *many*, as discussed by Westerståhl (1985) and illustrated by (13):

(13)    There are many native speakers of Dutch.

(13) can be a true statement if a speaker in the European parliament tries to make the point that all proceedings need to be translated into Dutch. But given that Holland is a small country, this statement will prove false when a speaker is trying to make the same point in a meeting of the United Nations. From one context to the next, the number of native speakers of Dutch does not change, but the size of the universe of discourse increases dramatically. If the number of individuals that counts as 'many' is a function of the number of positive instances compared to the size of the universe of discourse of the model, we can account for the different truth values of (13) in different contexts. *Many* is thus an example of a strongly context-dependent determiner, which may even lose the property of extension in some of its uses.

The combination of Conservativity and Extension leads to a strong version of conservativity, dubbed Conservativity$^+$ by van Benthem (1986):

- Conservativity$^+$
  For all $A, B \subseteq U$: $Q_U(A, B) \Leftrightarrow Q_A(A, A \cap B)$

Extension guarantees that we do not need to take into consideration individuals which are not in $A$ or $B$, for the meaning of the determiner is independent of the size of the universe. Conservativity tells us that individuals that are in $B$, but not in $A$, do not play a role in determining the truth value of the proposition, because the determiner is 'left leaning'. Strong conservativity thus effectively restricts the universe of discourse to the left-hand argument. Neither elements in $B - A$, nor individuals in $U - (A \cup B)$ are taken into account when the sentence is evaluated.

Another useful property of determiners is *Quantity*. Quantitative determiners are insensitive to the individual characteristics of the members of $A$ and $B$. The truth value of the sentence depends only on the number of elements in A and $A \cap B$. Quantity is formally defined as closure under permutation of individuals:

- Quantity
  For all $A, B \subseteq U$ and all permutations $m$ of $U$:
  $Q_U(A, B) \Leftrightarrow Q_U(m[A], m[B])$

A permutation $m$ is an operation which maps a set $X$ onto another set $X'$ by relating every member of $x$ with some member of $X'$. $X'$ has the same number of elements as $X$, because permutation affects only the identity of the members. Closure under permutations means that the quantifier does not care which individuals are in A and B, as long as the same number of individuals remains in each set. Most well-known determiners are quantitative in nature, for example *some* in (14a):

(14)    a.    Some students are lazy.
            b.    Mary's bike has been stolen.

(14a) is true if and only if the set of lazy students is not empty. It does not matter which students are lazy, but there must be at least some. We can mix up the set of students and the set of lazy individuals without any change in truth value as long as the intersection remains non-empty. Not all determiners are quantitative. Possessive determiners such as the one in (14b) are not closed under permutation. For (14b) to be true it is not enough that there be at least one bike which has been stolen, it has to be Mary's bike. We cannot apply just any permutation, because the determiner is sensitive to a specific property of the individual bike, namely that it is owned by Mary. So possessives are not quantitative determiners.

The relational interpretation of quantified NPs can be pictured in a Venn diagram. The combination of the three properties of Conservativity, Extension and Quantity makes the interpretation of the determiner only

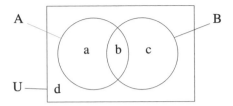

Figure 8.5: Constraints on determiner denotations

dependent on the cardinality of $A - B$ and $A \cap B$, that is $a$ and $b$ in the Venn diagram in figure 8.5.

The Venn diagram shows that the combination of the three general constraints greatly simplifies the interpretation of the determiner, because we can leave out two of the four subsets of the universe U as irrelevant, and for the two remaining sets we only need to know the number of elements in these sets. This effectively reduces the contribution of determiners that satisfy the three general constraints to a relation between two numbers: the number of individuals in the set $A$ and the number of individuals in the set $A \cap B$.

## 8.3 Subclasses of determiners

Certain properties do not characterize natural language quantifiers in general, but are particular to subclasses of quantifiers, such as the weak/strong distinction, definiteness and monotonicity.

### 8.3.1 The weak/strong distinction

The weak/strong distinction plays a role in the interpretation of existential *there*-sentences and related constructions, as observed by Milsark (1977), Barwise and Cooper (1981), de Jong (1987) and Keenan (1987). Consider:

(15) a.   There is a cat in the garden.
     b.   *There is the cat in the garden.
     c.   There are some/two/many/no cats in the garden.
     d.   *There is every/neither cat in the garden.
     e.   *There are most/not all/both cats in the garden.

(16)  a.  Mary has a sister.
     b.  *Mary has the sister.
     c.  Mary has two/several/many/no sisters.
     d.  *Mary has most/both/not all sisters.
     e.  *Mary has every/neither sister.

(17)  a.  We walked a mile.
     b.  ?We walked the mile.
     c.  We walked ten/several/many miles.
     d.  ?We walked most/not all/both miles.
     e.  ?We walked every/neither mile.

The contrast between the (a)- and (b)-sentences of (15)–(16) suggests
that indefinite NPs are admitted in existential sentences because the function of such constructions is to predicate existence. As pointed out in
section 5.4.2, indefinite NPs introduce new individuals into the universe
of discourse, which then become available for further reference. (17b) is
not downright ungrammatical, but it gets a very different interpretation
from (17a). (17a) is typically used to measure the distance we covered,
whereas (17b) can only be used if we somehow have a particular mile in
mind and assert that we walked (rather than biked, or drove) that particular mile. The measuring interpretation is subject to the same restrictions
as the existential contexts in (15) and (16). For definite NPs, existence
is presupposed, so they are not felicitous in constructions which introduce
new individuals. Milsark (1977) points out that this distinction needs to
be further generalized in view of examples (c)–(e) of (15)–(17). It is not so
clear what is indefinite about *no*, for instance, which would allow it to occur
in existential constructions whereas *neither* is not allowed. Similarly, it is
hard to explain what is definite about *most* which blocks it from existential
contexts, whereas *many* is possible. Therefore Milsark replaces the defi-
nite/indefinite contrast with a more general distinction between weak and
strong NPs. The weak/strong distinction plays an important role in the
study of syntactic and semantic properties of indefinite NPs, for instance in
the characterization of generic and partitive interpretations of indefinites
in a generalized quantifier perspective (see de Hoop 1992 for discussion).

One way to determine the strength of a determiner is the following test,
proposed by Barwise and Cooper (1981):

(18)  Det N is a N/ are Ns

According to Barwise and Cooper, a determiner is positive strong if this
statement is a tautology in every model in which the quantifier is defined.
A determiner is negative strong if it is a contradiction, and it is weak if the

truth of the statement depends on the model. This correctly classifies the following determiners:

(19)  a.  Every cat is a cat.                [pos. strong]
      b.  Both cats are cats.                [pos. strong]
      c.  Not all cats are cats.             [neg. strong]
      d.  Neither cat is a cat.              [neg. strong]
      e.  Many cats are cats.                [weak]
      f.  Ten cats are cats.                 [weak]
      g.  Some cats are cats.                [weak]
      h.  No cats are cats.                  [weak]

We have to be careful, for the judgments are not always very intuitive. (19a) and (c) are easy to classify, because the universal quantifier comes out true even on an empty domain, so the negation of the universal quantifier always comes out false. As a result, *every* is positive strong, and *not all* is negative strong.

The determiners in (19b) and (d) are positive and negative strong respectively, because they are definite (see section 8.3.2 below for a more precise definition of definiteness in generalized quantifier theory). Definite NPs are only defined when their presupposition is fullfilled. This means that (19b) and (d) are exclusively defined in models in which there are exactly two cats. Obviously, in such a model, (19b) is a tautology, and (d) a contradiction. The characterization of *many* in (19e) as a weak determiner is based on its behavior in models which contain less than 'many' cats (whatever the context-dependent number happens to be). In such a model the sentence comes out false, but of course in all other models it is true. If the sentence is sometimes true, sometimes false, it is neither a tautology nor a contradiction, so the determiner is classified as weak. (19f) is another example of a weak determiner. The sentence is true in a model which contains ten cats or more, false in a model in which there are less than ten cats. The argumentation for *some* and *no* in (19g) and (h) is similar, but may be somewhat harder to see. (19g) is always true, except in a model in which there are no cats, in which the sentence comes out false. Compare this with sentence (19h), which is always false, except when we evaluate it in models with no cats. Because of this one exceptional case, the determiners *some* and *no* count as weak.

We can use this to explain the distribution of determiners in existential sentences in the following way. Existential sentences are taken to predicate existence of the subject noun phrase. If we assume a predicate $E$ for 'existence in the universe of discourse $U$', we can write the quantificational structure of existential sentences as $Q(A, E)$. Because of Conservativity this statement is equivalent to $Q(A, A \cap E)$, which is in turn equivalent to

$Q(A, A)$, because all sets are a subset of the set of individuals that exist in the universe of discourse. Notice that $Q(A, A)$ is the quantificational structure of the sentences in (19). The claim is then that strong quantifiers are blocked from existential sentences because it would make them express a tautology or a contradiction.

There are two general problems with this line of explanation. One is that the definition of the weak/strong distinction proposed by Barwise and Cooper is not very intuitive. In particular, we have to accept that *some* and *no* are weak because of their behavior in models where the denotation of the common nouns is the empty set. In some sense, this is not what we would like to take as the basis of our linguistic theory. Furthermore, natural language usually does not rule out tautologies and contradictions as ungrammatical, as illustrated by the well-formedness of a sentence like (20):

(20)   There are less than zero cats in the garden.

There is no doubt about the contradictory character of (20): gardens do not contain negative numbers of cats. Even so, the sentence is fully grammatical (and understandable as a contradiction). Barwise and Cooper's characterization of the weak/strong distinction has been criticized for these reasons, but the general insight that there is a semantic difference between weak and strong determiners which explains their distribution in existential sentences has been preserved. Keenan (1987) exploits the property of symmetry to define a group of determiners as existential. Symmetry is one of the well-known properties of the theory of relations we studied in section 4.1.4. It has been observed that weak, but not strong determiners are symmetric. *Some* is symmetric, because we know that if some linguists are Spanish, then some Spanish are linguists. *No* is symmetric, for if no Stanford student is from Holland, then no one from Holland is a student at Stanford. Similarly, we can determine that *at least five, at most five, many* and *few* (in their cardinal interpretation) are symmetric. In combination with conservativity, the property of symmetry implies that only the intersection of A and B determines the truth value of the sentence:

(21)   $Q(A, B) \Leftrightarrow Q(B, A)$                    (symmetry)
       $Q(A, B) \Leftrightarrow Q(A, A \cap B)$              (conservativity)
       $Q(B, A) \Leftrightarrow Q(B, B \cap A)$              (conservativity)
       Thus:
       $Q(A, B) \Leftrightarrow Q(A, A \cap B) \Leftrightarrow Q(B, B \cap A)$
       As a result:
       $Q(A, B) \Leftrightarrow Q(A \cap B, A \cap B)$

The equivalencies in (21) show that determiners that are both conservative and symmetric are such that only the number of elements in the intersection of $A$ and $B$ plays a role in determining the truth value of the sentence. This can help us explain the constraints on existential sentences in the following way. We assume that in existential sentences the first argument of the quantifier is $E$, the predicate 'exist', which is satisfied by every individual in the universe of discourse $U$. Taking the part *cats in the garden* in (16) to denote the intersection of the set of cats and the set of individuals in the garden, we can write the quantificational structure of existential sentences as $Q(E, A \cap B)$. For conservative and symmetric quantifiers, this is equivalent to $Q(A, B)$, according to the following reasoning:

(22) $Q(E, A \cap B) \Leftrightarrow Q(E \cap A \cap B, E \cap A \cap B)$
(see above)

$Q(E \cap A \cap B, E \cap A \cap B) \Leftrightarrow Q(A \cap B, A \cap B)$
($A, B$ are subsets of $E$)

$Q(A \cap B, A \cap B) \Leftrightarrow Q(A, B)$
(see above)

So we know that for symmetric quantifiers $Q(E, A \cap B)$ is equivalent to $Q(A, B)$. Keenan (1987) defines existential determiners as determiners which satisfy exactly this equivalence. Existential determiners are the only determiners which allow an existential interpretation of *there*-constructions. Let us consider some examples. Because of the symmetry of the determiner, (23a) and (23b) are equivalent, and (23a) is appropriately characterized as an existential sentence. (23c) and (23d) are not equivalent, because *every* is not symmetric. Whatever interpretation we may be able to cook up for (23c), it will not qualify as an existential sentence:

(23)   a.   There are five cats in the garden.
      b.   Five cats are in the garden.
      c.   There is every cat in the garden.
      d.   Every cat is in the garden.
      e.   There are less than zero cats in the garden.
      f.   Less than zero cats are in the garden.

Finally, we observe that (23f) is as contradictory as (23e), but the two sentences are clearly equivalent. This appropriately characterizes *five* and *less than zero* as weak, existential determiners, and *every* as a strong, non-existential quantifier. Keenan's analysis correctly captures our intuitions about the meaning of the sentences in (23). It is also appropriate for cases such as (19), which do not involve ungrammaticality, but the unavailability of certain interpretations. It is harder to determine whether this purely semantic account also explains the lack of syntactic well-formedness of the (b), (d) and (e) examples in (15)–(16). The analysis explains why determiners that are not existential resist existential interpretations, but it does not explain why these determiners yield ungrammatical sentences. So there is more to be said about existential *there*-sentences.

The study of the distribution of NPs in existential contexts is a first illustration of the general approach in generalized quantifier theory. We study subclasses of determiners which have certain characteristics definable in terms of the theory of relations. On the basis of those properties and the universal constraints of conservativity, extension and quantity, we provide a semantic explanation of the behavior of certain classes of NPs.

## 8.3.2   Partitivity

We can explain the general constraints on partitive noun phrases of the form 'NP of NP' in similar ways. The data in (24) suggest that the NP embedded under the preposition *of* must be definite:

(24)  a.   Some of the students brought a gift.
      b.   Each of these two linguists has a theory about partitives.
      c.   The children ate all of the cake.
      d.   One of them must have committed the murder.
      e.   *Some of all students brought a gift.
      f.   *Each of most linguists has a theory about partitives.
      g.   *The children ate all of no cake.

The issue of which NPs can appear in the partitive construction bears on the meaning of the NP as a whole. Furthermore, we observe that the partitive and non-partitive members of the pairs in (25) are quite similar in interpretation, the main difference being that in the case of partitives, the quantification appears to be over some specific, non-empty, contextually fixed set, here a particular set of students:

(25)  a.   some of the students
          some students

      b.   few of the students
          few students

      c.   none of the students
          no students

In cases where both constructions are felicitous, the main difference between partitive and non-partitive NPs resides in the status of the set of individuals quantified over. In order to account for this intuition, Barwise and Cooper (1981) propose an interpretation of the partitive use of the preposition *of* as an operator which maps NP-denotations (sets of sets) onto CN-denotations (sets) by taking the intersection of all the sets in the generalized quantifier. Once *of* has applied, we have obtained a set again, which any determiner can combine with. There is a further restriction though, namely that the partitive construction is felicitous only in case the intersection of all the sets in the generalized quantifier denotation is a subset of the set of individuals denoted by the common noun. This requirement translates as the following claim: $\cap[\![NP]\!] \subseteq [\![CN]\!]$. Interestingly, the NPs which satisfy this constraint in a non-trivial way (i.e. in such a way that the intersection of all sets in the NP is not the empty set) are exactly those which satisfy Barwise and Cooper's definition of definite NPs. According to Barwise and Cooper, an NP is definite iff it has a non-empty set $B$ which is a subset of every set in the denotation of the generalized quantifier. This set $B$ is called the *generator* of the definite NP. It is clear from the diagram in figure 8.6 that the generator of a definite NP such as *the students* is the set of all students.

Figure 8.6: The students danced

The comparison with figure 8.3 above illustrates that an indefinite NP like *some students* does not have a unique generator set.

Note that the constraint on partitive NPs is stricter than strength. An NP like *most students* is strong, but it does not have a unique generator set. Universally quantified NPs like *every student* do have a unique generator set, namely the empty set, which, by definition is a subset of every set. Given that the generator set of a definite NP should be a non-empty set, universally quantified NPs do not satisfy the definition of definite NPs, and they do not satisfy the partitivity constraint in a non-trivial way. According to Barwise and Cooper, it is the ability of definite NPs to uniquely determine the generator set that allows the NP to play the role of a common noun and recombine with a determiner. The additional information that is supplied by the definite determiner is just that the set being quantified over is non-empty. This accounts for the intuition that in partitive constructions we quantify over some specific, contextually determined set of individuals (e.g. the set of students in 25). Further restrictions are necessary in order to explain why (26a) is good, whereas (26b) is not:

(26)  a.  One of the two books was sold out.
      b.  *One of both books was sold out.

Ladusaw (1982) points out that the main difference between these two NPs is that *the two* N has a group-level denotation, whereas *both* N does not. This is supported by the data in (27), which involve a group-level predicate:

(27)  a.  The two students are a happy couple.
      b.  *Both students are a happy couple.

A property like *to be a happy couple* is typically not ascribed to individuals, but to groups of individuals. The ungrammaticality of (27b) comes about as a result of the semantic nature of *both* N. This NP requires a distributive interpretation in which each of the two individuals has the property denoted by the VP. A property like *to be a happy couple* is typically not ascribed to individuals, but to groups of individuals. The relevance of a restriction to group-denoting expressions also explains some apparent counterexamples to the partitive constraint as in (28):

(28)  a.  John was one of several students who arrived late.
      b.  That book could belong to one of three people.

The sentences in (28) are felicitous only in contexts in which the speaker has a particular group of individuals in mind. The capacity of indefinite NPs to set up discourse referents available for further reference plays a role here (compare our informal discussion of discourse anaphora in chapter 5). It would lead too far to discuss all the intricate details of the partitive construction here, so the reader is referred to de Jong (1987) and de Hoop (1997) for further discussion.

## 8.3.3  Monotonicity

Monotonicity involves the possibility of inference to supersets or subsets of the set under consideration. As usual, we are interested in entailment relations, because of their impact on valid reasoning patterns in which the truth of some statement (the conclusion) follows from the truth of one or more other statements (the premises). This motivates a general interest in inference patterns.

Following Barwise and Cooper (1981) and Zwarts (1981, 1986), we define upward monotonicity as follows:

- A quantifier Q is monotone increasing (*mon* ↑) if:
  $Q(A, B)$ and $B \subseteq B'$ implies $Q(A, B')$

Some examples:

(29)    *Mon* ↑ quantifiers
    a.   All children came home late → All children came home
    b.   Most children came home late → Most children came home
    c.   At least five children came home late → At least five children came home

Not all quantifiers are monotone increasing. For instance, the inferences do not go through in the following cases:

(30)   a.   No children came home late ↛ No children came home
    b.   Not all children came home late ↛ Not all children came home
    c.   Less than five children came home late ↛ Less than five children came home

Some of these quantifiers have the related property of downward monotonicity:

- A quantifier Q is monotone decreasing (*mon* ↓) if:
  $Q(A, B)$ and $B' \subseteq B$ implies $Q(A, B')$

Some examples:

(31)    *Mon* ↓ quantifiers
    a.   No children came home → No children came home late
    b.   Not all children came home → Not all children came home late
    c.   At most five children came home → At most five children came home late

So monotonicity properties typically tell you that you can make inferences towards larger or smaller sets. In other words, they correspond to closure under superset or (finite) subset formation, respectively. Not all quantifiers are either monotone increasing or monotone decreasing. Some non-monotonic quantifiers are the following:

(32)   Non-monotonic quantifiers
    a.   Exactly two children came home late $\not\to$
       Exactly two children came home

    b.   An even number of children came home late $\not\to$
       An even number of children came home

    c.   More than two but less than five children came home late
       $\not\to$
       More than two but less than five children came home

One of the contexts in which the property of monotonicity plays a role is in the explanation of conjunction and disjunction reduction, as argued by Zwarts (1981, 1986). Consider the sentences in (33):

(33)   a.   Sara sang and danced.
      b.   Sara sang and Sara danced.
      c.   Sara sang or danced.
      d.   Sara sang or Sara danced.

For transformational grammarians in the '60s and '70s, the relations between reduced and unreduced sentences were a puzzle. At first sight, it looks attractive to transformationally derive (33a) from (33b). After all, the two sentences are equivalent. Similarly, we could try to derive (33c) from (33d) on the basis of the equivalence between the two sentences. However, it turns out that not every sentence of the form (34a) is equivalent to one of the form (34b):

(34)   a.   NP VP$_1$ and/or VP$_2$
      b.   NP VP$_1$ and/or NP VP$_2$

As far as quantified NPs are concerned, the equivalence works in examples like (35a). It works in (35b) if we switch *or* into *and*. It reduces to a one-way implication in cases like (35c), (d) and (e), and it breaks down entirely in cases like (35f):

(35)  a.  Every student sang and danced ↔
          Every student sang and every student danced

      b.  No student sang or danced ↔
          No student sang and no student danced

      c.  At least two students sang and danced →
          At least two students sang and at least two students danced

      d.  At most two students sang and danced ←
          At most two students sang and at most two students
          danced

      e.  At most two students sang or danced →
          At most two students sang and at most two students
          danced

      f.  Exactly two students sang and danced ↮
          Exactly two students sang and exactly two students danced

The observation that the sentences in (35) share the same syntactic structure, but participate in different inference patterns supports the claim that a purely syntactic approach to conjunction reduction is not the right line of explanation. If the only difference between the sentences in (35) is the choice of the NP, it is likely that conjunction and disjunction reduction are somehow dependent on the semantic properties of the NP. The property of monotonicity springs to mind, because of the similarities between entailment relations (defined on propositions) and inference to subsets and supersets (defined on sets). In chapter 3, we discussed entailment relations between conjoined/disjoined statements and the atomic propositions making up the complex propositions. These entailment relations have set-theoretical counterparts we can appeal to in our treatment of the examples in (35). If we assume that the conjunction of two VPs is interpreted as intersection of the two sets involved, and disjunction of two VPs is interpreted as set union, we obtain the following statements about relevant subset and superset relations:

- $[\![\,\text{VP}_1 \text{ and } \text{VP}_2\,]\!] \subseteq [\![\,\text{VP}_1\,]\!]$ and
  $[\![\,\text{VP}_1 \text{ and } \text{VP}_2\,]\!] \subseteq [\![\,\text{VP}_2\,]\!]$ because
  $[\![\,\text{VP}_1]\!] \cap [\![VP_2\,]\!] \subseteq [\![\,\text{VP}_1\,]\!]$ and
  $[\![\,\text{VP}_1]\!] \cap [\![VP_2\,]\!] \subseteq [\![\,\text{VP}_2\,]\!]$

- $[\![\,\text{VP}_1\,]\!] \subseteq [\![\,\text{VP}_1 \text{ or } \text{VP}_2\,]\!]$ and
  $[\![\,\text{VP}_2\,]\!] \subseteq [\![\,\text{VP}_1 \text{ or } \text{VP}_2\,]\!]$ because
  $[\![\,\text{VP}_1\,]\!] \subseteq [\![\,\text{VP}_1]\!] \cup [\![VP_2\,]\!]$ and
  $[\![\,\text{VP}_1\,]\!] \subseteq [\![\,\text{VP}_1]\!] \cup [\![VP_2\,]\!]$

We know that monotone increasing quantifiers are closed under super-set formation, whereas monotone decreasing quantifiers are closed under subset formation. These properties are related to conjunction/disjunction reduction in a straightforward way. If a quantifier is monotone increasing and a conjunction of two properties is a member of the quantifier, each of these properties will be a member of the quantifier. After all, the conjunction is a subset of both, and the quantifier licenses the inference to a larger set. For the same reason we expect the disjunction of two properties to be a member of a monotone increasing quantifier if either one of the properties is. For monotone decreasing quantifiers, the inferences go the other way around, because they license inferences to smaller sets:

(36)    $Mon \uparrow$ quantifiers
    a.    $Q(A, B \cap C) \rightarrow Q(A, B)$ and $Q(A, C)$
    b.    $Q(A, B)$ or $Q(A, C) \rightarrow Q(A, B \cup C)$

(37)    $Mon \downarrow$ quantifiers
    a.    $Q(A, B)$ and $Q(A, C) \rightarrow Q(A, B \cap C)$
    b.    $Q(A, B \cup C) \rightarrow Q(A, B)$ and $Q(A, C)$

The patterns in (36) and (37) explain the one-way inferences in (35c), (35d) and (35e). They also rule out any implication relation between the two sentences in (35f): non-monotonic quantifiers do not allow this kind of inference pattern. Because there is no inference relating one sentence to the other, we cannot derive one sentence from the other by means of conjunction reduction. The general properties of monotone increasing and monotone decreasing quantifiers also explain one half of the inferences in (35a) and (35b). The inference from left to right in (35a) follows from the interpretation of conjunction as set intersection, just like in (35c). The inference from right to left in (35b) follows from the definition of disjunction as set union, just like in (35d).

In order to explain the equivalences in (33), (35a) and (35b), we still need to account for the other half of the inferences. This requires a more refined semantic analysis of the quantifiers involved. It turns out that we can define several linguistically interesting subsets of monotone increasing and decreasing quantifiers. The inference patterns in (36) and (37) follow directly from the monotonicity properties of the quantifiers involved. However, they cannot replace the original definition of monotone increasing and decreasing quantifiers given above, for they impose a weaker constraint on the quantifier denotation. In particular, we find that a subset of the set of mon $\uparrow$ quantifiers also licenses the inferences in (37). Such quantifiers are called *filters*. Furthermore, a subset of the set of mon $\downarrow$ quantifiers licenses the inferences in (36). They are called *ideals*. The formal definition of filters and ideals is as follows:

- filters
  $X \in Q$ and $Y \in Q$ iff $(X \cap Y) \in Q$

- ideals
  $X \in Q$ and $Y \in Q$ iff $(X \cup Y) \in Q$

Natural language expressions which have filter structure are universal quantifiers, definite NPs and proper names, as we can see from the following equivalences, repeated from (33a) and (35a):

(38)   a.   Every student sang and danced ↔
                Every student sang and every student danced

         b.   Sara sang and danced ↔
                Sara sang and Sara danced

Ideals in natural language are negative universal quantifiers like *no* (35b) and the negation of definite NPs and proper names. The full range of equivalences and one-way implications in (35) is now accounted for. The equivalence in (33b) requires a further refinement, for this pattern is valid for a subset of the set of filters only. Compare (33b), repeated here as (39a) with the one-way inference in (39b):

(39)   a.   Sara sang or danced ↔
                Sara sang or Sara danced
         b.   Every student sang or danced ←
                Every student sang or every student danced

The inference from right to left is licensed by the monotone increasing nature of the quantifier. The inference from left to right is licensed only for ultrafilters. Examples of ultrafilters are proper names and definite descriptions. The formal definite of an ultrafilter is as follows:

- ultrafilters
  $X \in Q$ or $Y \in Q$ iff $(X \cup Y) \in Q$

The examples discussed in this section show that conjunction and disjunction reduction can fruitfully be explained if we take a semantic approach to natural language and describe the properties of determiners in a mathematically precise way.

## 8.3.4  Negative polarity

Another application of the property of monotonicity to natural language semantics is the treatment of the phenomenon of *negative polarity items*. Negative polarity items are expressions in natural language which only occur in contexts with a negative flavor, compare:

(40)  a.  Susan did not say anything.
     b.  *Susan said anything.
     c.  I do not think that John has ever read a paper in philosophy.
     d.  *I think that John has ever read a paper in philosophy.
     e.  Jim did not lift a finger to help us.
     f.  *Jim lifted a finger to help us.

At first sight, one might say that negative polarity items are expressions that need to occur in a 'negative' environment. Negation can be provided by sentence negation, but it could also be some negative quantifier like *nobody* or *never*. Compare:

(41)  a.  Susan never says anything.
     b.  *Susan often says anything.
     c.  No student in linguistics ever read a paper in philosophy.
     d.  *Every student in linguistics ever read a paper in philosophy
     e.  Nobody lifted a finger to help us.
     f.  *Everybody lifted a finger to help us.

We would have to stretch our use of negation even further to account for the following contrasts:

(42)  a.  Susan seldom says anything.
     b.  *Susan always says anything.
     c.  At most five students in linguistics ever read a paper in philosophy.
     d.  *At least five students in linguistics ever read a paper in philosophy.
     e.  Few people lifted a finger to help us.
     f.  *Many people lifted a finger to help us.

We would have to explain why *at least five*, *often* and *many* are 'positive' and *at most five*, *few* and *seldom* are 'negative' rather than the other way round. We could try to reanalyze *few* as 'not many' and *seldom* as 'not often', but that would be begging the question why *many* is not reanalyzed as 'not few', and *often* is not reanalyzed as 'not seldom'. Also, the fact that one can say things like (43) suggests that *many* and *few*, and *often* and *seldom* are not exactly each other's negation:

(43)   a.   There are not many majors in linguistics, but not few either.

        b.   This child does not pray often, but not seldom either.

This argumentation is reminiscent of the discussion of the distribution of NPs in existential contexts. Intuitively, existential contexts are sensitive to the definite/indefinite distinction, but in order to account for a broader range of determiners, we generalized this to a notion of weakness and strength. As far as negative polarity items are concerned, there is an intuitive explanation in terms of negation, but it needs to be generalized in order to account for all the relevant cases. One line of explanation which has been explored by Ladusaw (1979), Zwarts (1986), van der Wouden (1997) and others is to assume that the constraint on negative polarity items is to be formulated in terms of monotonicity rather than strict negation. More specifically, the claim is that negative polarity items are restricted to downward entailing contexts. Obviously, negation is a downward entailing environment, but the definition includes a large number of other licensing contexts as well. The restriction to downward entailing contexts provides an interesting semantic explanation of the distribution of negative polarity items in (41)–(43). Compare Ladusaw (1996) and references therein for more discussion of syntactic, semantic and pragmatic aspects of negative polarity.

So far we have only defined monotonicity for the right argument of the quantifier (the VP-argument). Examples like those in (44) show that we also need to have access to the monotonicity properties of the determiner with respect to the first argument of the quantifier (the nominal argument):

(44)   a.   Every student who has ever studied logic takes a semantics class.

        b.   No student who has ever studied logic fails to take a semantics class.

As argued above, *every* is a monotone increasing quantifier. It can easily be shown that this is true for the rightward argument only. In its left argument *every* is monotone decreasing:

(45)   a.   Every student left for spring break →
            Every linguistics student left for spring break

        b.   No student left for spring break →
            No linguistics student left for spring break

The generalization of the definitions of right monotonicity to left monotonicity is straightforward:

- A quantifier Q is left monotone increasing ($\uparrow mon$) if:
  Q(A,B) and $A \subseteq A'$ implies Q(A',B)

- A quantifier Q is left monotone decreasing ($\downarrow mon$) if:
  Q (A,B) and $A' \subseteq A$ implies Q (A',B)

As expected, and shown in (44), left monotone decreasing quantifiers license negative polarity items in their first argument.

In this chapter, we have seen that the theory of generalized quantifiers provides insight into a wide range of natural language quantifiers in different constructions. Furthermore, the theory can be extended in various ways. The theory does not only apply to determiners, but can account for quantification in the adverbial or verbal domain as well (compare Bach, Kratzer and Partee eds. 1995). De Swart (1991) takes adverbs of quantification like *sometimes, always, never, often* to denote relations between sets of events, and studies their semantic properties in a generalized quantifier perspective. Similarly, Hoeksema (1983) and others discuss monotonicity properties of comparative constructions, and Sánchez Valencia, van der Wouden and Zwarts (1994) use monotonicity patterns to study the semantics of temporal connectives like *since* and *before*.

The flexibility of the framework of generalized quantifiers and its wide range of applications have generated an impressive literature on this topic. The interested reader is referred to van Benthem and ter Meulen (eds.) (1984), van Benthem (1986), Zwarts (1986), Gärdenfors (ed.) (1987), Westerståhl (1989), van der Does and van Eijck (eds.) (1996), Keenan (1996) and Keenan and Westerståhl (1997) for further discussion, empirical studies and relevant overviews of logical and linguistic aspects of generalized quantifier theory.

## 8.4 Exercises

1.! Show in a model with four entities that *John's books* is not a quantitative determiner whereas *every book* is.

2.! The general constraints on determiner denotations (conservativity, extension and quantity) allow us to represent the space of possible determiner concepts in natural language graphically by means of a *tree of numbers*. Let A and B be sets, let $a =| A - B |$, and let $b =| A \cap B |$. Then we can construct a tree of numbers corresponding to the possible pairs $\langle a, b \rangle$:

| $a+b=0$ | | | | $0,0$ | | | | |
| $a+b=1$ | | | $1,0$ | | $0,1$ | | | |
| $a+b=2$ | | $2,0$ | | $1,1$ | | $0,2$ | | |
| $a+b=3$ | $3,0$ | | $2,1$ | | $1,2$ | | $0,3$ | |
| $a+b=4$ | $4,0$ | $3,1$ | | $2,2$ | | $1,3$ | | $0,4$ |
| $\cdots$ | | $\cdots$ | | | | | | |

To illustrate, the determiner *both* is represented by the point $\langle 0,2 \rangle$ on the tree, since in any sentence containing the form 'Both As are B', the number of A's that are not B is 0, and the number of A's that are B is 2.

(i) Indicate how the following determiners can be represented on the tree of numbers:

    a!   *neither*             b!   *every*

    c.   *most*                 d.   *at most two*

    e.   *not all*            f.   *exactly one or exactly three*

(ii) Show how determiners with the following properties can be represented on the tree of numbers:

    a! right monotone increasing

    b. left monotone decreasing

    c. symmetry

3. Give truth conditions for the following sentences, interpreting the (complex) determiner as a relation between sets. Illustrate with a Venn diagram:

(i)! Some but not all Dutchmen are good sailors.

(ii) Every student but John got an A+.

(iii) At most five students got an A.

(iv) Few babies cried.

4. Use inference patterns like the ones in (30)–(32) and (45) to determine the left and right monotonicity properties of the determiners in the following sentences. Make sure to discuss both cardinal and proportional interpretations for the determiners for which that is appropriate:

(i)! Many babies cried.

(ii) The baby cried.

(iii) Neither baby cried.

(iv) Few babies cried.

(v) A few babies cried.

As argued in section 8.3.4, monotonicity properties play a role in the distribution of negative polarity items. Explain which determiners in (i)–(v) license negative polarity items in their first and/or second argument and illustrate your results with examples.

5. Give an example of a natural language determiner which has the following properties. Motivate your answer with examples which illustrate the relevant properties:

(i)! left-monotone increasing and right-monotone decreasing

(ii) left-monotone decreasing and weak

(iii) right-monotone decreasing and strong

Explain why the quantifier you give in (i) must be strong, and the one in (ii) must be right-monotone decreasing. Show for your example that this is indeed the case.

6. (i)! Formulate a linguistic constraint on coordination of NPs with conjunction which explains the following well-formed and ill-formed expressions in terms of semantic properties of the NPs involved:

    a. Susan invited every linguistics student and most philosophy students.

    b. No books by Chomsky and not all books by Quine were on the reading list.

    c. ??Susan xeroxed no articles on quantifier raising and all articles on Cooper storage.

    d. ??Susan visited most of her cousins and neither of her sisters.

(ii) Give examples of coordination with *but* and compare them with the results for *and*. Formulate a linguistic constraint which captures your findings.

7. In the relational perspective on determiners, we can study the properties of determiners that are familiar from the theory of relations. In (i)–(iv) a number of these properties are defined. For each of these properties, give an example of a natural language determiner that does and that does not have this property. Motivate your choice.

$(!)reflexivity:$     $Q_U(A, A)$
$irreflexivity:$     $\neg Q_U(A, A)$
$antisymmetry:$     $((Q_U(A, B) \wedge Q_U(B, A)) \rightarrow A = B)$
$transitivity:$     $((Q_U(A, B) \wedge Q_U(B, C)) \rightarrow Q_U(A, C))$

# Chapter 9

# Worlds and times

Not all natural language constructions can be handled by the extensional theory we have developed so far. In this chapter, we make the interpretation function dependent on times in order to account for verbal tense, time adverbials and temporal connectives. Furthermore, we introduce possible worlds to model intensions, modal adverbs and modal auxiliaries.

## 9.1 Time and tense

So far we have developed a purely *extensional* view of semantics. We have individuals in a universe of discourse, we know which properties they have in our model, properties themselves have been modelled as sets of individuals, relations as sets of pairs of individuals, etc.

In this chapter, we will investigate constructions in natural language which resist an extensional analysis, and we will define a richer theory which can deal with at least a number of *intensional* contexts. The approach we adopt is to extend rather than replace the semantic theory built up so far. In particular, we will enrich our interpretation function by introducing more indices with respect to which the interpretation of an expression is evaluated.

The reference to individuals, sets, and set-membership relations that our universe of discourse $U$ and interpretation function $I$ provide create

a very 'static' picture. Things are the way they are, and our model does
not incorporate the notion of change. Suppose we have a set of students,
then we know exactly who is a member of that set in our model. In real
life, the set of students is fluctuating a lot. But our interpretation function
does not allow us to let the set of students grow with every new incoming
student and shrink with every student who graduates. We could respond
that a theory of natural language does not necessarily need to model that
kind of fluctuation, which after all has to do with the real world, rather
than with the meaning of the words as such. Given that our model is a
rather abstract picture of the real world, we need not take into account
everything happening out there. This argument is valid only as long as the
natural language we are trying to model with our logical language is not
sensitive to this kind of development over time. If we find expressions that
refer to changes, developments, and fluctuation in properties over time,
we need to develop a semantic theory which models that kind of information. Examples of expressions which indicate the dependence of truth
on a temporal parameter are verbal tenses, time adverbials and temporal
connectives. Consider the following sentences:

(1)  a.   Susan went to the movies yesterday.
     b.   Bill gave Susan a book for her birthday.
     c.   Susan will become a great linguist.
     d.   John became famous after he made this statue.
     e.   I didn't turn off the stove.
     f.   Frege was a great logician.

These are all well-formed sentences of English. But if we want to evaluate their truth value in the model, we have to do something more than
just say that Susan is a member of the set of individuals who went to the
movies. One possibility would be to say that Susan is a member of the
set of individuals that went to the movies yesterday, whereas, say, Paul is
a member of the set of individuals that are going to the movies tonight.
But that might give us two entirely disjoint sets, and it establishes no relation whatsoever between the two properties. This runs against our general
enterprise of developing a compositional analysis of meaning in natural language. Intuitively, (1a) means something like 'at a certain point in time,
namely a day before the speech time, the proposition that Susan goes to
the movies is true'. Similar observations can be made for (1b), even though
in the absence of a specific time adverbial the past tense reference is vague
as to the location in time of the event. The set of triples that stood in
the give-relation at Susan's birthday last year need not share any member
with the set of triples which stand in that relation this year. We want our

semantic theory to capture the intuition that the same three-place relation is involved, but that its extension at different times need not be the same.

A slightly different case is exemplified in (1d): the connective *after* is like conjunction in that it requires both sentences to be true, but not at the same time of course. In order to capture the semantics of the temporal connective, we need to be able to establish a relation between the times at which each of the two propositions is true. If we cannot refer to the time at which a proposition is true, there is no way we can specify the different relations established by *before, after, while,* etc.

Partee (1973) provides the example in (1e). She argues that it is appropriate to utter this sentence in a situation in which the whole family started off for a holiday and is just out on the highway. In such a situation, we want to relate the failure to turn off of the stove to some contextually relevant time, like the time right before they left. We definitely do not want to claim that the person in question is irresponsible to the extent that (s)he never turns off the stove, so the scope of the negation should be restricted to a contextually relevant interval, rather than ranging over all times preceding the speech time. Examples like this one show that the introduction of reference to time raises a number of complex semantic problems all of which we cannot address. We will not talk here about new individuals being born and other individuals dying, so we will assume throughout that the universe of discourse is fixed for all times and that we know at every moment in time what our individual constants refer to. This means that we will not give a complete account of (1f), which is in the past tense because Frege happens to be no longer among us. The analysis in this section focuses on the examples in (1a)–(d). These sentences show that tense morphemes, time adverbials and temporal connectives have a semantics of their own, which a general theory of meaning of natural language needs to account for. We will build up the semantics of these expressions step by step, starting with the introduction of some technical notions.

We can begin to account for the dependence on location in time by extending our model with a set $T$ of times or instants, and make the interpretation of the proposition dependent on the time with respect to which it is evaluated. More precisely, we add the time with respect to which the sentence is evaluated as an index on the interpretation function. This is similar to the way in which assignment functions are indices on the interpretation function (compare chapter 4). So now we interpret an expression $\alpha$ with respect to a model $M$, an assignment $g$ and a time $t$. This is written as $[\![\alpha]\!]^{M,g,t}$.

Adding a set $T$ of times to our model is of course begging the ontological question of what times are and how time is structured. There are different views on temporal structure, but there are a number of relatively straightforward and widely shared assumptions. The first assumption is that we view times as *instants*, that is, as objects which have no duration, which do not take time. This correlates with the idea that tense is not discrete, but continuous: there are no 'gaps' between moments in time. This suggests that we order our set of times like the set of $\mathbb{R}$ of real numbers. Furthermore, we distinguish between past, present ('now') and future, and assume that time has a specific directionality, as illustrated by figure 9.1.

Figure 9.1: Flow of time

The intuition of the flow of time is formally captured by the introduction of a precedence relation on the set of times. This guarantees that past times are earlier than future times. The set $T$ is thus ordered by a reflexive, transitive and anti-symmetric relation $\preceq$, which makes $\langle T, \preceq \rangle$ a partial order:

- The set $T$ is ordered by a relation $\preceq$ which has the following properties:

  (i) $\preceq$ is reflexive: $\forall t \, (t \preceq t)$
  
  (ii) $\preceq$ is transitive: $\forall t_1 \, \forall t_2 \, \forall t_3 \, ((t_1 \preceq t_2 \wedge t_2 \preceq t_3) \rightarrow (t_1 \preceq t_3))$
  
  (iii) $\preceq$ is anti-symmetric: $\forall t_1 \, \forall t_2 \, ((t_1 \preceq t_2 \wedge t_2 \preceq t_1) \rightarrow t_1 = t_2)$

Further restrictions one can impose on the temporal structure of the model are connectedness (the requirement that all instants be connected to each other) and density (no 'gaps'):

- (i) connectedness: $\forall t_1 \, \forall t_2 \, (t_1 \preceq t_2 \vee t_2 \preceq t_1)$

  (ii) density: $\forall t_1 \, \forall t_2 \, ((t_1 \prec t_2) \rightarrow \exists t_3 \, (t_1 \prec t_3 \wedge t_3 \prec t_2))$
  where $\prec$ is defined as:
  $\forall t_1 \, \forall t_2 \, ((t_1 \preceq t_2 \wedge \neg t_2 \preceq t_1) \rightarrow (t_1 \prec t_2))$

If you believe that time stretches infinitely far into the past and into the future, you may want to add the requirement that there be no smallest or greatest element in the temporal structure:

- (i) no smallest element: $\forall t_1 \, \exists t_2 \, (t_2 \prec t_1)$

(ii) no greatest element: $\forall t_1 \exists t_2 (t_1 \prec t_2)$

If there is no smallest element, there is no beginning to the flow of time. If there is no greatest element, there is no end to the flow of time. We can add further properties and constraints to develop temporal structures as rich as necessary for our purposes. But almost all models will share the kernel of temporal structure as a partial order (see van Benthem 1991, Landman 1991).

$[\![\alpha]\!]^{M,g,t}$ allows us to fix the interpretation of any expression $\alpha$ relative to a particular time $t$. So our interpretation function gives us for any time $t$ the possibility to evaluate the statement that Susan went to the movies at $t$, for instance. Obviously, the set of individuals that went to the movies yesterday need not have any members in common with the set of individuals that go to the movies today. But we still have a systematic relation between the two sets, because we have not changed the interpretation of the predicate (which is still given by the interpretation function $I$), we have just added an extra (temporal) index to the interpretation function. This enrichment of the interpretation function allows us to define the extension of the predicate at different times.

Now that we have added a set of times to our semantics, we can start interpreting expressions that are dependent on reference to time. We start with the interpretation of tense morphemes. The past tense of sentence like (1a) and (b) conveys the information that the situation holds at some time earlier than the speech time. The future tense in (1c) requires the proposition to be true at some time later than the speech time. One way of evaluating tensed sentences is to interpret tenses in natural language as operators on formulas (Prior 1967). These operators quantify over the times $t$ with respect to which a proposition is evaluated. We introduce two new propositional operators: **P** for 'past' and **F** for 'future'. These propositional operators can be prefixed to any well-formed formula to yield a new well-formed formula. This gives us the following extension of first order propositional (or predicate) logic:

- Syntax

    (i) If $\phi$ is a wff then $\mathbf{P}\phi$ is a wff
    (ii) If $\phi$ is a wff then $\mathbf{F}\phi$ is a wff

Intuitively, the operators **P** and **F** can be read as 'It was the case at some time in the past that $\phi$' and 'It will be the case at some time in the future that $\phi$'. We can use these operators to translate the sentences in (1b) and (c) as in (2a) and (b) respectively:[1]

---

[1] For the sake of transparency, we will ignore the internal structure of the proposition.

(2) a. Bill gave Susan a book for her birthday.
    **P**(Bill give Susan a book for her birthday)

  b. Susan will become a great linguist.
    **F**(Susan become a great linguist)

With the help of our extended interpretation function we can make the semantics of **P** and **F** more precise:

- Semantics
  - (i) $[\![ \mathbf{P} \ \phi ]\!]^{M,t,g} = 1$ iff there exists a $t' \in T$ such that
    $$t' \prec t \text{ and } [\![\phi]\!]^{M,t',g} = 1$$
  - (ii) $[\![ \mathbf{F} \ \phi ]\!]^{M,t,g} = 1$ iff there exists a $t' \in T$ such that
    $$t \prec t' \text{ and } [\![\phi]\!]^{M,t',g} = 1$$

The definition of **P** and **F** is clearly related to the interpretation of the existential quantifier defined in chapter 4. The main difference is in the domain of quantification: the quantifier $\exists$ binds an individual variable $x$ and involves quantification over individuals, whereas the tense operators **P** and **F** involve quantification over times.

In general (though not always), sentences like those in (2) are evaluated with respect to the time of the speech situation. In such cases, the index $t$ on the interpretation function is identified with the utterance time. The dependence on the time of the speech situation shows that tense is an essentially deictic category. We often give the speech time a special index, e.g. $t_0$, to highlight the indexical nature of the tense system of natural language. The meaning of the examples in (2) is spelled out in (3):

(3) a. $[\![ \mathbf{P}(\text{Bill give Susan a book for her birthday}) ]\!]^{M,t_0,g} = 1$ iff there exists a $t \in T$ such that $t \prec t_0$ and $[\![$ Bill give Susan a book for her birthday $]\!]^{M,t,g} = 1$

  b. $[\![ \mathbf{F}(\text{Susan become a great linguist}) ]\!]^{M,t_0,g} = 1$ iff there exists a $t \in T$ such that $t_0 \prec t$ and $[\![$ Susan become a great linguist $]\!]^{M,t,g} = 1$

The interpretations in (3) capture the intuition that sentences in the past tense refer to propositions which are true with respect to some time $t$ in the past of the moment of speech $t_0$. Sentences in the future tense are true with respect to some time $t$ later than the speech time $t_0$.

Given that tense operators are propositional in nature, they can be iterated. This is useful in the treatment of complex tenses in sentences like (4):

(4)   a.   (In 1976, Susan was told that) she would be a famous lin-
            guist.
            **PF**(Susan is a famous linguist)

      b.   (By that time) John will (already) have left.
            **FP**(John leaves)

One of the problems with the operator approach to tense morphemes
is that the iteration of tense operators in the logic is much more powerful
than what we find in natural language. For instance, English has a past
of a past (the Pluperfect for instance in 'Susan had left'), which we could
write as **PP**$\phi$.[2] However, it does not have a future of the future, so there is
no natural language counterpart to **FF**$\phi$. Languages generally have more
elaborate tense systems to refer to the past than to the future (Comrie
1985). This may be due to more general differences between the past and
the future. The past seems to be fixed forever (we cannot go back and
change our actions), whereas the future is open, and we do not (always)
know which course of action will be realized. Our conceptualization of time
is not symmetric, as suggested in figure 9.1 above. If we want to respect
the undetermined nature of the future, we can adopt a branching model of
time, as in figure 9.2.

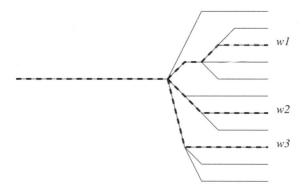

Figure 9.2: Branching future

The picture of time as a branching structure shows the time axis to be
a straight line up until the present (the moment of speech). After that
moment, any of the lines could be the continuation of the 'real' world. It
depends on what happens whether the real world turns out to be $w_1$, $w_2$

---

[2]Note that this treatment of the Pluperfect raises certain problems if we assume that
time is tense. See exercise 1 for discussion.

or $w_3$. The fact that we can anticipate different courses of events comes close to the notion of possible world we will define in section 9.2 below. The close and intricate connections between tense and modality are an important argument for discussing them in one chapter.

The view of time as branching towards the future has some interesting consequences for the interpretation of future tenses like (5a) and (b):

(5)  a.  He will die.
     b.  He is going to die.

(5a) has a trivial reading which just claims that man is not immortal. It can also have a stronger "predicting" kind of reading, which may still be in the faraway future, though. (5b) does not have the trivial reading. Moreover, it strongly suggests that the dying is near and somehow unavoidable: we have evidence from context and situation that this is about to happen, it is not just a mere possibility we are envisaging. The contrast in (5) illustrates how modal notions involving knowledge and evidence come into play when we interpret future tenses. Future and modality are closely tied together, because there is not yet a clear distinction between what the real world is and what is just a possible way it could be. On the basis of this observation, some people argue that we cannot really distinguish between worlds and times in the future. This leads to the claim that future tenses are not really tenses, but are in fact purely modal constructions. The observation that many languages use a modal auxiliary to express the future tense supports this position. English *shall, will* and Dutch *zullen* are good examples of this tendency. The discussion of the relation between future time reference and modality goes back to the classical Greek philosophers (see Øhrstrøm and Hasle 1995 for a historical overview). It would lead too far to discuss this issue in any detail here. Note however that there is at least some evidence that times and worlds are distinct, even in the future. The evidence comes from the comparison of the modal force of a sentence like (6a) and the one of (6b–d):

(6)  a.  It will rain tomorrow.
     b.  It will possibly rain tomorrow.
     c.  It will probably rain tomorrow.
     d.  It will necessarily rain tomorrow.

(6a) shares with (6d) the requirement that the situation becomes true in the real world. This need not be the case for (6b) and (c). However, we hesitate to characterize every future tense sentence as a necessary truth. Intuitively, a futurate sentence refers to whichever branch in figure 9.2 the real world develops into. Unlike modal operators like *possibly, necessarily,* the interpretation of the future tense is not dependent on other possible worlds besides the real one. We conclude that even though we do not have epistemic access to the real world after the speech time, the future tense cannot be purely described in terms of quantification over possible worlds.

Now that we have added times and tense operators to our semantics, we can specify the interpretation of time adverbials such as *yesterday, at six o'clock, in April*. These expressions provide more specific information on the time at which the proposition is claimed to be true. We can treat temporal nouns as predicates over times and interpret (7a) as (7b):

(7)  a.  Susan left at six o'clock.

     b.  $[\![ \mathbf{P}$ Susan leave at six o'clock$]\!]^{M,t_0,g} = 1$ iff there exists a $t$ such that $t \prec t_0$ and Six-o'clock$(t)$ and $[\![$ Susan leave $]\!]^{M,t,g} = 1$

Temporal connectives such as *before* and *after* express relations between the times at which two propositions are evaluated. Landman (1991) proposes the following definition for two simple past sentences related by *after*:

- $[\![ \mathbf{P}\phi$ After $\mathbf{P}\psi]\!]^{M,t,g} = 1$ iff there is a $t'$ such that $t' \prec t$ and $[\![\phi]\!]^{M,t',g} = 1$.
  Furthermore there is a $t''$ such that $t' \prec t'' \prec t$ and $[\![\psi]\!]^{M,t'',g} = 1$.

We can use this definition, to assign (8a) the interpretation in (8b):

(8)  a.  Susan came home after Bill left for the movies.

     b.  $[\![$ Susan came home after Bill left $]\!]^{M,t,g} = 1$ iff there is a $t'$ such that $t' \prec t$ and $[\![$ Susan comes home $]\!]^{M,t',g} = 1$. Furthermore there is a $t''$ such that $t' \prec t'' \prec t$ and $[\![$ Bill leaves for the movies $]\!]^{M,t'',g} = 1$

This model of interpretation can be extended in a straightforward way to other tenses, time adverbials, and connectives, so the extension of our semantics with a set of times $T$ increases the empirical coverage of our theory. This does not mean that all natural language sentences can be easily captured in Priorian tense logic. A well-known problem is raised by the fact that in Priorian tense logic there is no operator for the present. A proposition $\phi$ is read as a present tense sentence 'It is the case that $\phi$. In some contexts, this is problematic, as illustrated by sentences like (9) and (10), first discussed by Kamp (1971):

(9) Someday you will be grateful for what I am doing now

(10)  a.  A child was born which would rule the world
      b.  A child was born which will rule the world

The *now* in (9) refers to the moment of utterance. Given that there is no operator for the present tense, the only operator in the sentence is the future tense operator **F**. But if we translate the sentence as **F**(you are grateful for what I am doing now), we do not obtain the intended interpretation. Similar problems arise in (10). In (10a), we can give the past tense operator **P** scope over the sentence as a whole, and propose the translation **P**(a child is born **F**(who rules the world)). However, this translation cannot deal with the anchoring to the speech time in (10b). The solution proposed by Kamp (1971) is to enrich tense logic with a new operator **N** for 'now'. The interpretation of **N** is that $N\phi$ is true at time $t$ if and only if $\phi$ is true at the speech time $t_0$. Under this interpretation sentences like (9) and (10b) are always anchored to the utterance time. For instance, (10b) gets the right interpretation when it is translated as **P**(a child is born **N** **F**(who rules the world)). The introduction of new tense operators opens up a whole new perspective on tense logic, and its applications to natural language. The resulting systems are considerably more complex, and cannot be discussed here (compare Kuhn 1989 for an overview). The complexity of the logic and the coverage of empirical data is one reason why many linguistic theories that are concerned with the analysis of tense and temporal reference have developed alternative approaches.

Certain fundamental questions concerning the objects temporal expressions refer to are raised by Bennett and Partee (1972). Bennett and Partee argue that an adequate semantics of temporal expressions in natural language cannot just be based on instants, but that we need *intervals* as well. One of the problems which arises concerns the interpretation of time adverbials which refer to longer periods of time. Even in an example like (11), we cannot assume that the time adverbial covers only the instant at which we locate the leaving:

(11) John left yesterday morning.

We interpret the sentence as describing John's leaving at some point within the period of time referred to by *yesterday morning*. This means that we need to describe the denotation of the time adverbial in terms of intervals rather than instants. Certain classes of predicates also involve evaluation with respect to intervals rather than instants. It may be possible to view the event of leaving in (11) as instantaneous, but this cannot be argued for cases like (12):

(12)  a.  The apples ripened.
      b.  Susan and Bill waltzed at the party.
      c.  Mary sang.

It takes time for apples to ripen, and it takes time to waltz, because we have to make at least three steps in order to perform this dance. If we evaluate Mary's action at the moment she just opens her mouth, we cannot be sure that she is singing, for she might just as well have opened her mouth to start talking, yawning, laughing, etc. The upshot is that we cannot evaluate verbs expressing action, change, or movement at 'frozen' moments in time, because they take time, and are therefore not defined at instants. The propositions in (12) are true for intervals, which cover longer periods of time, but they cannot be evaluated at durationless instants. Given that we do not want to lose the insights from the instant-based approach, we define intervals in terms of instants. More precisely, we define intervals as *convex sets* of instants. The notion of convex set means that if two instants are in the interval, every instant between those two instants is also in the interval. Formally:

- A set of instants $I$ is a convex set (an interval) iff:
  $\forall t \, \forall t' \in I$ and $\forall t'' \in T$ it is true that, if $t \preceq t'' \preceq t'$ then $t'' \in I$.

We can expect interval structures to be richer in properties than instant structures, because we can define relations of temporal overlap, inclusion, etc. between intervals, which were not available for instants (van Benthem 1991). For instance:

- Properties of interval structures
    (i)    complete precedence:   $i \prec i'$ iff $\forall t \in i \, \forall t' \in i' \, (t \prec t')$
    (ii)   temporal overlap:   $i \circ i'$ iff $i \cap i' \neq \emptyset$
    (iii)  temporal inclusion:   $i \subseteq i'$ iff $\forall t \, (t \in i \rightarrow t \in i')$

One of the important advantages of the introduction of intervals is that we can model change as something happening over time. Change implies a transition between something being the case at some point in time, while it wasn't the case at some earlier point in time. For instance, (12a) involves the process which changes the apples from unripe into ripe fruits. We can describe this process as happening over an interval $I$ which extends from the initial point $t_1$ at which the apples are not ripe to the final point $t_2$ at which the apples are ripe, as illustrated in figure 9.3.

The move from instants to intervals is often compared to the relation between the 'static' notion of looking at pictures in an album and the 'dynamic' notion of watching a movie. On the other hand, it has been

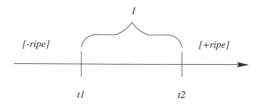

Figure 9.3: Ripening of an apple

argued that intervals still give us a rather 'static' view of change, because change is reduced to different propositions holding at different moments of time. As it stands, figure 9.3 does not give us much insight into what happens during the interval $I$. The intuition that the world is a dynamic system of changing processes then suggests the introduction of changes or *events* as the basic constituents of time as proposed by Davidson (1967), Kamp (1979) and others. For instance, we can locate a moment where the door was open before the moment where the door is closed, because we observed or are able to postulate an event of change leading from the state where the door was open to the state where the door was closed. This approach reflects the intuition that our awareness of time passing by is closely related to things happening: time flies when a lot of things are happening at once, whereas the hours crawl by when nothing is going on. Temporal systems which use events as the primitives of temporal structure are called *event semantics*. In event semantics, the definition of overlap, inclusion and precedence relations between events in an event structure is used as the basis from which interval structure and instant structure are derived. Recent theories of event semantics include Krifka (1989), Parsons (1990), Kamp and Rohrer (1983) and Kamp and Reyle (1993).

In this section, we restricted ourselves to a treatment of tense in terms of tense operators **P**, **F**, etc. The advantage of this system for the exposition of this chapter is that Priorian tense operators are very similar to the modal operators we will introduce in section 9.5 below. However, for linguistic applications, tense operators are not always the most appropriate choice. An alternative approach has been developed by Reichenbach (1947). It involves a representation of natural tenses in terms of three points: speech time (S), event time (E) and reference time (R). It would lead too far to discuss the Reichenbachian system of tense in any detail here. Some recent examples of linguistic analyses of tense that use the Reichenbachian approach are Partee (1984), Hinrichs (1986), Hornstein (1990) and Kamp and Reyle (1993).

## 9.2  Intension and extension

Once we add a set of times to our model, we can make the truth of sentences like (13) dependent on the moment in time with respect to which it is evaluated:

(13)  a.  Bill Clinton is the president of the U.S.
      b.  George Bush is the president of the U.S.

At any point in time, there is only one individual who is referred to as the president of the U.S. But given that no one remains in office for more than a few years, different individuals will satisfy the definite description over time. (13a) comes out true if the sentence is evaluated in 1997, whereas (13b) was true in 1990.

The sentences in (13) also illustrate a more general difference between proper names and definite descriptions. Both can be used to pick out a certain individual, but unlike proper names, definite descriptions come with a descriptive content which characterizes the individual as having a certain property. As Frege (1892) pointed out, this suggests that the meaning of a definite description is more than its reference (the individual it refers to). This intuition is confirmed by the comparison of the following sentences:

(14)  a.  The morning star is the morning star.
      b.  The morning star is the evening star.
      c.  The morning star is Venus.
      d.  The evening star is Venus.
      e.  Venus is Venus.

(14a) and (e) are uninformative statements: they tell us something which can never be false. They are appropriately characterized as tautologies. (14b), (c) and (d) are informative statements. (14b) tells us that the last star we see in the morning is in fact the same one as the first star we see in the evening. This star happens to be Venus (14c,d). Given that it so happens that the morning star and the evening star refer to the same individual, we cannot distinguish between the propositions expressed by (14a) and (14b). In the referential theory of definite descriptions, both cases make a statement which boils down to the claim that Venus is Venus (14e). Intuitively, however, there is more to the meaning of the definite description than its reference. It is possible that someone is not familiar with the truth of the statement made in (14b). But anyone who knows the language will know that (14a) is true, even a person who does not know which planet is referred to with the description, or even how to pick out the morning star in the sky. These observations suggest that a purely referential theory of definite descriptions does not capture the full informational value of the statements in (14). This conclusion is further supported by the behavior of referential descriptions in embedded contexts. The referential theory of definite descriptions predicts that if we have two coreferential descriptions, we can always replace one description with another, because they refer to the same individual. This prediction yields the right results in contexts like (15):

(15)   a.   I saw the president of the United States this morning.
       b.   I saw Hillary Rodham Clinton's husband this morning.

Given that the (current) president of the United States is married to Hillary, the two descriptions refer to the same individual, namely Bill Clinton. And if I have seen the referent of the description in (15a), this entails the truth of (15b). The truth of the proposition is thus purely dependent on the referent of the definite description, not on the way the individual is described. However, not all contexts allow substitution of coreferential definite descriptions. Observe that (16a) is odd in ways in which (16b) and (16c) are not, and the information contributed by (17a) is trivial in ways in which (17b) and (17c) are not:

(16)   a.   Susan didn't know that the morning star is in fact the morning star.
       b.   Susan didn't know that the morning star is in fact the evening star.
       c.   Susan didn't know that the morning star is in fact Venus.

(17)   a.   I told Susan that the morning star is identical to the morning star.
       b.   I told Susan that the morning star is identical to the evening star.
       c.   I told Susan that the morning star is identical to Venus.

It can be useful to inform people of the identity of the morning star and the evening star (17b), or to tell them what the actual referent of the description is (17c). But it does not make sense to inform someone of the identity of the morning star and the morning star (17a), because this statement is a tautology. If we cannot describe the difference in informational value between the statements in (14), (15), (16) and (17) in an extensional theory, we should build an intensional theory which has more to say about the difference between proper names and definite descriptions, and about the difference between the informational content of an expression and its reference.

The following example further supports the view that the meaning of an expression is more than just reference to its denotation. Suppose the two sentences (18a) and (b) are both true in our model:

(18)  a.  Chomsky is a linguist.
      b.  Paris is the capital of France.

If both sentences are true, they have the same reference, namely the truth value 1. If reference is all there is to meaning, we expect the two sentences to be equivalent. But that does not fit in with our intuitions. What we really want to say is that sentences may denote a certain truth value, but in addition they describe a certain situation or state of affairs. Just as in the case of definite descriptions discussed above, reference per se is not enough, and we need access to the informational content of the proposition if we want to say something more interesting about its meaning.

Frege (1892) modelled the distinction between informational content of an expression and the object it picks out as the contrast between *Sinn* and *Bedeutung*. These German terms are often translated as *sense* and *reference*. The reference of a proposition is its truth value, its sense is the thought it expresses, the state of affairs it describes, etc. The reference of a one-place predicate is a set of individuals, its sense is a property. The reference of a definite description is the individual which satisfies the description, its sense is the descriptive content, the uniquely identifying concept.

In later literature, the distinction between sense and reference is referred to as the distinction between *intension* and *extension*. These notions have informally come up when we discussed the interpretation of properties and relations in model-theoretic semantics. In chapter 4, we proposed to model properties extensionally as the sets of individuals that have those properties. It was pointed out that we could also try to give an intensional definition of properties, which would give the criteria an individual has to fit in order to satisfy the property. The intensional definition attempts to capture the sense of the predicate. We can now say that the sense of a noun or a verb phrase is the concept associated with the predicate. Its extension or reference is the set of individuals that have that property. Once we understand Frege's basic insights, the intuitive distinction between intension and extension is straightforward enough. The question that arises at this point is how we can incorporate these insights into the model of interpretation we have developed so far. Just as we have done for the temporal cases, we will handle intensional constructions by enriching the interpretation function, making it dependent on more indices than just time.

A formal way to account for the difference between the extension and the intension of natural language expressions is to distinguish between the reference of the expression at some index, and the function from indices to referents at that index. This gives us the set of all the different possible referents a particular expression can denote at any index. For an example like (13), it would be enough to identify indices with times: the concept of being the one and only president of the U.S. is realized by different individuals over time. For the other examples discussed in this section, variation over time is not very relevant. This means that we need to introduce some other index, which is not dependent on time. It has become customary to use the notion of *possible world* to describe this index. In most of the examples discussed above, the referent of the definite description could have been some other object if the facts of the world had been different. We all have the intuition that things could have been different in countless ways. We call any possible way the world can be, could be or might be, a possible world. Possible worlds are then viewed as states of affairs. We single out one world as the 'actual' or 'real' world. Other possible worlds describe alternative states of affairs, which are more or less different from what is the case in the actual world. Note that possible worlds are not some kind of exotic entities. They are purely abstract objects, which we postulate when we need them: possible worlds are *stipulated*, not *discovered* by powerful telescopes or other physical instruments. The semantic theory that uses the notion of possible worlds is referred to as *possible world semantics*. Possible world semantics originates in the logics developed by Carnap (1947), Kripke (1963, 1972) and others. It was introduced in a more linguistically oriented semantic framework by Montague (1970a, 1970b, 1973).

We can now do the same thing as we did for times and introduce a separate index for evaluation of our expressions with respect to some particular world $w$. We add a set $W$ of worlds to our semantics and interpret any proposition $\phi$ with respect to a model M, an assignment $g$, a time $t$, and a world $w$: $[\![\phi]\!]^{M,g,t,w}$. We often give the real world a special index like $w_0$. Our interpretation function gives us an interpretation of natural language expressions for every pair $\langle w, t \rangle$ of a world $w$ and a time $t$. We will assume for simplicity that individual constants get the same interpretation in every world and that the universe of discourse is the same for the whole set $W$. Whether this is so or not is debatable. It is known as the problem of 'transworld identity'. There is also the problem of non-existing objects which have names, such as Pegasus and Santa Claus. We want them to exist only in certain possible worlds (such as the worlds of stories and myths), not in the real world. The reader is referred to Kripke (1972) and Lewis (1968, 1973, 1986) for further discussion and rather different solutions to the problems of existence, reference and identity across worlds.

The notion of possible world allows us to model the distinction between intension and extension as follows. The extension of an expression is its referent as we have defined it in the extensional theory developed so far. The intension of an expression is a function from possible worlds to its extension. For instance, the extension of a definite description is an individual: it is the individual the definite description picks out in the world with respect to which the expression is evaluated. The intension of a definite description is a concept: it is a function from possible worlds to individuals. It is possible that the solar system could have been slightly different so that the last star we see in the morning was actually not Venus but Saturn. So we postulate a possible world which differs from the actual one in that in that world *the morning star* refers to Saturn. Assume also that in that world *the evening star* still refers to Venus. We can then account for the difference between sentences like (14a) and (b). Obviously, the concept of *the morning star* is identical to the concept of *the morning star*, that is, in no possible world will these two have different extensions, different individuals they refer to. But the concept of *the morning star* is not identical to the concept of *the evening star*, because we can postulate a possible world in which the referent of the two expressions is not the same: one picks out Saturn, the other one Venus. An identity statement between two expressions that share the same concept corresponds to a tautology. The discovery that two concepts have the same reference in a particular world is a non-trivial accomplishment, which accounts for the informative value of the statement in (14b). Furthermore, we can preserve the generalization that definite descriptions that refer to the same individual can be substituted for one another in contexts like (15). Substitution is licensed because of the extensional nature of the embedding context. Since the object of our vision is an individual, not concepts, we are clearly dealing with extensions here, not intensions. Given that the two descriptions pick out the same individual, the extension of the one is identical to the extension of the other. We conclude that two different but coreferential descriptions can be freely substituted for one another in extensional contexts. The impossibility of substituting *the morning star* for the definite description *the evening star* in (16) and (17) is due to the intensional nature of the context. Substitution in intensional contexts requires not only identity of extension (reference), but also identity of intension (sense) of the expression involved. Accordingly, we will argue in section 9.4 that attitude verbs like *know, believe, tell* embed propositions rather than truth values.

Similar observations can be made about properties. The extension of a predicate is a set of individuals: the set of individuals in our universe of discourse which satisfy the predicate. The intension of a predicate is a property, that is, a function from possible worlds to sets of individuals. The intensional definition of predicates as denoting properties comes in useful in contexts where an extensional definition is not appropriate. In chapter 7 it was pointed out that not all adjectives and adverbs can be taken to operate on the extension of a common noun or a verb phrase. A fake golden ring is not a golden ring, and if Bill allegedly killed John, it may not be true that he actually killed him. A full theory of the semantics of modifiers treats adjectives and adverbs like *fake, former, allegedly*, ... as modifiers which operate on the intension, rather than the extension of the expression they modify (see Keenan and Faltz 1985 for such an analysis).

An intensional semantic theory also provides a more insightful view of propositions. The extension of a sentence is its truth value. The intension of a sentence is a proposition, which is defined as a function from possible worlds to truth values.

The generalization from the idea of truth at a particular index to truth at different indices solves the rather strange problem brought up in relation to (18). Even though the two sentences have the same truth value at a particular index (namely, the real world in 1997), they do not necessarily have the same truth value at all other indices we could take into consideration. In particular, it is easy to imagine a possible world in which Chomsky is not a linguist, but Paris remains the capital of France. We define equivalence as a relation between the intension of sentences (that is, propositions), rather than their extension (that is, truth values). As a result, the observation that (18a) and (b) have the same denotation in the real world does not imply that they are equivalent.

Now that we have enriched our semantics with the notion of possible world, we can discuss the meaning of a number of intensional constructions which were outside the scope of the extensional theory of meaning we have developed so far. In the next two sections, we will discuss the analysis of counterfactuals and modal adverbs and auxiliaries in possible world semantics.

## 9.3   Counterfactuals

Counterfactuals exploit our capacity to talk about things being different from what they are in the real world. Consider the following statements:

(19)   a.   If Chris wins the lottery tonight, he will be rich.
       b.   If Chris were rich, he would probably not be here today.
       c.   If Susan had been in Wednesday's class, she would have learnt some French.

(19a) is a regular conditional: if Chris does not win the lottery tonight, but instead inherits a fortune (because his rich uncle died), he will still end up being a rich man. So even if the antecedent is false, the consequent can still be true. But if Chris does win the lottery, then it must also be true that he becomes a rich man. As long as we do not have information about the truth or falsity of the antecedent, the truth value of the consequent is not determined. (19b) also has the form of a conditional statement, but its meaning is somewhat different from (19a). (19b) speculates about a situation in which Chris is somehow rich, and draws certain inferences from this situation. But at the same time the sentence conveys the information that Chris is not rich. (19c) both conveys that Susan did not go to class Wednesday and makes the claim that if the world had been different and she would have come to class, then she would have learnt some French. Statements such as (19b) and (c) are called *counterfactuals*. A counterfactual is a conditional the antecedent of which describes something which is not true in the actual world. The problem that counterfactuals raise is that, as far as the standard interpretation of material implication goes, we can conclude anything from the falsehood of the antecedent: the conditional as a whole is always true when the antecedent is false. But somehow, counterfactuals express something stronger. Although we evaluate the antecedent in a situation in which it is false, we somehow want to play the game as if we assumed it was true, and everything else remained the same. Intuitively, we evaluate the conditional in a world very much like the world we live in, except that certain facts are slightly different.

In order to analyze counterfactuals, it is not enough to introduce a set of times and assume that we evaluate propositions at different times. (19b) is a counterfactual which tells us something about other ways the present situation could have been, (19c) tells us about the past. The contrast between (19b) and (19c) shows that we cannot do without our set of times, but evaluation with respect to a different time is not enough to explain the specific phenomenon of counterfactual statements. The crucial property of counterfactuals is that we evaluate the antecedent in a context in which we know that the antecedent is false. We can formalize this by saying that the counterfactual is true in a world $w$ if and only if all the worlds where the antecedent is true and *that most closely resemble* $w$ are such that the consequent is also true. The definition of counterfactuals implies that the set of worlds is structured by a *similarity* relation. Some worlds are more similar to, say the real world than others. A world $w_2$ in which Chris is rich and the moon is made out of green cheese is not as similar to the real world $w_0$ as a world $w_1$ in which Chris is rich and nothing else is different from the situation in the real world $w_0$. Intuitively, counterfactuals invite us to stay as close as possible to the real world. This means that we are expected to interpret a sentence like (19b) with respect to $w_1$, rather than $w_2$. We can account for the similarity relation by adding an *ordering source* for our set of worlds $W$. In the case of counterfactuals, we want a realistic ordering source, which orders the possible worlds according to certain standards of similarity to the real world. The generalization to an ordering source leaves open the possibility that other contexts order the set of worlds $W$ according to some other relation. The introduction of a similarity relation is not only useful for counterfactuals, but also for probability statements like (20):

(20)   a.   Susan will probably be home now.
       b.   There is a slight chance of rain tomorrow.

Adverbs like *probably* and locutions like *a slight chance* require that we determine the relative weight of several alternatives. They claim that some propositions have higher chances of including the real world in their denotation than others. We can capture this by saying that worlds ranked 'higher' in the set of alternatives will have a higher degree of probability than worlds 'lower' in the ranking. The reader is referred to Lewis (1973, 1986), Kratzer (1989) and Franck (1996) for various approaches to counterfactuals and ordering relations in modal constructions.

## 9.4   World-creating predicates

In chapter 1, we pointed out that there are predicates which describe situations in some mental world which is not necessarily identical to the real world:

(21)   a.   Sally dreamt that Robert Redford kissed her on the lips.
       b.   Imagine that we were all alone on a desert island, just the two of us, and the sun would always shine, and we would always be happy.
       c.   I wish that I did not have to take the exam.

We called those predicates *world-creating* predicates. One important difference between predicates like *dream, imagine, think, wish* and the counterfactual statements in (19) is that the predicates in (21) carry no implication with them as to the truth of the embedded proposition in the real world. In counterfactuals we know that the antecedent is actually false in the real world. With world-creating predicates, the question whether the embedded sentences is true or false is not always resolved. We may think that the situations dreamt of and imagined in (21) are unlikely to become true in the real world, but the sentence as a whole is not committed to either truth or falsity. The status of the embedded proposition depends on the semantics of the embedding predicate, as illustrated by the sentences in (22):

(22)  a.  Susan knows that Clinton is the new president.
      b.  Polly believes that Clinton won the elections.
      c.  Jim believes that fairies ruined his garden last night.

We assume that one can only know true things, so if (22a) is true, then it follows that Clinton is the new president. In belief contexts the embedded proposition may come out either true or false, depending on what the facts are. The embedded proposition in (22b) happens to be true in the real world. However, most people believe that fairies do not exist. Thus the embedded sentence of (22c) may be true in Jim's belief world, but it is not true in the real world. The existence of world-creating predicates provides another argument in favor of the distinction between extensions and intensions of sentences. Even if we do not know what the truth value is of the embedded sentence, we can determine the truth value of the sentence as a whole. Predicates like *dream* and *believe* thus make it clear that what we embed under a world-creating predicate is a proposition, not a truth value.

This interpretation of world-creating predicates gives us a handle on the contrast between *know* and *believe*, for instance. Both can be described as relations between individuals and propositions. But in the case of *know* the actual world is in the set of worlds to which the individual is related, whereas this need not be the case with *belief* (even though the believer thinks so). For instance, if Susan knows that Clinton is the new president, then we may infer from this that in the real world Clinton is the new president, although there may be other possible worlds in which he was not. If Polly believes Dole won the elections we may **not** infer from this that Dole won the elections in the real world of 1996, although there may be other possible worlds in which he actually did.

## 9.5   Modal auxiliaries and adverbs

Another important set of data which calls for a more complex analysis than what we have been doing so far concerns modal auxiliaries and modal adverbs. Some examples of modal adverbs are given in (23):

(23)  a.  Spinsters are necessarily unmarried.
      b.  Necessarily, $2 + 2 = 4$.
      c.  It will possibly not rain tomorrow.
      d.  Possibly, John will tell me tomorrow that he is not going to the party.

(23a) reflects the fact that, whichever way the world may look in other respects, you will find that the set of spinsters is a subset of the set of unmarried people. The necessary nature of the statement is a result of the definition of the word *spinster*. Given that the unmarried status of the individual is part of the concept of being a spinster, not just part of the extension, it constrains the admissible models of interpretation for the language (see chapter 2 for more discussion on meaning postulates). In the same way we assume that mathematical truths are necessary: they are true by virtue of the way the algebra is set up. If we translate this again as constraints on admissible models of interpretation for the language, there is no way in which (true) mathematical statements can be made false. As a result, they are necessarily true statements.

The sentences in (23c) and (23d) do not have this inherently necessary character. They explicitly introduce a certain way the world might be, leaving open the possibility that it looks different. According to (23c), one way of viewing the real world at a time later than the speech time is that it is not raining. This leaves open the possibility that a rainstorm suddenly comes in overnight and that it is raining tomorrow.

The examples in (23) illustrate that the evaluation of adverbs like *necessarily* and *possibly* requires us to take into account other possible states of affairs than just the real world. We can spell out the interpretation of adverbs of possibility and necessity in possible world semantics if we introduce new operators over propositions. Just as we exploited the extension of the model with a set of times to define operators **P** and **F** quantifying over times, we can use the extension of the model with a set of worlds to define new operators quantifying over possible worlds. We define two new propositional operators, the modal operators $\Box$ for necessity and $\Diamond$ for possibility. The syntax is straightforward; we can prefix any proposition with a modal operator and get a new proposition:

- Syntax

    (i) If $\phi$ is a wff then $\Box\phi$ is a wff

    (ii) If $\phi$ is a wff then $\Diamond\phi$ is a wff

$\Box\phi$ is to be read as ' it is necessarily the case that $\phi$'; $\Diamond\phi$ is to be read as 'it is possibly the case that $\phi$'. The introduction of modal operators allows us to translate sentences like (23a) and (c) as in (24a) and (b):[3]

---

[3] In order to keep the formulas more readable, we do not spell out the internal structure of the proposition.

(24)  a.  Spinsters are necessarily unmarried.
          □(spinsters are unmarried)

      b.  It will possibly not rain tomorrow.

      c.  $\Diamond(\mathbf{F}(\neg(\text{it rains})))$

Modal operators are propositional operators, so they combine with tense operators and logical connectives as expected in (24b). The enriched interpretation function allows us to interpret modalized statements in the following way:

- Semantics
  (i)   $[\![\Box\phi]\!]^{M,w,i,g} = 1$ iff for all worlds $w' \in W$ such that $w'$ is accessible from $w$, $[\![\phi]\!]^{M,w',i,g} = 1$
  (ii)  $[\![\Diamond\phi]\!]^{M,w,i,g} = 1$ iff for at least one world $w' \in W$ such that $w'$ is accessible from $w$, $[\![\phi]\!]^{M,w',i,g} = 1$

These definitions make it clear that □ is interpreted like the universal quantifier and ◇ is like the existential quantifier. The main difference to the well-known quantifiers ∀ and ∃ from first-order predicate logic is that these quantifiers bind individual variables $x$ and quantify over individuals, whereas □ and ◇ range over possible worlds. The way in which modal operators are defined in a possible world semantics makes it a straightforward extension of first-order logic. Note that the definitions refer to worlds *accessible* from the world with respect to which we are interpreting our proposition.

The notion of accessibility has to do with the way we structure our set of worlds $W$. When we added a set of times to our model, we argued that we had to impose a certain order on $T$ to capture the directionality of the flow of time. As far as $W$ is concerned, we argued that we need an ordering source in order to account for counterfactuals and probability statements. The accessibility relation imposes further structure on the set of worlds by imposing restrictions on the worlds that are taken into consideration in the evaluation of the modal statement. The simplest view is that all worlds are accessible to all other worlds, and this is indeed the accessibility relation that we adopt here. However, if you study modal logic, you will see that the definition of the accessibility relation on worlds is a quite intricate question, because the definition of different accessibility relations leads to different inference patterns on modal statements. In depth introductions to modal logic can be found in Hughes and Cresswell (1968) and van Benthem (1988).

The translations in (24) show that all examples involving *necessarily* are represented in terms of formulas introduced by a $\Box$ operator, and the $\Diamond$ operator is used as the translation of *possibly*. We can also use the modal operators $\Box$ and $\Diamond$ to give an interpretation of modal auxiliaries like those in (25):

(25)   a.   Spinsters must be unmarried.
           $\Box$(spinsters are unmarried)

       b.   Shoes must be worn.
           $\Box$(shoes are worn)

       c.   Susan must be home by now.
           $\Box$(Susan is home by now)

       d.   Paul can read French.
           $\Diamond$(Paul reads French)

       e.   You can go home now.
           $\Diamond$(you go home now)

       f.   Susan can be home now.
           $\Diamond$(Susan is home now)

The use of modal auxiliaries like *must, can, should, might, may, could,* etc. implies that we cannot evaluate the truth of the statement just with respect to the real world as it is. *Must* is like *necessarily* in that it involves universal modal force. The translation of *must* (25a) in terms of the $\Box$ operator gives us the interpretation that in all possible worlds spinsters are unmarried. *Can* is like *possibly* in that it involves existential modal force. If John can read French, this means that there is a possibility of him doing so. There is no implication that John is involved in reading French at this time, although that is not ruled out either. The translation of *can* in (25d) in terms of the $\Diamond$ operator leads to an interpretation in which John reads French in some possible world.

What the modal auxiliaries illustrate even more clearly than the adverbs is that modalities come in different classes. The examples in (24), (25a) and (25d) exemplify the 'root' or 'circumstantial' use of the modal adverb. By this we mean that they require a background constituted by relevant facts or actual circumstances. The other examples in (25) show that natural language expresses a wider range of modalities. (25b) is not a necessity based on facts, but a *deontic* necessity. A deontic necessity expresses an obligation to act in a certain way. Someone who is invested with moral authority can request that there be no other way of envisaging the real world than the one in which you wear shoes in this place. If you don't do that, you will not be incoherent (as in 25a), but you will be kicked out of the place. This illustrates that quantification in deontic contexts is not about realistic states of affairs, but ideal or admissible states of affairs. (25e) is also a deontic modality, but it corresponds to a possibility operator, rather than a necessity operator, and as a result it expresses permission, rather than obligation.

(25c) is an instance of *epistemic* modality. Epistemic modalities rely on knowledge of the facts, over and above the facts themselves. (25c) means something like: 'as far as my knowledge goes (she has had plenty of time, no bad weather, etc.), there is no way in which I can imagine the world otherwise than that Susan is home right now (so why does she not answer the phone when I am trying to call her?). (25f) is also an epistemic modality, and it opens up the possibility that, in view of background knowledge etc, the person is at home right now. Because of the change from *must* to *can*, this sentence does not support the implication that Susan is indeed home right now, but considers this a mere possibility.

The advantage of the representations in (25) is that we get a unified translation of all uses of *must* and *can*. The drawback of this approach is that the translations in (25) do not reflect the various meaning effects that the different modalities give rise to. The modal operators □ and ◇ are just concerned with the quantificational force of the statement, and do not specify the nature of the modality expressed. We can preserve the translations in (25) but add the information about the modality expressed being a root, deontic or epistemic modality by introducing different *conversational backgrounds*, as proposed by Kratzer (1979, 1981).

A conversational background is conceived of as a set of propositions. This set of propositions constitutes the background with respect to which the sentence is evaluated. The background for a root interpretation is a set of relevant facts or actual cirumstances that are relevant for the evaluation of the sentence. In evaluating mathematical statements for instance, we want to quantify over all possible worlds. But we might choose our background differently. A deontic modality sets up a set of 'ideal' or 'morally admissable' propositions as the conversational background. These are usually dependent on some notion of authority: someone is invested with the power of deciding what the rules are. Keeping such a background in mind, the statement 'Shoes must be worn' can be translated in terms of universal quantification over all possible worlds which fit in with admissible standards of behavior. Similarly, 'You can go home now' gives the addressee permission to do something. That is, the sentence tells the addressee that with respect to the set of ideal or desirable worlds it is a possibility to go home now. In other words, it is not forbidden (impossible, excluded) for that person to go home now. Epistemic modals result from the interpretation of a sentence against the conversational background of a particular knowledge base. For instance, (25c) means that in all worlds compatible with the set of propositions which constitutes my knowledge of this afternoon's traffic, Susan's work schedule, etc, it is the case that Susan is home. (25f) makes the much weaker statement that in at least one of these worlds Susan is home.

Formally, conversational backgrounds are defined as the intersection of the set of propositions that are taken to be true in a certain context. Remember that propositions are interpreted as functions from possible worlds to truth values. A function that maps entities onto truth values is called a *characteristic function*. The mapping onto truth values essentially determines for each of the entities the function applies to whether the output is true or false. We can unite all the entities which yield 'true' in a set, and all the entities which yield 'false' in another set. This accounts for the observation that all characteristic functions can be modelled as sets, namely the set of entities for which the function yields the value 'true'. Under the view that propositions are functions from possible worlds to truth values, the application of this general procedure to the particular case of propositions implies that we can model propositions as sets of worlds. Set-theoretically, propositions correspond to the set of those worlds in which the sentence comes out true. If we take the intersection of a set of propositions to give us the conversational background, we need to take the intersection of the set of worlds denoted by each proposition. Thus our conversational background consists of a set of worlds in which each of the propositions in the conversational background comes out true. One way to fix the conversational background in a particular context is to extend the use of the assignment function $g$. Normally, $g$ maps free variables onto some value in the model. We can extend its use and assume that it also picks out a certain set of worlds that determines the conversational background for the modal.

Not all modalized statements in natural language are expressed by explicit modal operators such as adverbs or auxiliaries. Statements about capacities, dispositions and inherent qualities are also expressed by adjectives such as *solvable, fragile, washable, conceivable* (26a), constructions which are known as 'middles' (26b), or even conditionals which somehow have the stronger flavor of a modalized implication (26c):

(26)  a.  This glass is fragile.
      b.  This glass breaks easily.
      c.  If you drop that glass, it will break.

The connection between the antecedent and the consequent in (26c) is much tighter than in a plain material implication. The sentence conveys that there is a necessary relation between the dropping of the glass and its breaking. The necessary character of the relation is due to certain inherent physical properties of the object. Along similar lines, (26a) and (26b) are analyzed as dispositional statements which describe the tendency or capacity of an object to act or to behave in a certain way in certain circumstances.

## 9.6 More about intensionality

Although possible world semantics has a number of interesting properties which shed light on the meaning of certain intensional expressions in natural language, there are also some problems related to this particular framework. Recall that the problem of definite descriptions like *the morning star* and *the evening star* was that we could not distinguish between the two in a purely extensional framework, because in the real world the two descriptions refer to the same object, namely Venus. The problem was solved by introducing possible worlds, because we can assume that the two definite descriptions do not have the same extension in all possible worlds.

This works fine for the cases at hand. But a problem arises with expressions that have the same extension in all possible worlds. The present framework predicts that we can still not distinguish between them, because they do not only have the same extension, but the same intension as well. Consider (27) and (28):

(27)   a.   Susan knows that $2 + 2 = 4$.
       b.   Susan does not know that there are infinitely many prime numbers.

(28)   a.   The teacher told the child that $2 + 2 = 4$.
       b.   The teacher told the child that there are infinitely many prime numbers.

As we pointed out in section 9.5 above, any true mathematical statement is necessarily true, that is, true in every possible world. In every model, there is just one necessarily true proposition, which is the set of all possible worlds. So on the possible world semantics account of propositions all true mathematical statements not only have the same truth value, they express the same proposition. If we take world-creating predicates such as *to know* to be relations between individuals and propositions, this predicts that if an individual knows any true mathematical statement, she knows them all. In other words, if (27a) is true, then (27b) cannot but be false. Similarly, the statement in (28a) makes perfect sense to describe a classroom situation in which (28b) would be way over the head of the child. However, in the theory under consideration, both statements make the same point. This is highly counterintuitive. Even if Susan happens to be a person who knows that both statements are true, we can easily imagine other people who don't. We often fail to notice that two statements are logically equivalent, or we are quite ignorant of their equivalence. Therefore we do not want to accept a relation of entailment between the two sentences in (27) and (28).

Ironically, the problem that possible worlds semantics faces in examples like (27) and (28) is just a variant of the exact same problem it was set up to solve. Just as a purely extensional theory cannot discriminate between different expressions which refer to the same individual in the actual situation, possible world semantics cannot discriminate between logically equivalent propositions. Possible world semantics seems to imply a logical omniscience that humans notably lack.

There are different ways one can go from here. Some people have taken the difficulty of handling problems involving mental states in a theory like possible world semantics as a primary motivation to adopt a mentalistic perspective and introduce a level of 'mental representations'. Others are reluctant to draw such drastic conclusions and keep trying to pursue a realistic approach. This requires getting rid of logical omniscience and developing a more fine-grained representation of the information content of a sentence. The problem of the undistinguishability of necessarily true propositions in possible world semantics is then an important motivation to develop theories of partial knowledge of the world. This has led to a number of fruitful developments in semantic theory. Important proposals include situation theory developed by Barwise and Perry (1983), a situation semantic analysis of counterfactuals developed by Kratzer (1989), a theory of interpreted logical forms as the object of attitude reports as developed by Larson and Ludlow (1993), etc.

## 9.7 Exercises

(1)! An obvious way to interpret the Pluperfect sentence in (i) in the tense-logical system developed in section 1 would be to translate it as (ii):

  (i) Susan had left.
  (ii) **PP**(Leave(s))

  The problem with this translation is that the combination of our definition of **P** in combination with the density of $T$ leads to a situation in which $\mathbf{P}\phi$ entails $\mathbf{PP}\phi$. Show this and explain why it is a problem. There are two ways out of this dilemma. We could either drop the density of $T$, or we could adopt another definition of the Pluperfect. Explore the pros and cons of dropping density and give suggestions for an alternative interpretation of the Pluperfect that avoids the problem sketched here.

(2)! Compare the inference patterns in (i) and (ii):

    (i) If Bill left at 2 pm, he is in Pittsburgh by now.
        If Bill is in Pittsburgh by now, Lefty has tipped off the feds.
        Therefore, if Bill left at 2 pm, Lefty has tipped off the feds.

    (ii) If Bush had been born in Palestine, he would be a PLO agent.
        If Bush were a PLO agent, he would be sending American defense secrets to Saddam.
        Therefore, if Bush had been born in Palestine, he would be sending American defense secrets to Saddam.

Are these arguments valid? Explain why they are or aren't. (Hint: determine which property of the *if ... then* construction the inference is built on, and find out how it is related to the indicative/counterfactual conditional. Then, for the counterfactual, look at the worlds in which the relevant premises are true, and how they differ from the real world.)

(3)! Consider the following sentences:

    (i)! Every person can read.

    (ii) A passport must be carried on your person.

For each example, give two different translations of the sentence in a first-order predicate logical language enriched with modal operators. Give informal paraphrases of the truth conditions these translations are associated with, in a way that makes clear whether they are equivalent or not. The account of scope ambiguities in (i) and (ii) can be extended to explain the ambiguity of sentences like (iii) and (iv):

(iii) Mary believes that a professor was caught shoplifting.

(iv) Chris wants to marry a Spanish linguist.

At this point, we do not have the tools to spell out the ambiguity of (iii) and (iv) in formal terms, but the intuition is that verbs like *believe* and *want* creat intensional contexts in ways similar to modal auxiliaries like *can* and *must*. Explain informally how the interpretation of the indefinite NP inside or outside the intensional context created by *believe* or *want* leads to different readings of the sentences in (iii) and (iv).

(4) Consider the following definition of a basic propositional tense logic:

- Syntax

  (i) $p$ is a well-formed formula.

  (ii) $\neg p$, $p \wedge q$, $p \rightarrow q$, and $p \leftrightarrow q$ are well-formed formulas.

  (iii) **P**$p$, **H**$p$, **F**$p$ and **G**$p$ are well-formed formulas.

  (iv) Nothing else is a well-formed formula.

- Semantics

  (i) $[\![\mathbf{P} \ \phi]\!]^{M,t,g} = 1$ iff there exists a $t' \in T$ such that $t' \prec t$ and $[\![\phi]\!]^{M,t',g} = 1$

  (ii) $[\![\mathbf{H} \ \phi]\!]^{M,t,g} = 1$ iff for all $t' \in T$ such that $t' \prec t$, $[\![\phi]\!]^{M,t',g} = 1$

  (iii) $[\![\mathbf{F} \ \phi]\!]^{M,t,g} = 1$ iff there exists an $t' \in T$ such that $t \prec t'$ and $[\![\phi]\!]^{M,t',g} = 1$

  (iv) $[\![\mathbf{G} \ \phi]\!]^{M,t,g} = 1$ iff for all $t' \in T$ such that $t \prec t'$, $[\![\phi]\!]^{M,t',g} = 1$

Answer the following questions on the basis of this tense logic:

4.1 Translate the following sentences into propositional tense logic. Give the key for the propositional variables you use. Represent as much as possible of the temporal structure. The parts in brackets are there to clarify the temporal structure; they need not be part of the translation.

    a! Jane was in love with Fred, but she kept it a secret.

    b. (Jane whispered to Fred:) "I will love you forever".

    c. Jane always wanted to study linguistics, but she never did.

    d. (The teacher told Jim that) he would never get his PhD this way.

    e. Susan is going to New York next week to visit her brother who moved there (two years ago).

4.2 Give examples of English sentences corresponding to the following tense logical formulas a! **PF**$p$

  b. **FP**$p$

  c. $p \vee \neg$**G**$p$

  d. **F**$(p \to$ **F**$p)$

4.3 Give equivalent formulas for the following statements, using other tense operators:

  a! $\neg$ **F**$p$

  b. **H**$\neg p$

  c. **G**$p$

  d. **H**$p \wedge$ **G**$p$

4.4 Consider the following formulas:

  a. **P**$p \to$ **GP**$p$

  b. **F**$p \to$ **HF**$p$

  Describe their meaning and discuss the implication of these statements for a system of tense logic which reflects our intuitions about time and temporal structure. Would you like to claim about one or both of these that they are true for every $p$? Motivate your answer.

(5) There are several ways to introduce events into the representation of sentences. A popular way is to suppose that verbal predicates come with an extra argument position, which is filled by an event variable (Davidson 1967). Existential quantification over this event variable allows us to locate the event in time. As a result, a sentence like (i) translates as in (i'):

  (i) Kate arrived.

  (i') $\exists e\, [\text{Arrive}(k, e) \wedge e < t_0]$ where $t_0$ is the speech point

One of the advantages of an event-based semantics is that it provides an interesting account of adverbs by translating them as predicates over events. Along these lines, (ii) translates as (ii'):

  (ii) Kate arrived late.

  (ii') $\exists e\, [\text{Arrive}(k, e) \wedge \text{Late}(e) \wedge e < t_0]$

On the basis of this analysis, we can predict a range of interesting entailment relations that arise with adverbial modification. Consider the sentences in (iii)–(vii):

(iii) Kate buttered the toast with a knife at midnight.

(iv) Kate buttered the toast with a knife and Kate buttered the toast at midnight.

(v) Kate buttered the toast with a knife.

(vi) Kate buttered the toast at midnight.

(vii) Kate buttered the toast.

Describe all the entailment relations in the set of sentences (iii)–(vii). Give translations of these sentences in first-order predicate logic enriched with event variables along the lines of (ii'). Explain how your translation accounts for all the entailment relations you observed.

(5) An important difference between stative and non-stative predicates is that sentences describing states (i) can be evaluated with respect to instants, whereas sentences describing processes (ii) or events (iii) need to be evaluated with respect to intervals:

(i) Susan was in the garden.

(ii) Susan ran.

(iii) Susan ran a mile.

We can generalize over all states, processes and events if we assume that all sentences are evaluated with respect to an interval, but there are different ways in which truth at the interval is related to truth at subintervals or instants. A stative sentence is true at an interval $I$ if and only if it is true at all instants that are member of $I$. For (i) this means that if Susan was in the garden at some interval $I$ then Susan was in the garden at every instant of that interval. Explain along similar lines how truth at the interval carries over to truth at subintervals or instants for sentences describing processes or events. Illustrate your statements with the examples (ii) and (iii). Show how your characterization of processes and events explains the inference patterns in (iv) and (v):

(iv) Susan is running → Susan has run

(v) Susan is running a mile ↛ Susan has run a mile

(8) Consider a model $M = \langle U, V, W \rangle$. The universe of discourse $U$ consists of the set of individuals { Jane, Molly, Chris, Bill }. In every possible world, the values of the individual constants $j, m, c, b$ are

exactly these individuals. $P$ is a one-place predicate 'to go to the party', $A$ is a two-place (symmetric) predicate 'to accompany to the party'. It will be assumed that you can only accompany someone to the party if you go to the party. The set of worlds $W$ consists of $\{w_1, w_2, w_3, w_4\}$. The facts in the different worlds are the following:

$w_1$: $P(b) = 0$ ; $P(c) = 1$ ; $P(j) = 1$ ; $P(m) = 0$ ; $A(j,c) = 1$

$w_2$: $P(b) = 1$ ; $P(c) = 1$ ; $P(j) = 0$ ; $P(m) = 0$ ; $A(b,c) = 1$

$w_3$: $P(b) = 1$ ; $P(c) = 1$ ; $P(j) = 0$ ; $P(m) = 1$ ; $A(c,m) = 1$ ; $A(b,m) = 1$ ; $A(b,c) = 1$

$w_4$: $P(b) = 0$ ; $P(c) = 0$ ; $P(j) = 1$ ; $P(m) = 1$ ; $A(j,m) = 1$

Evaluate the following propositions in this model:

(i)! It is impossible for Bill to go to the party.

(ii) Possibly, Chris is going to the party.

(iii) Chris is not necessarily going to the party.

(iv) If Jane goes to the party, she must be accompanied by someone other than Chris.

(v) Whoever is going to the party must be accompanied by someone else.

(vi) It is not possible for anybody to accompany Molly to the party.

# Appendix

## A.i  Example of an exam

> This is an example of an exam based on the materials developed in
> chapters 1 through 7.

A linguistic theory ought to account for the semantics of adjectives and
comparatives illustrated in (ia-c):

(i)  a. Phil is tall.
     b. Phil is taller than Elisa.
     c. Phil is as tall as Elisa.

We can define the semantics of comparatives in terms of degrees which
correspond with points on a scale. In (i), we have the scale of tallness.
If the point $d_1$ on the scale indicates the degree of tallness that holds for
Phil, and $d_2$ indicates the one for Elisa, we can say that (ib) is true for the
diagram in figure A.1.
Somewhat more formally, we define a scale as a set S ordered by a relation
$\leq$ which is reflexive, transitive and anti-symmetric. We define a function $d$
which maps each individual onto their degree of S-ness on a given scale S.
For instance $d_1 = d_{tall}(p)$ tells us that $d_1$ is the degree to which Phil is tall.
The semantics of comparatives and superlatives can then be formulated in

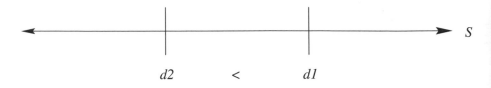

Figure A.1: Scale

terms of relations between degrees. For instance, the comparative *-er* than denotes the $>$ relation between degrees on the relevant scale. Accordingly, the sentence in (ib) is true iff $\exists d_1 \exists d_2 [d_1 = d_{tall}(p) \land d_2 = d_{tall}(e) \land d_1 > d_2]$.

1. Give similar diagrams for (ia), (ic) and (id):

   (i) d. Elisa is short.

   Spell out the corresponding truth conditions for the sentences in terms of first-order logic with quantification over degrees. Discuss the possible entailment relations among (ia), (ib), (ic) and (id).

2. Use the terminology introduced to explain why sentences like (ii) are infelicitous in normal use:

   (ii) a. ??Helen is more pregnant than Jane.
        b. ??Klaus is as German as Sabine.

   Indicate what kind of contextual reinterpretation can make these sentences acceptable. Show how this confirms the general analysis of comparatives outlined above.

3. Use the two-place relations T (for: as tall as) and S (for: stronger than) to translate the following sentences into first-order predicate logic:

   (iii) a. Phil is as tall as himself.
         b. No one is stronger than himself.

   Use the semantics developed for comparatives to explain why these sentences are necessarily true.

4. Superlatives are related to comparatives. Sentences involving superlatives often create ambiguities because there is more than one way to construct the comparison. Consider (iv):

(iv) Phil climbed the highest mountain.

(iv) can either mean that there is no one who climbed a mountain higher than the one Phil climbed (without implying that he climbed the highest mountain in the world) or that there is no mountain higher than the one Phil climbed (without implying that he was the only one doing so). Spell out the two interpretations of (iv) in terms of quantification over degrees on a scale, in such a way that your analysis makes the different types of comparison explicit.

5. We can extend the analysis of comparative adjectives to comparative determiners. Give the truth conditions of the following sentences in terms of relations between sets:

   (v) a. More students than teachers came to the party.
       b. More students steal bikes than teachers buy cars.

6. Explain why comparative determiners license negative polarity items as in:

   (vi) a. Phil reads more books than any other student.
        b. Elisa is taller than almost any boy.

Illustrate your argument with the relevant inference patterns.

# A.ii   Answers to exam questions

1.    a. Diagram for (ia):

Figure A.2: Scale for 1.a

Truth conditions: $\parallel$ Phil is tall $\parallel = 1$ iff $\exists d\,[d = d_{tall}(p) \wedge d > t]$, where $t$ is the point which separates not-tall people from tall people.

   c. Diagram for (ic):
      Truth conditions:
      $\parallel$ Phil is as tall as Elisa $\parallel = 1$ iff $\exists d_1\,\exists d_2\,[d_1 = d_{tall}(p) \wedge d_2 =$

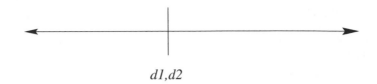

*d1,d2*

Figure A.3: Scale for 1.c

$d_{tall}(e) \wedge d_1 = d_2]$.

If you prefer to interpret *as tall as* as 'at least as tall as', you can replace the '=' sign by a '$\geq$' sign. This will change the entailment relations.

d. Diagram for (id):

$d \quad < \quad s$

Figure A.4: Scale for 1.d

Truth conditions:
$\parallel$ Elisa is short $\parallel = 1$ iff $\exists d\,[d = d_{tall}(e) \wedge d < s]$.

Note that (ia) requires that the degree to which Phil is tall is higher than the point $t$ which separates not-tall people from tall people. If Elisa is short, the degree to which she is tall must be lower on the scale than the point $s$ which separates short people from not-short people. Pairs of adjectives like *short/tall* typically come with a neutral area in the middle, which counts as neither short nor tall. Comparatives like *as tall as* or *taller than* do not make reference to either $t$ or $s$. Therefore, (ib) and (c) do not allow us to infer either that Phil is tall or that Elisa is short. However, the conjunction of (ia) and (ic) allows us to infer that Elisa is tall; similarly the conjunction of (ic) and (id) allows us to infer that Phil is tall.

2. Normally, we regard adjectives like *pregnant* or *German* as absolute rather than gradable adjectives. That is, an individual has or does not have the property in question, but does not have it to some degree. In appropriate contexts, we can reinterpret absolute adjectives as involving some sort of gradation. For instance Helen may have a

bigger belly than Jane and therefore look 'more pregnant'. Similarly, we can argue that Klaus has more properties of a typical German than Sabine, and therefore he appears 'more German' than she does. Note that in both cases, the contextual reinterpretation introduces a notion of degree to which the individual has the property in question, and that these degrees must be ordered on a scale. This fits in with the general analysis of comparatives in terms of relations between degrees on a scale.

3. (iiia) Phil is as tall as himself: $T(p, p)$ This is a tautology because the semantics of 'as Adj as' is defined in terms of identity of degrees, which makes the relation $T$ reflexive. This means that $\forall x\, T(x, x)$. The sentence is derived from this by universal instantiation.

 (iiib) No one is stronger than himself: $\neg \exists x\, S(x, x)$ or $\forall x \neg S(x, x)$
    This is a tautology, because the semantics of comparative 'more Adj than' is defined in terms of a relation of $>$ between degrees on a scale, which makes the relation $S$ irreflexive. This means that $\forall x \neg S(x, x)$, which is exactly what the translation for the sentence is.

4.   a. reading 1: no one climbed a mountain which is higher than the mountain Phil climbed.
    $\exists x\, \exists d_1\, (\text{Mountain}(x) \wedge d_1 = d_{high}(x) \wedge \text{Climb}(p, x) \wedge$
    $\forall y\, \forall z\, \forall d_2\, ((\text{Mountain}(z) \wedge z \neq x \wedge d_2 = d_{high}(z) \wedge$
    $\text{Climb}(y, z)) \rightarrow d_2 < d_1))$

   b. reading 2: there is no higher mountain than the one Phil climbed.
    $\exists x\, \exists d_1\, (\text{Mountain}(x) \wedge d_1 = d_{high}(x) \wedge \text{Climb}(p, x) \wedge$
    $\forall z\, \forall d_2\, ((\text{Mountain}(z) \wedge \wedge z \neq x\ d_2 = d_{high}(z)) \rightarrow$
    $d_2 < d_1))$
    Note: a translation into first-order predicate logic is not strictly required, so a more informal version of this is also acceptable, as long as the interpretation comes out right.

5.   a. More students than teachers came to the party is true iff:
    | Student ∩ Come | > | Teacher ∩ Come |

   b. More students steal bikes than teachers buy cars is true iff:
    | Student ∩ {$x$ | $\exists y\ \text{Bike}(y) \wedge \text{Steal}(x, y)$} | >
    | Teacher ∩ {$x$ | $\exists y\ \text{Car}(y) \wedge \text{Buy}(x, y)$} |

Note that the comparison is now between cardinalities of the sets involved, as it befits a determiner.

6. Negative polarity items are licensed by monotone decreasing quantifiers which allow inferences to a smaller set. The (right) downward entailing properties of comparatives are illustrated by the following kind of inferences:

    a. More students danced than teachers sang $\longrightarrow$
       More students danced than teachers sang a ballad

    b. More students danced a tango than teachers $\longrightarrow$
       More students danced a tango than nutty teachers

    c. Elisa is taller than either Phil or Peter $\longrightarrow$
       Elisa is taller than Phil and Elisa is taller than Peter

Comparatives are not downward entailing in their left argument.

# References

ABUSCH, D. 1994. The scope of indefinites. Natural language semantics 2.83–136.

AKMAJIAN, A., R. DEMERS, A. FARMER, and R. HARNISH. 199. Linguistics. an introduction to language and communication. Cambridge, MA: MIT Press. third edition.

AOUN, J., and Y. LI. 1993. Syntax of scope. Cambridge, MA: MIT Press.

ASHER, N. 1993. Reference to abstract objects in discourse. Dordrecht: Kluwer.

——, and A. LASCARIDES. 1995. Lexical disambiguation in a discourse context. Journal of Semantics 12.69–108.

AUSTIN, J. 1962. How to do things with words. Oxford: Oxford University Press.

BACH, E. 1980. Informal lectures on formal semantics. Albany, NY.: Suny Press.

—— 1986. The algebra of events. Linguistics and Philosophy 9.5–16.

—— 1989. Informal lectures on formal semantics. Albany, NY: Suny Press.

——, E. JELINEK, A. KRATZER, and B. PARTEE. 1995. Quantification in natural languages. Dordrecht: Kluwer.

BARWISE, J. 1987. Noun phrases, generalized quantifiers and anaphora. In Generalized quantifiers, ed. by P. Gärdenfors, 1–30. Dordrecht: Reidel.

——, and R. COOPER. 1981. Generalized quantifiers and natural language. Linguistics and Philosophy 4.159–219.

——, and J. ETCHEMENDY. 1987. The liar. Oxford: Oxford University Press.

——, and J. PERRY. 1983. Situations and attitudes. Cambridge, MA: MIT Press.

BEAVER, D. 1997. Presuppositions. In Handbook of logic and language, ed. by J. van Benthem and A. ter Meulen, 939–1008. Amsterdam: Elsevier.

BEGHELLI, F., and T. STOWELL. 1997. Distributivity and negation: the syntax of *each* and *every*. In Ways of scope taking, ed. by A. Szabolcsi, 71–197. Dordrecht: Kluwer Academic Press.

BENNETT, M., and B. PARTEE. 1972. Tenses and aspect as functions on verb-phrases. ms. distributed by the Indiana University Linguistics Club, ms.

VAN BENTHEM, J. 1986. Essays in logical semantics. Dordrecht: Reidel.

—— 1988. Manual of intensional logic. Stanford: CSLI publications.

—— 1991. The logic of time. Dordrecht: Kluwer. second edition.

——, and A. TER MEULEN (EDS.). 1984. Generalized quantifiers in natural language. Dordrecht: Foris.

BLOOMFIELD, L. 1933. Language. New York: Holt, Rinehart and Winston.

—— 1936. Language or ideas? Language 12.89–95.

BRÉAL, M. 1900. Semantics. New York: Henry Holt. translation of the French (1899) *Essai de Sémantique*.

BROWNE, A. 1986. Univocal *or* again. Linguistic Inquiry 17.751–754.

BÜRING, D. 1997. The great scope inversion conspiracy. Linguistics and Philosophy 20.175–194.

CANN, R. 1993. Formal semantics. Cambridge: Cambridge University Press.

CARNAP, R. 1947. Meaning and necessity. Chicago: University of Chicago Press.

CHIERCHIA, G. 1992. Anaphora and dynamic binding. Linguistics and Philosophy 15.111–183.

—— 1993. Questions with quantifiers. Natural language semantics 1.181–234.

—— 1995. Dynamics of meaning. Chicago: University of Chicago Press.

——, and S. MCCONNELL-GINET. 1990. Meaning and grammar. Cambridge, MA: MIT Press.

CHOMSKY, N. 1957. Syntactic structures. The Hague: Mouton.

—— 1965. Aspects of the theory of syntax. Cambridge, MA: MIT Press.

—— 1970. Remarks on nominalization. In Readings in English transformational grammar, ed. by R. Jacobs and P. Rosenbaum. Waltham: Ginn.

—— 1977. Essays on form and interpretation. New York: North-Holland.

—— 1982. Some concepts and consequences of the theory of government and binding. Cambridge MA: MIT Press.

—— 1986. Knowledge of language: its nature, origin, and use. New York: Praeger.

COMRIE, B. 1985. Tense. Cambridge: Cambridge University Press.

COOPER, R. 1975. Montague's semantic theory and transformational syntax. University of Massachusetts at Amherst dissertation.

—— 1979. The interpretation of pronouns. In Syntax and semantics, ed. by F. Heny and H. Schnelle, 61–92. New York: Academic Press.

—— 1983. Quantification and syntactic theory. Dordrecht: Reidel.

—— 1996. Head-driven phrase structure grammar. In Concise encyclopedia of syntactic theories, ed. by K. Brown and J. Miller, 191–196. Oxford: Elsevier Science.

CRUSE, D. 1986. Lexical semantics. Cambridge: Cambridge University Press.

DALRYMPLE, M., M. KANAZAWA, S. MCHOMBO, and S. PETERS. 1994. What do reciprocals mean? In Proceedings of SALT, volume 4, Ithaca, NY. Cornell University Press.

DALRYMPLE, M., R. KAPLAN, J. MAXWELL III, and A. ZAENEN (EDS.). 1995. Formal issues in lexical-functional grammar. Stanford CA: CSLI publications.

DAVIDSON, D. 1967. The logical form of action sentences. In The logic of decision and action, ed. by N. Rescher, 81–120. Pittsburgh: Pittsburgh University Press.

DEKKER, P. 1993. Transsentential meditations: ups and downs in dynamic semantics. University of Amsterdam dissertation.

DIESING, M. 1992. Indefinites. Cambridge MA: MIT Press.

VAN DER DOES, J. 1994. Formalizing e-type anaphora. In Proceedings of the ninth Amsterdam Colloquium, Amsterdam. ILLC publications.

—, and J. VAN EIJCK (EDS.). 1996. Quantifiers, logic and language. Stanford CA: CSLI publications.

DOWTY, D. 1991. Thematic proto-roles and argument selection. Language 67.547–619.

——, R. WALL, and S. PETERS. 1981. Introduction to Montague semantics. Dordrecht: Reidel.

EGLI, U. 1979. The stoic concept of anaphora. In Semantics from different points of view, ed. by U. Egli, R. Bäuerle, and A. von Stechow. Berlin: Springer.

ENGDAHL, E. 1986. Constituent questions. Dordrecht: Reidel.

EVANS, G. 1977. Pronouns, quantifiers and relative clauses (i) and (ii). The Canadian journal of philosophy 7.467–536, 777–797. reprinted in G. Evans (1985) Collected Papers, Foris, Dordrecht.

—— 1980. Pronouns. Linguistic Inquiry 11.337–362. reprinted in G. Evans (1985) Collected Papers, Foris, Dordrecht.

FARKAS, D. 1997. Evaluation indices and scope. In Ways of scope taking, ed. by A. Szabolcsi. Dordrecht: Kluwer Academic Press.

FILLMORE, C. 1968. The case for case. In Universals in linguistic theory, ed. by E. Bach and T. Harms, 1–90. New York: Holt, Rinehart and Winston.

FODOR, J., and I. SAG. 1982. Referential and quantificational indefinites. Linguistics and Philosophy 5.355–398.

FODOR, J. A. 1975. The language of thought. New York: Crowell.

FODOR, J.D. 1977. Semantics: theories of meaning in generative grammar. New York: Crowell.

FOX, B. 1987. Discourse structure and anaphora. Cambridge: Cambridge University Press.

240 / REFERENCES

FRANCK, A. 1996. Context dependence in modal constructions. University of Stuttgart dissertation.

FREGE, G. 1879. Begriffsschrift. Halle: Verlag Louis Nebert.

—— 1892. Über Sinn und Bedeutung. Zeitschrift für Philosophische Kritik 100. reprinted in: G. Patzig (ed.) (1962). *Function, Begriff, Bedeuting: fünf logische Studien*, Vanden Hoeck, Göttingen. English translation in P. Geach and M. Black (1960) *Translations from the philosophical writings of Gottlob Frege*, Blackwell, Oxford.

GAMUT, L.T.F. 1991. Logic, language and meaning. Chicago: University of Chicago Press. volume 1: Introduction to logic; volume 2: Intensional logic and logical grammar.

GÄRDENFORS, P. (ed.) 1987. Generalized quantifiers. Dordrecht: Reidel.

—— 1994a. Frameworks for properties. Sémiotiques 6–7.99–120.

—— 1994b. Three levels of inductive inference. In Logic, methodology and philosophy of science, ed. by D. Prawitz, B. Skyrms, and D. Westerståhl, 427–449. Amsterdam: Elsevier Science B.V.

GEACH, P. 1962. Reference and generality. Ithaca, NY: Cornell University Press.

GOLDBERG, A. 1995. Constructions: a construction grammar approach to argument structure. Chicago IL: University of Chicago Press.

GRICE, H. P. 1975. Logic and conversation. In Syntax and semantics 3: Speech acts, ed. by P. Cole and J. L. Morgan, 41–58. New York: Academic Press.

GROENENDIJK, J., and M. STOKHOF. 1984. Studies on the semantics of questions and the pragmatics of answers. University of Amsterdam dissertation.

——, and ——. 1990. Dynamic Montague grammar. In Papers from the second symposium on logic and language, ed. by L. Kálmán en L. Pólos, 3–48. Budapest: Akadémiai Kiadó.

——, and ——. 1991. Dynamic predicate logic. Linguistics and Philosophy 14.39–100.

——, and ——. 1997. Questions. In Handbook of logic and language, ed. by J. van Benthem and A. ter Meulen, 1055–1124. Amsterdam: Elsevier.

GROSZ, B., and C. SIDNER. 1986. Attention, intentions and the structure of discourse. Computational Linguistics 12.175–204.

GRUBER, J. 1965/67. Lexical structures in syntax and semantics. New York: North Holland.

HAMBLIN, C. 1973. Questions in Montague English. Foundations of language 10. reprinted in: B. Partee (ed.) (1976). *Montague Grammar*, New York, Academic Press.

HARRIS, R.A. 1993. The linguistic wars. Oxford: Oxford University Press.

HEIM, I. 1982. The semantics of definite and indefinite NPs. University of Massachusetts, Amherst dissertation.

—— 1990. E-type pronouns and donkey anaphora. Linguistics and Philosophy 13.137–178.

—— 1991. Artikel und Definitheit. In Semantics: an international handbook, ed. by A. von Stechow and D. Wunderlich, 487–535. Berlin: De Gruyter.

HENDRIKS, H. 1993. Studied flexibility. University Amsterdam dissertation.

HERBURGER, E. 1997. Focus and weak noun phrases. Natural language semantics 5.53–78.

HIGGINBOTHAM, J. 1985. On semantics. Linguistic Inquiry 16.547–593.

—— 1996. The semantics of questions. In Handbook of contemporary semantic theory, ed. by S. Lappin, 361–384. Oxford: Blackwell.

HINRICHS, E. 1996. Temporal anaphora in discourses of English. Linguistics and Philosophy 9.63 82.

HOBBS, J. 1979. Coherence and coreference. Cognitive Science 3.67–90.

——, M. STICKEL, D. APPELT, and P. MARTIN. 1993. Interpretation as abduction. Artificial Intelligence 63.69–142.

HOEKSEMA, J. 1983. Negative polarity and the comparative. Natural language and linguistic theory 1.403–434.

DE HOOP, H. 1992. Case configuration and noun phrase interpretation. University of Groningen dissertation. published 1995 by Garland, New York.

—— 1997. A semantic reanalysis of the partitive constraint. Lingua 103.151–174.

——, and J. SOLÀ. 1996. Determiners, context sets and focus. In Proceedings of the fourteenth West coast conference on formal linguistics, ed. by J. Camacho, L. Choueiri, and M. Watanabe, 155–167. Stanford: CSLI publications.

HORN, L. 1972. On the semantic properties of logical operators in English. University of California at Los Angeles dissertation.

—— 1989. A natural history of negation. Chicago: University of Chicago Press.

—— 1996. Presupposition and implicature. In The handbook of contemporary semantic theory, ed. by S. Lappin, 299–319. Oxford: Blackwell.

HORNSTEIN, N. 1990. As time goes by: tense and universal grammar. Cambridge MA: MIT Press.

HUGHES, G., and M. CRESSWELL. 1968. An introduction to modal logic. London: Methuen.

JACKENDOFF, R. 1972. Semantic interpretation in generative grammar. Cambridge MA: MIT Press.

—— 1983. Semantics and cognition. Cambridge MA: MIT Press.

—— 1990. Semantic structures. Cambridge MA: MIT Press.

—— 1996. The proper treatment of measuring out, telicity, and perhaps even quantification in English. Natural language and linguistic theory 14.305–354.

JANSSEN, TH.M.V. 1997. Compositionality. In Handbook of logic and language, ed. by J. van Benthem and A. ter Meulen, 417–473. Amsterdam: Elsevier.

JOHNSON-LAIRD, P. 1983. Mental models. Cambridge: Cambridge University Press.

DE JONG, F. 1987. The compositional nature of (in)definiteness. In The representation of (in)definiteness, ed. by E. Reuland and A. ter Meulen, 270–285. Cambridge MA: MIT Press.

——, L. OVERSTEEGEN, and H. VERKUYL. 1990. Betekenis en taalstructuur. Dordrecht: Foris.

KADMON, N. 1989. On unique and non-unique reference and asymmetric quantification. University of Massachusetts at Amherst dissertation.

KAMEYAMA, M. 1996. Indefeasible semantics and defeasible pragmatics. In Quantifiers, deduction and context, ed. by M. Kanazawa, C. Pi nón, and H. de Swart, 110–138. Stanford: CSLI Publications.

KAMP, H. 1971. Formal properties of *now*. Theoria 31.237–273.

—— 1979. Events, instants and temporal reference. In Semantics from different points of view, ed. by R. Bäuerle, U. Egli, and A. von Stechow, 367–417. Berlin: Springer.

—— 1981. A theory of truth and semantic representation. In Formal methods in the study of language, ed. by J. Groenendijk, T. Janssen, and M. Stokhof. Amsterdam: Mathematisch Centrum. reprinted in J. Groenendijk, T. Janssen and M. Stokhof (eds.) (1984). *Truth, interpretation and information*, pp 1–41, Foris, Dordrecht.

——, and U. REYLE. 1993. From discourse to logic. Dordrecht: Kluwer Academic Publishers.

——, and C. ROHRER. 1983. Tense in texts. In Meaning, use and interpretation in language, ed. by R. Bäuerle, C. Schwarze, and A. von Stechow, 250–269. Berlin: De Gruyter.

——, and A. ROSSDEUTSCHER. 1994. Remarks on lexical structure and DRS construction. Theoretical linguistics 20.97–164.

KARTTUNEN, L. 1976. Discourse referents. In Syntax and semantics vol. 7, ed. by J. McCawley, 363–385. New York: Academic Press.

—— 1977. Syntax and semantics of questions. Linguistics and Philosophy 1.3–44.

KATZ, J., and J. A. FODOR. 1964. The structure of semantic theory. In The structure of languages, ed. by J. A. Fodor and J. Katz, 479–518. Englewood Cliffs, NJ: Prentice-Hall.

KEENAN, E. 1987. A semantic definition of "indefinite NP". In The representation of (in)definiteness, ed. by E. Reuland and A. ter Meulen, 286–317. Cambridge MA: MIT Press.

—— 1996. The semantics of determiners. In The handbook of contemporary semantic theory, ed. by S. Lappin, 41–63. Oxford: Blackwell.

——, and L. FALTZ. 1985. Boolean semantics for natural language. Dordrecht: Kluwer Academic Publishers.

——, and D. WESTERSTÅHL. 1997. Generalized quantifiers. In Handbook of language and logic, ed. by J. van Benthem and A. ter Meulen, 837–893. Amsterdam: Elsevier.

KRAHMER, E., and R. MUSKENS. 1995. Negation and disjunction in discourse representation theory. Journal of Semantics 12.357–367.

KRATZER, A. 1977. What "must" and "can" must and can mean. Linguistics and Philosophy 1.337–355.

—— 1989. An investigation of the lumps of thought. Linguistics and Philosophy 12.607–653.

—— 1995. Stage-level and individual-level predicates. In The generic book, ed. by G. Carlson and F. Pelletier, 125–175. Chicago: University of Chicago Press.

KRIFKA, M. 1989. Nominal reference, temporal constitution and quantification in event semantics. In Semantics and contextual expressions, ed. by R. Bartsch, J. van Benthem, and P. van Emde Boas, 75–115. Dordrecht: Foris.

——, F. PELLETIER, G. CARLSON, A. TER MEULEN, G. CHIERCHIA, and G. LINK. 1995. Genericity: and introduction. In The generic book, ed. by G. Carlson and F. Pelletier, 1–124. Chicago: University of Chicago Press.

KRIPKE, S. 1963. Semantical considerations on modal logic. Acta philosophica Fennica 16.83–89.

—— 1972. Naming and necessity. In Semantics of natural language, ed. by D. Davidson and G. Harman, 253–355. Dordrecht: Reidel. reprinted in A. Martinich (ed.) The philosophy of language, Oxford, Oxford University Press.

LADUSAW, W. 1979. Polarity sensitivity as inherent scope relations. University of Texas at Austin dissertation.

—— 1982. Semantic constraints on the English partitive construction. In Proceedings of WCCFL, volume 1, Stanford. CSLI publications.

—— 1996. Negation and polarity items. In The handbook of contemporary semantic theory, ed. by S. Lappin, 321–341. Oxford: Blackwell.

LAKOFF, G., and M. JOHNSON. 1980. Metaphors we live by. Chicago: University of Chicago Press.

LAMBRECHT, K. 1994. Information structure and sentence form. Cambridge: Cambridge University Press.

LANDMAN, F. 1991. Structures for semantics. Dordrecht: Kluwer Academic Publishers.

—— 1996. Plurality. In Handbook of contemporary semantic theory, ed. by S. Lappin, 425–457. Oxford: Blackwell.

LAPPIN, S., and N. FRANCES. 1994. E-type pronouns, i-sums and donkey anaphora. Linguistics and Philosophy 17.391–428.

LARSON, R., and P. LUDLOW. 1993. Interpreted logical forms. Synthese 95.305–355.

LARSON, R., and G. SEGAL. 1995. Knowledge of meaning. Cambridge MA: MIT Press.

LASERSOHN, P. 1995. Plurality, conjunction and events. Dordrecht: Kluwer Academic Publishers.

LEVIN, B., and M. RAPPAPORT HOVAV. 1995. Unaccusativity: at the syntax-lexical semantics interface. Cambridge MA: MIT Press.

LEVINSON, S. 1983. Pragmatics. Cambridge: Cambridge University Press.

LEWIS, D. 1968. Counterpart theory and quantified modal logic. Journal of philosophy 65.

—— 1973. Counterfactuals. Oxford: Blackwell.

—— 1986. On the plurality of worlds. Oxford: Blackwell.

LINK, G. 1983. The logical analysis of plurals and mass terms, a lattice-theoretic approach. In Meaning, use and interpretation of language, ed. by R. Bäuerle, C. Schwarze, and A. von Stechow, 302–323. Berlin: de Gruyter.

—— 1991. Plural. In Handbook of semantics, ed. by A. von Stechow and D. Wunderlich, 418–440. Berlin: de Gruyter.

LIU, F-H. 1990. Scope dependency in English and Chinese. University of California at Los Angeles dissertation.

LØNNING, J.-T. 1997. Plurals and collectivity. In Handbook of logic and language, ed. by J. van Benthem and A. ter Meulen, 1009–1053. Amsterdam: Elsevier.

LYONS, J. 1995. Linguistic semantics. Cambridge: Cambridge University Press.

MAY, R. 1977. The grammar of quantification. MIT, Cambridge dissertation.

—— 1985. Logical form: its structure and derivation. Cambridge MA: MIT Press.

MCCAWLEY, J. 1993. Everything that linguists have always wanted to know about logic but were ashamed to ask. Chicago: University of Chicago Press. Second edition.

MILSARK, G. 1977. Toward an explanation of certain peculiarities of the existential construction of English. Linguistic Analysis 3.1–29.

MONTAGUE, R. 1970a. English as a formal language. In Linguaggi nella società e nella tecnica, ed. by B. Visentini et al. Milan: Edizioni di Communità. Reprinted in Thomason, R. (ed.) (1974). *Formal philosophy, selected papers of Richard Montague*, pp 247–270, Yale University Press, New Haven.

—— 1970b. Universal grammar. Theoria 36. Reprinted in Thomason, R. (ed.) (1974). *Formal philosophy, selected papers of Richard Montague*, pp 247–270, Yale University Press, New Haven.

—— 1973. The proper treatment of quantification in ordinary English. In Approaches to natural language: proceedings of the 1970 Stanford workshop on grammar and semantics, ed. by J. Hintikka, J. Moravcsik, and P. Suppes, 221–242. Dordrecht: Reidel. Reprinted in Thomason, R. (ed.) (1974). *Formal philosophy, selected papers of Richard Montague*, pp 247–270, Yale University Press, New Haven.

—— 1974. Formal philosophy, selected papers of Richard Montague. New Haven: Yale University Press. Edited by R. Thomason.

MUSKENS, R. 1996. Combining Montague semantics and discourse representation. Linguistics and Philosophy 19.143–186.

——, J. VAN BENTHEM, and A. VISSER. 1997. Dynamics. In Handbook of logic and language, ed. by J. van Benthem and A. ter Meulen, 587–648. Amsterdam: Elsevier.

NEALE, S. 1990. Descriptions. Cambridge Massachusetts: MIT Press.

NEIDLER, C. 1996. Lexical functional grammar. In Concise encyclopedia of syntactic theories, ed. by K. Brown and J. Miller, 223–231. Oxford: Elsevier Science.

NUNBERG, G. 1995. Transfers of meaning. Journal of Semantics 12.109–132.

OBENAUER, H.-G. 1983. Une quantification non-canonique: la "quantification à distance". Langue Française 58.66–88.

OBENAUER, H.-G. 1994. Aspects de la syntaxe a-barre. effets d'intervention et mouvements des quantifieurs. Paris: University of Paris 8. Thèse de doctorat d'Etat.

ØHRSTRØM, P., and P. HASLE. 1995. Temporal logic: from ancient ideas to artificial intelligence. Dordrecht: Kluwer Academic Publishers.

PARTEE, B. 1973. Some structural analogies between tenses and pronouns in English. Journal of Philosophy 70.601–609.

—— 1984. Nominal and temporal anaphora. Linguistics and Philosophy 7.243–286.

—— 1987. Noun phrase interpretation and type shifting principles. In Studies in discourse representation theory and the theory of generalized quantifiers, ed. by J. Groenendijk, D. de Jongh, and M. Stokhof, 115–144. Dordrecht: Foris.

——, A. TER MEULEN, and R. WALL. 1990. Mathematical methods in linguistics. Dordrecht: Kluwer Academic Publishers.

PINKER, S. 1994. The language instinct. New York: William Morrow and Company.

POLLARD, C., and I. SAG. 1994. Head driven phrase structure grammar. Chicago: University of Chicago Press.

PRIOR, A. 1967. Past, present and future. Oxford: Clarendon Press.

PUSTEJOVSKY, J. 1995. The generative lexicon. Cambridge, MA: MIT Press.

PUTNAM, H. 1975. The meaning of "meaning". In Language, mind and knowledge, ed. by K. Gunderson. Minneapolis, Minn.: University of Minneapolis Press.

—— 1988. Representation and reality. Cambridge, MA: MIT Press.

REICHENBACH, H. 1947. Elements of symbolic logic. Berkeley CA: University of California Press.

REINHART, T. 1982. Pragmatics and linguistics: an analysis of sentence topics. Distributed by the Indiana University Linguistics Club, ms.

—— 1983. Coreference and bound anaphora: a restatement of the anaphora question. Linguistics and Philosophy 6.47–88.

—— 1997. Quantifier scope: how labor is divided between QR and choice functions. Linguistics and Philosophy 20.335–397.

ROBERTS, C. 1989. Modal subordination and pronominal anaphora in discourse. Linguistics and Philosophy 12.683–721.

—— 1996. Anaphora in intensional contexts. In The handbook of contemporary semantic theory, ed. by S. Lappin, 215–246. Oxford: Blackwell.

RUSSELL, B. 1905. On denoting. Mind 14.479–493. reprinted in B. Russell (1956) Logic and Knowledge edited by R.C. Marsh, pp 41–56, Allen and Unwin, London/Macmillan, New York.

SADLER, L. 1996. Lexical functional grammar. In Concise encyclopedia of syntactic theories, ed. by K. Brown and J. Miller, 259–265. Oxford: Elsevier Science.

SAINT-DIZIER, P., and E. VIEGAS. 1995. Computational lexical semantics. Cambridge: Cambridge University Press.

SÁNCHEZ VALENCIA, V., A. VAN DER WOUDEN, and F. ZWARTS. 1994. Polarity, veridicality and temporal connectives. In Proceedings of the Amsterdam Colloquium, volume 9, 587–606, Amsterdam. ILLC Publications.

VAN DER SANDT, R. 1992. Presupposition projection as anaphora resolution. Journal of Semantics 9.333–377.

DE SAUSSURE, F. 1916. Cours de linguistique générale. Paris: Payot. edited by Ch. Bally and A. Séchehaye.

SCHA, R. 1981. Distributive, collective and cumulative quantification. In Formal methods in the study of language, ed. by J. Groenendijk, T. Janssen, and M. Stokhof. Amsterdam: Mathematisch Centrum. reprinted in J. Groenendijk, T. Janssen and M. Stokhof (eds.) (1984). Truth, interpretation and information, pp 131–158, Foris, Dordrecht.

SCHIFFRIN, D. 1994. Approaches to discourse. Oxford: Blackwell.

SCHUBERT, L., and F. PELLETIER. 1989. Generically speaker or using discourse representation theory to interpret generics. In Properties, types and meaning, ed. by B. Partee G. Chierchia and R. Turner, volume II, 193–268. Dordrecht: Reidel.

SCHWARZSCHILD, R. 1996. Pluralities. Dordrecht: Kluwer Academic Publishers.

SEARLE, J. 1969. Speech acts. Cambridge: Cambridge University Press.

—— 1979. Metaphor. In Metaphor and thought, ed. by Andrew Ortony, 92–123. Cambridge: Cambridge University Press. reprinted in: A. Martinich (ed.) (1990) *The philosophy of language*, second edition, Oxford: Oxford University Press, 408–429.

DE SWART, H. 1991. Adverbs of quantification: a generalized quantifier approach. University of Groningen dissertation. published by Garland New York in 1993.

—— 1992. Intervention effects, monotonicity and scope. In Proceedings of SALT, volume 2, 387–406, Columbus Ohio. Ohio State University Press.

SZABOLCSI, A. 1997. Strategies for scope taking. In Ways of scope taking, ed. by A. Szabolcsi, 109–154. Dordrecht: Kluwer Academic Press.

——, and F. ZWARTS. 1993. Weak islands and an algebraic semantics for scope taking. Natural language semantics 1.235–284.

TARSKI, A. 1944. The semantic conception of truth and the foundations of semantics. Philosophy and Phenomenological Research 4.341–375.

VALLDUVÍ, E. 1994. Detachment in Catalan and information packaging. Journal of Pragmatics 22.573 601.

VERMEULEN, C. 1994. Explorations of the dynamic environment. University of Utrecht dissertation.

WEBBER, B. 1991. Structure and ostension in the interpretation of discourse deixis. Language and Cognitive Processes 6.107–135.

WESTERSTÅHL, D. 1985. Logical constants in quantifier languages. Linguistics and Philosophy 8.387–413.

WESTERSTÅHL, D. 1989. Quantifiers in formal and natural languages. In Handbook of philosophical logic iv, ed. by D. Gabbay and F. Guenther, 1–131. Dordrecht: Reidel.

VAN DER WOUDEN, A. 1997. Negative contexts. collocation, negative polarity and multiple negation. London: Routledge.

ZWARTS, F. 1981. Negatief polaire uitdrukkingen I. Glot 4.35–62.

—— 1983. Determiners: a relational perspective. In Studies in model-theoretic semantics, ed. by A. ter Meulen, 37–62. Dordrecht: Foris.

—— 1986. Categoriale grammatica en algebraïsche semantiek: een studie naar negatie en polariteit in het nederlands. University of Groningen, Groningen dissertation.

ZWARTS, J., and H. VERKUYL. 1994. An algebra of conceptual structure: an investigation into Jackendoff's conceptual semantics. Linguistics and Philosophy 17.1–28.

# Subject Index

# Name Index

Janssen, 39
Johnson, 11
Johnson-Laird, 5
de Jong, 178, 185

Kadmon, 141
Kameyama, 13, 147
Kamp, 21, 134, 140, 144, 205, 208
Karttunen, 49, 126, 130
Katz, 24
Keenan, 178, 181, 193, 214
Krahmer, 141
Kratzer, 93, 140, 193, 216, 221, 224
Krifka, 140, 208
Kripke, 212
Kuhn, 206

Ladusaw, 185, 192
Lakoff, 11, 24
Lambrecht, 149
Landman, 55, 201, 205
Lappin, 134
Larson, 6, 224
Lascarides, 28, 148
Lasersohn, 55
Levin, 21
Levinson, 11, 12, 37
Lewis, 212, 216
Li, 98
Link, 55
Liu, 109
Lønning, 55
Ludlow, 224
Lyons, 18

May, 98, 101, 102
McCawley, 24, 65
ter Meulen, 65, 193
Milsark, 178
Montague, 10, 39, 103, 109, 142, 169, 212
Muskens, 126, 141, 145

Neale, 134
Neidler, 21
Nunberg, 148

Obenauer, 112
Øhrstrøm, 204

Parsons, 208
Partee, 65, 140, 141, 193, 199, 206, 208
Pelletier, 142
Perry, 11, 224
Peters, 142, 160
Pollard, 10, 21, 109
Postal, 24
Prior, 201
Pustejovsky, 21
Putnam, 15

Rappaport Hovav, 21
Reichenbach, 208
Reinhart, 149, 150
Reyle, 134, 140, 208
Roberts, 141
Rohrer, 140, 208
Ross, 24
Roßdeutscher, 21
Russell, 133, 161

Sadler, 21
Sag, 10, 21, 109, 141
Saint-Dizier, 21
Sánchez Valencia, 193
van der Sandt, 140
de Saussure, 22
Scha, 55
Schiffrin, 146
Schubert, 142
Schwarzchild, 55
Searle, 11, 49
Segal, 6
Solà, 175
Stokhof, 49, 110, 130, 142, 144
Stowell, 109
de Swart, 112, 141, 193
Szabolcsi, 109

Tarski, 40, 48

Vallduví, 150